BEAR
TALES

for the Ages

from Alaska and Beyond

By
Larry Kaniut

COVER PICTURE STORY

An old boar stood at the base of the falls, head submerged for minutes at a time before emerging with a sockeye salmon between his jaws. Holding the fish in his forepaws, he devoured it before submerging for another. Before long a huge boar emerged from the woods and entered the pool. They met in the middle of the river and eyed each other. The newcomer advanced as the old timer wheeled around on hind legs without warning and smacked him in the face with a right hook. Snarling viciously, he struck again, knocking saliva from the interloperís mouth and lifting him from the river, razor sharp claws peeling back pink meat and exposing bone. Bleeding badly, the challenger regained his feet and fled into the woods, hoping for safe eating elsewhere. (Note: saliva around head and missing ear)

—Photographer Mike Swanson,
    owner of D & M Photo in Anchorage.

—Illustrations by the author.

© 2001
ISBN 0-9709537-0-4
Library of Congress 2001116825
Subjects: 1. Bears 2. Bear-man interaction
3. Nature 4. Adventure 5. Survival

PAPER TALK
Anchorage, Alaska

From the den of Larry Kaniut

Best wishes from Larry and Friends

TABLE OF CONTENTS

DEDICATION

I enthusiastically dedicate this volume to the special memory of Frank H. Morgan. A voracious reader who loved learning, he always shared his books, ideas and the name of someone I might contact for a story. He enjoyed baking and cooking and provided us his jerky, mincemeat and bread recipes.

Frank was our friend and my college dorm mate at Linfield College in Oregon. After college he moved to Kodiak and imparted his math knowledge, humor and sincerity to students–many kept in touch with him over the years.

Frank was a wood worker and nature lover. This book is something that he would have enjoyed, because he especially loved learning about history and animals. He donated most of his books to libraries including the one in Willamina, Oregon not far from his retirement farm. Always considerate and thoughtful, he kept us posted on his activities and remembered ours. He was an all-around good guy.

During his last years he interacted regularly with his extended family–helping his elderly parents and spending time with his sister Nancy and her daughters, fondly teasing them as only Uncle Frank could.

Frank left us in an untimely manner in late 2000 due to an unfortunate accident. And we have lost a true friend.

Frank Morgan

ACKNOWLEDGEMENTS

Since beginning my first bear book in 1975, a number of people have shared personal stories or referred me to family, friends or companions with stories. I am grateful for all who helped and supported me and my family and our dreams over the years (I wish there were a better way to express my gratitude to them). When *Alaska Bear Tales* was published, it was very exciting to see it on a news rack the first time. It is humbling to see my five books being sold. I thank all of you who were kind enough to purchase these books and/or to send them to family and friends throughout the world since 1983.

I wish to thank all those contributors who shared these stories and to those who took the effort to record and print them. This book would not be possible without them.

A huge "thank you" to others who helped with this volume:

• Jill and Ben Kaniut for your suggestions and encouragement.

• Brad, Ginger and Sarah Risch for your enthusiastic support, web site and hard work.

• Dennis Confer for the suggestion to self-publish and for your time advising.

• Off the Wall for distributing the book–owners Russ Miller and Bill Kellogg and for Renea Pickett who took on the marketing challenge.

• Owners Glenn and Teresa Bracale and Jon Brophy at Professional Colorgraphics for printing this book and their competent staff including Molly Beich, Julie Christensen and Noreen Folkerts.

• All the others over the years who have told me to "keep writing" and encouraged us to self-publish.

And most importantly, I wish to thank my wonderful "editor-in-chief" wife Pam, whom I have adored since first meeting her in 1960 on our college campus in Portland, Oregon.

INTRODUCTION

I love bears. From a very young age I've been captivated by stories about this grand creature. After graduate school in 1966, I began purchasing books about bruin. I had a job that I loved and was perfectly content reading others' bear books, never dreaming I'd some day write one.

Grizzly Country was one of my first purchases. On Friday nights during our first four years in Anchorage, my wife Pam and I journeyed to Aurora Village Mall to spend our budgeted $20 a week for food. She went to grocery shop while I scooted to the Book Cache to read yet another chapter in *Grizzly Country*. Since I couldn't afford the book, I eagerly awaited each week's installment because it was captivating. After several months of that activity and upon completion of it, I decided I needed to acquire the necessary $7.95 for its purchase. It has become a favorite.

As a result of efforts to convince publishers of my classroom need for a good anthology of Alaskan adventure, a publisher suggested "we think you can do a bear book." Thus began my "writing career."

With the release of *Alaska Bear Tales* my family and I, the contributors, editor and publisher were rewarded with very kind and encouraging feedback. I've always attributed the book's success to the fact that: 1) the stories come from the hearts of the contributors; 2) the tales are in their own words; 3) the stories were not embellished; 4) a good editor (Jim Rearden) polished the text; 5) the publisher built a great cover and 6) Alaskans (who probably knew many of the people in the book) shared it with family and friends, both here and Outside.

You are the wonderful reading public whom we thank for your kind support and for purchasing our books. One of the greatest rewards of my writing experience is the privilege of meeting thousands of individuals–contributors, their families, "referrers", printers, publishers and the public. I owe my writing career to all of you and to the One who "breathed" us into being.

Because I have written about bears, it seems only natural for people to ask me, "What's your favorite bear story?"

This is a difficult question to answer because I've heard so many, every story has something different or special and the term "favorite" means different things to different people.

For this volume I've selected 28 stories, primarily from my collection of over fifty bear books, focusing on the sagacity of the bear clan and the indomitable human spirit. Over seventy-five percent of these tales come from out of print sources; and it is my hope that their inclusion here provides a new generation a crack at these amazing stories. Some are classics. Many great bear stories are in my previous books and will not be addressed again.

Collecting bear tales for nearly half a century has been rewarding. It is our hope to continue providing quality reading on various subjects that you will be proud to possess.

And now, I invite you to throw another log on the fire, snuggle into your favorite easy chair, turn the page and enjoy reading these *Bear Tales for the Ages.*

Author by kitchen fireplace March 2001.

Photo by Pam Kaniut, author's wife.

BEAR TALES

TALES

for the Ages

A BAD ONE

*Quickly dismounting, Henry rushed to attend Joe who
lay half-conscious, torn and bloody, on the ground.*

This phenomenal tale is about a cunning grizzly, a
shepherd's protective attitude and his determination to save
his sheep. Since the original source is out of print, I have
rewritten it below.

A maelstrom of confusion enveloped the
bleating sheep as they ran frantically about in the black of
night. Earlier that evening the sheep had bedded down on an open
flat near the herder's campsite. Josif heard the disturbance. Josif
Chincisian was a wiry little sixty-five-year old Rumanian sheep
herder as tough as rawhide, who herded two thousand sheep for Dick
Mosher.

Probably that darn bear again. This was not the first night the
grizzly had come calling. He'd invaded the flock and killed some of
Joe's sheep the previous couple of nights.

Joe lived in a wagon on a long grassy ridge. On one side was a
small coulee while Cuniff Creek tinkled by on the other. Winding
down from the hills, the creek was lined with a grassy bottom and
choked with thick willow thickets as high as fifteen feet along its
near level route. At the foot of the ridge below Chincisian's camp
was a homesteader's vacant, tumbledown, one-room log cabin.

Joe chose to leave the dogs in the wagon. He grabbed a flashlight, his herder's cane and his .30/40 Krag, a battered old weapon
that had seen much service, and started for the commotion.

Most people would shy away from the chore of walking outdoors
to face a grizzly *any time*, but to do so voluntarily in the indigo night

was a true measure of the herder's dedication and courage. Josif had no fear of bears.

Shining his flashlight onto the worn sheep trail and following it to the bottom, Joe walked down off the ridge away from his wagon. Unbeknownst to him the sheep-killing grizzly lay in the darkness feeding on its latest victim. The bear had dropped the animal on the far side of the creek and carried it across closer to the wagon, laying it on a gravel bar. The silvertip fed noisily, tearing, chomping and slurping.

When the little herder rounded a willow clump within twenty feet of it, the grizzly exploded in an all out charge, covering the distance between them in two jumps and reaching Joe within a second.

Josif frantically shouldered his Krag and his rifle spoke with its yellow tongue. But it was a wayward shot. He didn't know that the round plowed into the gravel, high and a little to the left of the target. As with most surprise encounters with grizzlies, Joe got off only the one quick shot–time did not permit him to bolt another round.

With one swat of its forepaw the brute knocked Joe down, broke his skull and scalped him. Joe's blood spattered onto the gravel bar. The bear clamped its jaws onto his upper right arm near the shoulder and dragged him across the rocky stream bed through a dense tangle of brush and dropped him, leaving four deep puncture wounds in the arm. While Joe lay unconscious, the animal raked leaves and earth over him and left him for dead.

When Joe regained consciousness during the night, his stamina and courage foiled the bear's plans. Joe kicked off the leaves and matter that covered him and crawled away.

He dragged himself across the creek bottom and as far as the homesteader's fallen-down shack, a hundred feet from where the bear had left him. Joe crawled inside, trailing blood onto the floor and smearing it onto the walls and bunk. Perhaps he realized that should the bear follow him, the shack provided little protection because the windows and door had long since disappeared.

He stayed there only long enough to recover sufficient strength and clear headedness to fortify himself for the challenge of climbing up the hill to his wagon.

As he toiled up the hill, splotches of blood marked his route back along the sheep trail. Once inside the wagon he left bloody handprints on the doors of a small cupboard where he had stumbled against it. Blood also smeared the covering of his bed. He lay on his bunk until his wounds clotted and the fresh blood dried. Then around noon, hours after the attack, discovering that help had not arrived and determined to save himself, Joe started his journey. Perhaps he was stronger, more lucid and/or perhaps pain and the desperation of his condition compelled him to leave.

He struggled to his feet in a moment of consciousness and staggered out the door and away from the wagon on his trek to the Heydweiller place, a mile and a half away. The agony of that effort will forever remain a mystery guessed at only from the evidence found along the way.

Traversing the familiar trail, Josif had covered a mile when he fell and could go no farther. It was here that rancher Henry Heydweiller found him, at the head of the coulee.

That Saturday morning, September 27, 1947, Henry had ridden his horse up into the hills above his ranch looking for signs of the sheep-killing bear, hoping to find and end its sheep raiding days. How could he have known that the previous night Josif had been frightfully mauled? About 5 o'clock that afternoon he was returning to his home place to take care of the evening milking. His ranch was on the North Fork of the Dearborn River south of Augusta, Montana.

Heydweiller came to America as a young man and a trained engineer from Germany. He'd worked in the kitchen of a Chicago hotel, moved on to a railroad survey job in Canada and finally settled on the Montana ranch. Henry and Josif had become good friends, perhaps in part because of their common European background. Heydweiller also had a smaller herd of sheep on his own place, and when a bear started giving Chincisian a bad time that fall, he undertook to help get rid of it, both as a neighborly gesture and to protect his own stock.

Over the years Josif had had his share of trouble with bears. The little herder waged an ongoing war between the wild beasts and the domestic animals in his care. Whether it was blacks or grizzlies, he had terminated a few of them while protecting the sheep. But this time things were different.

When the bear first showed up, the sheep were moved down out of the mountains to a safer location near the ranch. However within a few nights the bear found the herd. Hearing the disturbance, Josif took his flashlight and rifle and went out to investigate. He saw something black moving among the white sheep, touched off a shot and killed his dog, one of the best he had ever owned. Although that was an unfortunate development, it proved to be only the beginning of tragic events.

Josif was an industrious, focused and reliable herder—not the kind to work for months on end before going into town to blow his earnings for a good time. He'd socked away enough money to purchase a farm in Minnesota. However a week after Joe shot his dog, Dick Mosher brought him the news that his barn in Minnesota had been struck by lightning and had burned to the ground.

Even though Joe was sorry and felt badly about his dog and the barn, those circumstances merely seemed to feed the idea that he was destined to die in the not too distant future. He had been giving away large sums of money and other things to friends. Whenever Mosher remonstrated, the herder's response was that he wouldn't need it.

Within a short period of time the bear struck again, requiring them to move the sheep a second time nearer to the ranch headquarters. Soon after that Heydweiller and Chincisian trapped a black bear nearby and hauled it to Dick's place in Henry's pickup, but none of them believed it was the sheep raiding bear.

Perhaps all these things were on Henry's mind as he rode towards his ranch. He pulled up short when he saw a man sprawled face down in the short grass at the head of a small timbered coulee half a mile from his house. Riding closer he could tell immediately that it was his friend Josif.

Quickly dismounting, Henry rushed to attend Joe who lay half-conscious, torn and bloody, on the ground. Henry noticed only a few wounds. Joe's body and legs were untouched and there were no claw marks on his arms. Joe's torn scalp and ear hung in a dried, bloody flap over his face. At the corner of one eye was a deep cut. It appeared that the four tooth marks and his head wounds were all the hurts he had suffered. *Maybe they are not serious injuries.*

However when Heydweiller bent over the herder, he noticed that a piece of skull the size of a silver dollar had been smashed out and torn away, exposing Josif's brain.

Joe seemed to recognize his friend and began to babble incoherently. How he had reached this spot, a full mile from his sheep wagon, nobody ever learned.

Heydweiller raced for the house, turned his horse into the corral and drove back in his pickup. He was a slight man with a bad hand and leg from an earlier accident with a horse thus he was incapable of lifting the half-conscious herder into the bed of the truck. He was able to get Josif up with his elbows propped on the tailgate, urged him to help and managed to boost him in. Then he drove like lightning for the Mosher place.

Mosher's crew was in the house for the supper hour. One of the ranch hands saw Henry drive into the yard with something lying in the back of the pickup and assumed he'd caught another bear. That would have been wonderful news for Josif.

When the ranch house emptied of men attempting to help, they noticed that Joe's torn scalp was too hardened to be put back in place. Nevertheless they laid damp bandages on his head and moved him to the back seat of a car. He kept moaning softly and running a hand over his bare, bloody skull.

The men observed that Joe's pain was extreme but they made him as comfortable as they could. One man held him on the seat and just before their departure for Deaconess Hospital in Great Falls, sixty-five miles away, Dick said to Josif, "Say your prayers, Joe. We're going to take you to the doctor."

Joe made no reply, but he lay back and folded his arms as if the pain had been eased. He was out cold when they reached the hospital.

The attack on Josif aroused the ranchers and locals. There were many unanswered questions and a strong desire to put an end to the bear that caused it all.

The immediate talk centered around the herder's dogged determination to defend his sheep and his interminable trek for survival. First the questions.

What happened that night?

How long did he lie beneath the flora and earthen matter before rising and making his way to the shelter shack?

How long did he stay in the homesteader's shack? In his wagon?

Just when did he start down the valley to the Heydweiller ranch, and how long did it take him to cover that long mile? Did he stagger or crawl toward the ranch house? No one knows.

He was weak from loss of blood. Perhaps he passed out numerous times as he struggled on, half conscious and in blinding pain. The dried scalp flap hanging over his eyes impaired Joe's vision. Perhaps he had to hold it back in order to see more clearly. He consciously forced himself along, willing one foot ahead of the other, inching a step at a time. Two fences blocked his pathway, one of woven wire, the other, four strands of barbwire. Because his pants legs were not torn and dirty as they would have been had he crawled, it appeared he managed to stay on his feet most of the way, staggering and falling, getting up and tottering on.

The agony Joe endured on his terrible trek can only be imagined by those who returned to the scene.

Right after breakfast the next morning Mosher led a party up to Josif's camp to piece together the details of what had happened. It wasn't difficult. The search party found two sheep the bear had killed, one a short distance up the creek, the second directly below Josif's camp. They found Joe's tracks where he had come down off the ridge.

His flashlight and cane, unstained with blood, lay where he had dropped them when the bear struck. There was no bear blood or evidence that Joe's single shot at the critter connected, though a bloody trail led back into a willow thicket.

No one was eager to take that trail, for they knew not whether they followed man blood or bear blood, or both. The tracks in the mud along the creek confirmed what they had suspected, that this was the work of a grizzly. It was entirely plausible that he might be lying in ambush just ahead in the willows, wounded, nursing a grudge and ready for a fight.

When the dogs they sent ahead stirred up no trouble, the men, crouching over with fingers on their rifle triggers and safeties, took the blood trail.

They followed it only twenty-five feet when they came upon a pile of leaves and ground litter. In that pile they found, too, the fragment of bone that had been torn from Josif's skull.

A Montana state game warden and former government trapper with almost fifty years' experience with bears carefully investigated the whole affair. Bruce Neal knew bear ways as well as any man in Big Sky Country and he contended that covering Josif was classic silvertip behavior and indicated it intended to return to eat its victim.

The searchers found Josif's rifle leaning against the creek bank where he had left it. Bloody handprints on the weapon evidenced that he had fumbled for and found it after leaving the "burial" spot. He'd tried to take it along but had found it too much and left it against the bank. The bolt of the Krag was open and the ejected shell lay nearby.

Even though it sounds preposterous, Dick Mosher insists that the next act in the drama occurred.

Before starting on Josif's fateful trip to the hospital, Dick instructed his ranch hands to move the sheep down to a corral and open shed a mile nearer the ranch buildings where there was a small shack. He sent a man into Augusta to request experienced herder Theodore Olsen to replace Josif to tend the herd. Dick left strict orders that Olsen was to remain indoors–and that the door of the shelter was to remain closed–all night regardless of any noise or other occurrence that might transpire.

It didn't take the bear long to find the sheep in their new location. Bruin came in around midnight, climbed over a four-foot board fence surrounding the corral and killed an ewe. Olsen heard the commotion but obeyed orders and remained inside the shack.

The bear carried the sheep back over the fence, the dragging entrails left hanging on the boards. Almost ceremoniously, the bear circled the corral within a few yards of the shack before taking it into a grove of quaking aspen behind the shed (as the bloody trail indicated the next morning). The bear deposited the dead sheep at the base of a tree, covered it with a few leaves and left it there. Next he made himself a bed against one corner of the shed, thirty feet away. For hours the bear lay near his kill as if waiting for something. He left some time before daybreak without feeding on the sheep.

Bruce Neal was convinced that the bear cunningly tried to draw Olsen out of the shack using the sheep as bait. The beast had attacked a man, had a chip on his shoulder, and, as strange as it seems, when he got scent of the herder, killed again and set up an ambush near the sheep carcass in the hope the man would accept the dare.

Fortunately, Olsen refused to take the bait.

Ten days after reaching the hospital, on Tuesday, October 7, despite brain surgery, the use of oxygen and everything the doctors could do, the little Rumanian sheepherder died. Because he never regained consciousness or spoke an understandable word after the mauling, his actions up to and following the bear mauling can only be explained by way of the existing evidence.

The hunt for the bear got under way the day after Josif was hospitalized. Many people, both those with and those without bear experience, joined the intense effort to terminate the grizzly. The hunt lasted all through the fall.

Two government trappers used bear dogs to trail the bear, following it into the hills for nearly six miles from the sheep wagon, but the track proved too old as the dogs lost it on bare ground and gave up.

Some believed that Josif's one shot wounded the grizzly and that it had crawled off into the willows and died. Mosher didn't swallow that idea because the dogs would have found the bear had it been hurt. All evidence at the scene indicated Josif's single shot had missed. A wounded bear would not take time to drag a man into the brush or cover him. And finally, a wounded bear surely wouldn't return to the sheep corral the following night to kill a sheep and try to outwit another herder in the shack.

Trappers brought in a couple small black bears not far from the sheep camp, but not the grizzly they sought. A female black, thin and in poor condition from a festering bullet wound in one hip, was trapped in the area later that fall. The trapper who caught her thought that he had exterminated the right bear, but the one that had left its tracks at the scene of the attack was obviously a grizzly.

While moving cattle up into the hills a couple of weeks after Josif was mauled, neighboring rancher Dick Bean, shot a big grizzly. Many thought it was the killer, however it was missing two middle toes on a front foot, compliments of an encounter with a trap. Because the stubs had healed, the foot had been pinched some time before the herder was attacked and the tracks seen along Cunniff Creek showed no sign of mutilation.

The commotion of the hunt apparently drove the bear into the hills, for he did not come back to feed on any of his three sheep kills, nor did he ever bother the herd again. Olsen stayed on as Dick's herder and they wintered the sheep at the corral where the grizzly had made his last raid, but they saw no more of him. And when they moved the herd back into the hills the following spring, they had no more bear trouble.

Mosher was convinced that, unless some hunter miles from the attack scene back in the mountains shot him later and was unaware of what he had bagged, the grizzly that struck down Chincisian that dark September night was never killed.

Long after, there was still disagreement around Augusta as to the outcome, but there was no doubt in Mosher's mind about what happened. They did their best to avenge Josif, but Mosher is convinced to this day that they did not succeed.

Although man with a weapon sometimes comes up on the short end, that is not always the case when a grizzly encounters a "well armed" animal that can account for itself.

Author hunting Kenai Mountains, 1978.
Photo by Randy Terry, from author's personal collection.

BATTLE OF GIANTS

*The moose struck the earth with his hoof and shook that mighty
rack of broad-pointed antlers, then charged uphill toward the bear.*

While reading the following story, I was amazed at the
sagacity of the two monstrous mammals involved. The
author's introduction stated, "Many good big-game stories
have been lost because when related they were not
recorded...My friend Charles Bunch once told me of a fight
between a Kodiak bear and a bull moose, a marathon
combat...Charlie never regretted that long day he and his
father spent witnessing, spellbound, this extraordinary
battle."

Even though he'd observed a number of man and animal
fights, Charlie later admitted that none ever measured up to
the drama and raw power of the one that unfolded before
him on the rim of Little White Horse Creek nearly a century
ago.

I, too, am glad that someone was present to observe the
event and that he had the presence of mind to record it.

The tale that F.M. Young called "The Bull Moose and the
Kodiak Bear," I've rewritten.

While living in Alaska in the early 1900s
Charlie's father invited him to accompany him to a gold-
quartz-mining claim that the elder Bunch had grubstaked. As was
his custom, Mr. Bunch took one of his sons with him on such occasions. The May weather was conducive to travel and they left
Seward, Alaska, aboard the Santa Anna Mail* sailing south-south-
west around the tip of the Kenai Peninsula and then north-north-
east through Cook Inlet for Anchorage.

Departing Anchorage by dog team they mushed to the trading station at Matanuska from whence they outfitted with saddle and pack horses. From there they had a journey of 110 miles to the Mabel Mine. Low bench land blanketed by birch and scattered spruce trees welcomed them as they followed Little White Horse Creek. Below them stretched a canyon a couple of hundred yards deep. A gradual slope ran from them to the creek and a rugged, rocky wall bordered the other side of the creek bottom.

The second morning out, the elder Bunch reigned in his horse and pointed to the ground and a large brown bear track telling his son, "There is a large bear ahead of us and not far away, so we must be on the alert." The riders followed the rim where they could better observe the canyon. Because there were few trees and little brush, their view was unobstructed thus enabling them to see just about everything below.

They'd traveled only a short distance more when the father pointed out a bear that resembled a load of hay, calling it a Kodiak. The animal strode along next to the creek in an unusual fashion. They surmised that it was stalking something. It ran a short distance, stopped, then repeated its action, all the while hiding wherever it could; then it moved ahead again. Sometimes it merely walked, always moving in a resolute manner.

A gentle breeze moved down-valley, masking the bear's approach to its quarry and carrying the riders' scent away from bruin–thus the bear's prey was unaware of it just as the bear was unaware of the men on horseback.

With eyes glued to the brownie the riders moved ahead. In no time at all they spotted the object of the bear's attention. A huge bull moose and two cows stood at the foot of the far canyon wall near a handful of trees. Recalling traditional stories about the great bear's stamina and reputation, both father and son anticipated a brief battle before the mighty brown bear claimed victory.

However, as they studied the bull, they gained renewed respect for this forest dweller. Armed with sharp hooves, a crown of broad and pointed antlers, sheathed in rippling, rock-hard muscle, the king of the deer family was no patsy.

As the boy and his father watched the scene below, the moose became aware of the bear and snorted a warning to the cows in his company. They took shelter in some nearby trees as the bull turned to face his antagonist. With eyes riveted on the bear and tracking his every move, the moose pawed the ground and shook his outsized antlers, almost as an invitation.

The brownie moved within three yards of the ungulate, popping his teeth and whining in a half woof as he rose on his hind legs, towering over his foe. At that moment the bull also rose on hind legs and lunged toward the bear. His massive antlers stretched fully as tall as the bear.

When the animals collided, the bear struck with a hay hook paw, ripping a hole in the moose's shoulder and side. The power of the blow sent the moose spinning for ten yards. The men wondered if the battle was over, but the moose regained his footing, took two quick jumps and was back in the midst of the fray. He speared the bear with his antlers.

The bruin took a few moments to free himself from the moose, then he swatted again at the bull.

Moving apart, the animals faced each other and watched for an opening.

The intensity of the battle mixed with the wild smell of bear and bull excited the horses, so the riders took their mounts back from the rim and tethered them to trees. Upon their return to the canyon lip, they noticed that the combatants had re-engaged and fought furiously. They expected the bear to put away the moose at any moment, however the moose's strength and determination surprised them. The bull was not ready to call it quits.

Charlie's father asked him how long he thought the battle would last. They had been so intent upon the event that they'd lost track of time. Fully expecting to see one of the combatants break off, turn tail and leave the scene in as dignified a manner as possible, father and son didn't see how the fight could continue much longer.

Both animals moved away from each other, the moose watching bruin slowly climb the rocky side wall of the canyon. The bear reached a vertical stone backdrop, stopped, turned and looked toward the moose as if issuing a challenge. Perhaps the bear chose the rock outcrop as a position of strength, but his choice proved otherwise.

The moose struck the earth with his hoof and shook that mighty rack of broad-pointed antlers, then charged uphill toward the bear. Thundering up the slope, the bull lowered his antlers and, just before the moment of impact, swung upward with as much power as he possessed, driving two brow tines into the side of the bruin. The moose drove the bear against the rock wall, stiffening his legs and driving the bulk of his energy into the bear.

Bruin let forth a howl of pain and rage and struggled to free himself. He champed his teeth and swung his paws at the bull, even digging at the moose with his hind paws. But the moose never faltered.

The combatants remained in that position as a full forty-five minutes ticked away on Mr. Bunch's watch. Although they needed to be going, the men could not tear themselves away from the unusual scene before them.

In time the bear's moaning died away to silence. Then the bull pulled back from the shaggy bruin, shook his head, snorted to clear away the blood from his nostrils and mouth, stepped back and watched as the bear's limp form tumbled end over end three or four times down the slope to the level ground below. The bull followed the bear and sniffed it momentarily before turning to limp toward the protective timber shielding the cows.

Spellbound for eight hours, the spectators on the rim were nearly speechless. They untied and mounted their horses then rode down the slope to the valley floor. Father and son dismounted and examined the carcass of the bear. From the tip of his tail to the tip of his nose, he measured 13-feet 6-inches. Because the hide was punctured so badly, they left it behind and rode off.

A week later while returning from the mining claim along the same route, they discovered a large bull moose carcass. All that remained were bones and some patches of hide, the skull and the antlers. Claw and tooth marks on the antlers evidenced that it was the same bull they'd watched kill the bear. They rode on, wondering whether the bull had died of injuries inflicted by the bear or had fallen to a pack of wolves that found the bull too weak to defend itself.

* In an effort to shed more light on the *Santa Anna Mail*, I contacted a couple of people on the Internet. My records show that I sent the following message Friday, November 10, 2000:

> I recently ran across a reference to *Santa Anna Mail*, I believe she's a ship plying West Coast waters at the turn of the century. The reference stated that she left Seward bound for Anchorage via Cook Inlet. Am wondering if you could verify whether it's a ship, approximate time of service and any other info...or point me to that source?

Three people responded, Laura Carroll, Gil P. Joynt and Tiger Avery. I am beholden to them for providing the following information within a couple of days:

> My McCURDY shows lots of entries for a Santa Ana, beginning in 1900. But no "Santa Anna Mail". There is a Grace liner, the Santa Ana, renamed Baranof by Alaska Steam, but no "Mail".
>
> —Gil P. Joynt

> My home resources are limited, nevertheless I doubt the name of the vessel that Mr. Kaniut cites. I can find no vessel named SANTA ANNA (with two Ns) near the turn of the century and the appended MAIL is problematic. "MAIL" vessels do not show up in Merchant Vessels of the United States (MVUS) until after World War II.
> There have been several SANTA ANAs, the Grace Line ship built under a different name in 1918, among them. But the one which you found in McCurdy, official number 116944, is the most likely candidate. As you now know, Hans Reed built her in 1900 at the J. Ross shipyard near Marshfield (Coos Bay), Oregon. She was a coal-fired wooden steam schooner, 1,203 tons gross, 730 tons net, 182.4- x 36.2- x 12.4-feet, 600 horsepower. After conversion to oil in 1914, her speed increased from seven to nine knots.

> A small photograph of SANTA ANA appears on page 113 of: Newell, Gordon and Williamson, Joe. "Pacific Coastal Liners." Seattle: Superior Publishing Co., 1950. After operating on the West Coast for many years under several different owners, she went to Florida in either 1929 or 1930. McCurdy's reference to 1924 looks to be in

error since MVUS (1929) still lists her as owned by Santa Ana Steamship Co., Seattle.

SANTA ANA stranded on the Mobile River mudflats where a fire destroyed her on February 2, 1940.
I could not find an email address for Kaniut and so trust either you or Laura to forward this message to him provided you feel that it is worthwhile. Should this be the vessel in which he is interested, we can provide a good deal more detail from McCurdy concerning its various owners and services.

—Tiger Avery

Author's note: I assume the reference *Santa Anna Mail* was a generic term for the Santa Ana, a ship that carried mail as well as passengers and cargo.

If a grizzly struggles for survival against a wild, well-equipped foe, one would have to wonder about a man's ability to survive a grizzly's fierce power in a knife to paw battle.

"THE LORD'S ON MY SIDE"

By
Gene Moe as told to Larry Kaniut

*I opened up two fingers with my teeth. Then I got a finger from
my left hand in and opened my right fist.*

Imagine a strapping, robust, 69-year-old guy swaggering up to you, ramrod straight, a black, short billed skipper's cap atop his head, a halo of white hair above his ears, a ruddy complexion and a big smile. That's Gene Moe. Solid as a rock at 6-foot-1 and tipping the scales at 220-pounds, he exudes confidence and competence. My former student and friend Matt Ketchum recently told me that, "Gene Moe is the quintessential Alaskan. He's as rugged as they come. A straight shooter and a hard worker. As fine a man as I ever met."

Gene grew up during the Depression in Minnesota where he and his brothers hunted and trapped–their catch providing funds for clothes (unable to afford long rifle bullets, they purchased shorts for 11-cents a box). Gene was 6-years old when his hunting career began ..."It was common for my mother to say, 'Boys, you've got to get us three partridge for supper tomorrow night.'" Gene always thought the Lord provided.

Gene is only one of half dozen men I know of who have stuck a knife into a grizzly and lived. Most of them lived in the 1800s when running into Old Ephraim was common on the Plains or in the Rockies, at a time when their weapons weren't as efficient as modern day firepower.

A cement finishing contractor, Gene is no easy mark for a bear. Not only did he take on a grizzly with a knife, but also, and more importantly, he owned that bear! Gene stood toe to toe with the animal, convinced he was going to win.

Getting "eaten" by a bear was probably the last thing Gene had on his mind that day his son Karl, Steve Fitzpatrick and Tom Frohlich hunted deer on Raspberry Island northwest of Kodiak Island. I was pleased to meet Gene and grateful for his permission to include his story which he shares here.

The boned out deer meat was on the plastic, preparatory to going into my pack. I had just cut away the heart and liver when I saw something coming real fast. It was as big as a Volkswagen. *Aaaahhhhh, aaahhhhhh!* Really growling and both forelegs digging towards me. I turned to face it.

I never leave my rifle more than two steps away when I'm butchering an animal. I thought of reaching for my gun but the bear was less than thirty feet. I figured I could pull one shot at him. If I hit him in the chest, I'm going to be dead anyhow because that bear isn't going to stop. I didn't shoot.

We were on our annual deer hunt. It's a real planned thing but with the pickup and everything, it looks like the Grapes of Wrath. The guys who coordinate the trip have an 18-foot skiff, a rubber boat and three motors. We drive to Homer, put it on the ferry and go to Kodiak. We off load in Kodiak then drive to Anton Larsen Bay where we put in. We've got a friend with a 40-some-foot boat who takes us across Marmot Staits to our campsite.

We make our Kodiak trip a hunt; we've got to shoot a buck with four points on a side. Usually we try to take one deer each a day. We bone out our meat and carry it to the beach, which reduces the problems with bears because it's harder to take care of a couple of deer at a time in different locations. Every evening when we get back to camp, we fry up liver and heart. Usually I take a little piece of liver, but this year I'd been eating a whole frying pan full each night.

To pass the time at night we play a little game called 20 questions—what did you see today in the woods? You'd be surprised what you find in the woods. Everybody tries to guess it because there isn't much to do until daylight at 8 o'clock next morning. We have a great time.

I'm really proud of these young people I hunt with. Everything is picked up and clean. I used to bury my stuff; they bring everything back out. If somebody else has been there ahead of us, we spend the first two hours cleaning up the mess.

Before hunting Kodiak I hunted Prince William Sound fourteen years with my good friend Martin Goresen, the man who captured goats near Seward and kept them in his basement before taking them to Kodiak to be transplanted.

I've been in Alaska about fifty-three years now, and hunted every year. I'm a meat hunter; I <u>don't</u> shoot the biggest moose. But I don't have to shoot anything to have a good time.

I think blacktailed deer is about the finest eating there is. A whitetail's got a tallow and a blacktail's got a fat. If you don't take the tallow off a whitetail, your deer meat gets rancid a lot faster than a blacktail. I rate the blacktail next to wild sheep as good a meat as you can eat.

The first of November 1999 found us looking at a depleted deer population. In three days I'd seen ten deer and ten bear. I've never seen so many bear. I saw one bear working on a group of elk. That was a big bear and I had no reason to go there. The bear should have been going into hibernation.

Bears need two things: berries and fish. Since deer and elk were transplanted to Kodiak fifty years ago, they have become part of the bear's diet. The winter before our hunt Kodiak received about 12-feet of snow that didn't melt completely, resulting in a poor berry year. When you don't have a good berry year or salmon producing fat, you're going to have trouble with bears.

We planned to cross the straits from Afognak and go down to Raspberry Island to Seleif Bay. Steve was going to hunt with me, and Tom would hunt with my boy Karl. We parked the skiff above high tide line and split up. (We usually take the skiff completely out of the water so the tide won't affect it.)

We worked our way up into pretty big 3-foot diameter spruce timber. The wind was wrong all morning. Although I'd seen one nice buck and I was trying to get Steve a deer, he hadn't seen a thing. I see a lot of game and bear all the time. A guy in Palmer used to say, "It must be your underwear that attracts bears." Hardly a day goes by at Kodiak or Lake Louise that I don't see a bear–it's just the craziest thing.

In the afternoon we had lunch then crossed a canyon and started working our way down to the beach. We've got to be there about 4 o'clock, 4:15 cause it's dark by 4:30; and we've got a long ways to run back to camp. We don't want to run into any of the numerous logs drifting in the strait that could punch a hole in the boat.

We have a shot signal system. Whichever partner gets to the skiff first, gives a sound shot. The other one sounds from his position. We've got it planned so that there isn't going to be anybody coming out in the dark.

It's afternoon now. I go out about 400 yards on a drive to bring a deer back to Steve. We are in bigger timber now because the snow has pushed these deer down the mountain a little bit. Snow was 2-feet deep on top and 6-inches on the beach. When I came back to Steve, he hadn't seen any deer and he has his earflaps down.

I asked him, "Can you hear good with those flaps down?"

"Oh, yeah."

So the next time I swing out, I saw two deer.

I thought, "It's 2 o'clock. I'd better shoot one and take it." After I shot one, I thought Steve would come, but he didn't. We use a hoot like an owl to communicate without alarming the game in the area, a carry-over from our Minnesota hunting days. I hooted, but Steve didn't answer. I know I have to dress and pack this deer by myself and be on the beach by 4 o'clock.

We carry a pack board and plastic. I lay down the plastic and I take the four quarters. Then I cut the deer down the backbone and take all the backstrap. Next I open up and get the two neck meats all the way up. Then I take what rib meat I can for hamburger. I turn the deer over and open up the diaphragm and take the tenderloins on the inside. Last I take the heart and liver. It takes me about thirty minutes to remove all the meat from a deer, put it in the pack board and leave.

So, there I was. I had all the meat on the plastic just prior to removing the heart and liver. I was bent over with my knife in my hand, when I saw the bear coming.

As the bear closed the distance and it became evident it was not going to stop, I said, "Lord I need help. Help me, Lord."

I swung around with my knife in my hand, thinking I'd put that knife down that bear's mouth. It was lathered and foam came out its mouth. It came right on me full force and didn't stop running. I turned sideways to my left with the 3-inch Buck folding knife in my right hand and my knife just missed its mouth. The knife grazed its skull and left a cut along the side of the head.

The bear bit my right arm, ripping it from mid-biceps to my wrist and clear to the bone. The flesh hung down off my wrist. The pain was so intense that it felt like the bear yanked my arm off.

Then I reached around the bear's head with my left hand and tried to put my finger in the eye. I missed its eye but put my left index finger up his ear. I jammed it up as far as my finger would go, and that bear didn't like that at all. He just shivered and quivered, backing away. Thinking I could break it down, I grabbed the bear by the neck with my left arm. But it flipped me like I was one of those TV wrestlers. I must have gone 5, 6, 8-feet in the air and landed 10 feet away; but I immediately reached my feet. You don't have any concept how strong they are.

I wasn't going to give my body up without a fight.

After watching me for thirty seconds from a broadside position 15-feet away, the bear rose on its hind legs and took a few steps towards me.

Although I didn't really have any feeling in my right arm, I gripped my knife with my right hand. As the bear approached me, I circled away, my knife thrust out in front of me. I could see the flesh from my right arm hanging down by my finger, but I didn't really have time to focus on it.

Because I believe that ninety percent of bears are right pawed, I watched his right paw. I've watched them dive into the water with both paws to catch a fish, but usually when they're standing down on all fours, the right paw rakes berries.

When that bear was circling, growling and coming, I constantly watched his right paw. When the bear got close, it swung its right paw at my head. Even though I pulled my head back, one claw creased the side of my face and cut my ear in two. Then his swinging left paw hit me on the legs, knocking me to the ground and tearing up my legs.

He lunged at me. With my big leather boots and my feet together, I kicked out and hit the bear right in the neck below the head, knocking it off sideways. I was on my feet before the bear was on his.

The bear again circled and came back. Now we had a little arena where we're fighting. But now, I'd decided I needed to get inside his paws some way because he was tearing me up.

This time the bear came on all fours. I knew that it could use its right paw better from a position on all fours.

As I stood sideways with my arm and knife out so he doesn't get my body, he came in like a rocket. When I saw his right paw come out, I stepped inside it and the paw went behind me.

I stuck my right leg out and the bear grabbed my leg in its jaws, right above my knee. That gave me a chance with my left arm. I put it around the bear thinking that I could bend the bear's head down, but I couldn't. Then I reached over its neck with my knife and hit it in the neck real hard. Next I got up close to the jawbone and I really buried the knife, chewing and digging it into the neck.

Even though I could feel the bear try to back away, it grabbed me on the left butt cheek with the right paw and lifted me up in the air. My knife was in its neck, so as it lifted me up, the knife lifted his head up. He couldn't get away. He tried to pull with that left foot down but couldn't get away until he put his right foot down.

When he lowered his right foot, I stood and swung the knife down on him as hard as I could. The knife hit something hard in his neck, probably the vertebrae. When the bear pulled away this time, his head was cocked sideways and blood was spurting out two to three feet all over me. When he went around some brush and out of our arena, I thought it was going to leave.

About thirty seconds later he came back again. Blood was squirting from his neck in gushes.

I remembered talking with the Fur Rondy sled dog musher Billy Sturdevant from the 1970s who lived down towards Homer. I always asked him, "Aren't you scared of these huskies eating you?"

He said, "I've got this club about two feet long, and I figure I can lick any animal if I hit it in the nose. You can take a pencil and hit a dog in the nose and they'll whimper."

For some reason this time the bear had his head cocked really sideways. I thought the fight was out of that bear and I told it to, "Come on. The Lords' on my side, come on!"

This time when it lunged toward me on all four feet and mouth open, it jumped from six feet away. I swung with my left fist and caught the bear some place in the nose below the eye. I hit it as hard as I've ever swung in my life, and of course it was 750-pounds coming towards me. The bear stopped right in mid air. It just vibrated. I hit the bear so hard that it went straight down, bouncing once.

It landed with its legs and feet were under him, his head buried in the moss. It never moved.

I knew that bear was dead. If you've ever shot an animal and hit the backbone or the brain, it dies that instant. I don't know if the knife damaged the vertebrate and I finished breaking its neck when I hit it, but that bear was dead.

I said, "I'm going to shoot that bear anyway." I stepped back and got the gun, but I couldn't open my right fingers. The flesh from my biceps dangled down off my right wrist.

The knife was frozen to that hand. The left hand was all white where I'd hit the bear. As of yet I have no feeling in my last two fingers in my left hand, but I'm starting to get a little feeling (5-months after the event).

I took my right hand and I opened up two fingers with my teeth. Then I got a finger from my left hand in and opened my right fist. I put the knife down and grabbed the gun. When I brought the gun up, the flesh hanging off my arm laid over the breech by my scope. I pushed the flesh off with my left hand and I shot the bear. Even though it never moved, I decided to shoot again.

The gun is a bolt action Winchester Model 70. My torn flesh fell over the bolt again so I raised the gun up in the air to cause the flesh to fall back in order to inject another shell. And I shot the bear again.

It never moved that time either. It gave me a good feeling to shoot that bear!

I checked myself over. My leg's and my arm were in bad shape. I've got claw marks all over. I took the gun and started for the beach. I knew I had about two miles to go and probably an hour and a half before darkness fell.

I got dizzy and was leaving a blood trail. The only way to replace it was by drinking fluids and stopping the blood flow.

When I reached the alders, the flesh from my arm wrapped around them. I kept unwrapping it. I took some plastic and tried to wrap that arm, but the plastic pulled off. I lay down to die and asked the Lord to take me home. I couldn't get up.

I ate snow and my dizziness left. Then I got up. After three times of lying down, eating snow and getting up to struggle on, I saw a little cut in the big timber. I could see Afognak on the other side. I didn't know where the boat was, but when I thought I was within 200 yards of it, I said, "I can't go anymore."

I yelled. Tom and Steve were at the boat and they came. When they looked at me, they saw blood all over me. The bear ripped my pants to ribbons and my suspenders held up the shredded remains. I just happened to have a pair of red underwear on and they were just torn down one leg.

I told Tom, "Tom, man I can't...shoot me, it hurts so bad."

He looked at me, gave me his coat and said, "If you're still here tomorrow, I will." That was kind of a joke. They pulled the skiff and brought it around and got me.

My boy was coming down with a big deer. They shot and he signaled. When they were yelling back and forth saying "bear," Karl thought there was a bear between us. So he didn't really come in right away.

A German couple, Peter and Barabel Guttchen, live in Selief. They have a kind of a little lodge. My son said to take me there because they had the only radio phone within forty, fifty miles–the only way to contact anybody. During the ten, fifteen years, we'd been hunting there, we'd always heard they were not good people.

We pulled into Selief Bay and Peter came out. Two from our boat shouted, "Hey, we got somebody tore up real bad. Can you help us?"

They tried to carry me, and that hurt worse than my crawling. With arm support I half walked, half crawled to the cabin.

We had to go around three sides to get into the cabin. When I came in, they took me into the living room and called the Coast Guard.

These two Germans are about the most gracious people I've ever met. The woman brought out two sleeping bags and they put me in them.

Our contractor business requires everybody to take CPR and First Aid. That's kind of an every day thing in our construction outfit. One or our cement finishers, Tom, who's worked with us for a long time, put my arm back together and of course, there were a lot of tendons and stuff that he tried to lay them in there–some of them were frayed. He pushed everything in with his thumbs. The flesh is not smooth inside, it's tore down to the bone and he put that thing together and Mrs. Guttchen added an ace bandage.

My boy tore strips from her apron to bind the flesh back in place on my leg. They really did a good job.

Normally it takes about forty minutes or so to warm up a helicopter, but they were going on maneuvers and were ten feet off the ground when they got the call, so they were there real quick. With his chainsaw Peter removed two studs and cut his siding out so they could slide the stretcher through the wall instead of taking it all the way around the house.

When would you ever find somebody to cut the side of their house out...it's like the story in the Bible about the men who removed the roof and lowered a sick man into the room and Jesus healed him. I learned that day to judge people for myself.

The Lord did many things for me. I know He helped me.

Kodiak has a new hospital, only two, three years old. Doctor Barry Goldsmith sewed on me for about seven hours. The woman nurse, Linda Koob, took the sleeping bags and washed them. Somebody gave us a car to use and a place to stay. I was so appreciative of the hospital staff and the good care they provided me.

About two days later the doctor asked me, "What medic put your arm together?"

And I said, "It was just a cement finisher."

The hospital staff kind of wondered, so I was very thankful that Tom did what he did.

The next day Karl, Tom, Steve and Lee Robbins, a friend who lives on Raspberry Island, retraced my steps into the woods to the site of the battle. They were able to follow my blood trail. They found my rifle part way up from the beach.

When the guys approached the dead animal, they found that it was a sow with 2-year old cubs. But they didn't have any problems. She had chased them away so that she could fatten up before going into hibernation–that's the reason I never saw them.

The boys took pictures of her with her legs under her just like I said. My boy skinned her out and saw the knife wounds in the neck. She was 13-years old.

That bear had a little bit of fat on her rear. She attacked me from hunger. Mr. Guttchen said no salmon had come up the river that summer. Although time didn't allow me to protect myself with my rifle, I was glad I had my knife and the physical stamina to face the bear with the Lord on my side.

All too frequently, however, a sow with cubs, a powder keg wrapped in a fur coat, is more than a handful, as you'll witness in the next story.

The 750-pound brown bear that Gene killed.

Photo from his private collection

4

LIFE FOR LIFE

*He spun around to behold a monster brownie closing
on him in a full out gallop within 15-yards.*

I've often been asked the value of a dog in bear country. What are the advantages and disadvantages of having a pooch along when encountering Mr. Bruin?

More than one dog has turned "retriever" when confronting a bear. That is, the dog flees the bear, "retrieving" bruin–in great bounds in the dog's wake–to its master.

There are a few dogs, however, that do their breed proud, either by warning their masters or by distracting the animal until the man reaches safety. A couple of such stories in this book are "Old Groaner" and "Bud's Faithful Kenai."

The story below honors Rex, a dog whose love of his master guided his actions, although he learned that chasing brownies is a health hazardous.

Had it not been for a man who took kindly to Rex's mother, Rex's biography would have ended before it started.

Alex Brogle was a fisheries technician and ski instructor. He began working Alaska's commercial fishery at Yakutat in 1961. Yakutat is a fishing village between Cordova and Juneau in southeast Alaska on the south end of Yakutat Bay. It hugs the beach, pinched between the Gulf of Alaska and the mountains, twenty miles to the east. Depending upon the season, emerald green to gray waters of the Gulf wash her shores. Wilderness circles the village–from the ocean floor to the forest. Black-green spruce trees sweep east to the foothills of the wild St. Elias Mountain Range. Yakutat is home to brown bears and long legged, gangly moose. Timber wolves roam the region, howling their songs at night.

Part of Alex's management endeavor for the Alaska Department of Fish and Game consisted of stream surveys that involved counting spawning salmon. When salmon arrived in significant numbers each summer, the bays and fishing areas were opened to the commercial fishermen who then scrambled to their nets. Sometimes the fish were "counted" from the air, sometimes from the ground.

It was a demanding and, often, thankless job. Because the fisheries employees' efforts determined when the season could begin, commercial fishermen often heaped abuse on the system. I know, because I worked for the ADF&G doing similar surveys during the summer of 1968. I was test fishing for salmon aboard the *Trout* out of Dillingham in Bristol Bay. I also walked streams counting salmon and toting a Browning 12 gauge auto shotgun, alternating magnum double ought buckshot with rifled slugs, 5 shots with the plug removed.

Normal procedures in the 1960s called for a summer temporary to count salmon on both sides of a river, tallying fish with a hand clicker for the first ten minutes of the hour then crossing the stream to count the first ten minutes the following half hour.

One day just prior to my arrival at the Igushik River fish camp, a brown bear sat near the fish counting tower. The two summer temporaries decided that they would not count the fish on that side of the river that day until he left. As I recall, they climbed the near tower, counted then doubled the count to compensate for the fish on the bear's side.

In some areas counting on streams necessitates hiking said stream. That was one of Alex Brogle's jobs. Clad in rain gear and hip waders when the occasion called for it, he crunched over the gravel bars of streams and waded the shallow portions where the hump-backed dorsal fins of pink salmon sliced the air.

Alex began patrolling Yakutat Bay in a Boston Whaler in 1967 and not long after spotted two dogs on the beach of Khantaak Island. It was a lonely, isolated stretch half- mile from the mainland. Alex drove his boat to shore and discovered that the pregnant black Labrador was friendly. Her male companion, a Siberian husky with mask-like facial markings, stood off to the side. Alex later learned

that the dogs' owners sometimes occupied a cabin there and had
been delayed for weeks on their return trip.

Alex was an experienced woodsman and felt strongly for
animals. He was worried about the condition of these dogs. Whereas
the bitch was gaunt and hungry, the male looked well fed, probably
resulting from beach combing, eating mussels and the like. She
gobbled the lunch Alex offered her. After that first day Alex stopped
at the island periodically to check on the dogs, visit and feed the
"orphaned" pair.

Weeks later when Alex checked on them, he discovered that the
Lab had whelped her pups. He followed her to the cabin and noticed
a hole in the wood floor. Claw and tooth marks in the wood around
the hole indicated that she had tried to get at something. He heard
nothing but reached into the hole. The hidey hole held seven dead
black pups. Evidently she'd deposited them there for their protection but was unable to retrieve the blind pups, and the little fur balls
had died of starvation and exposure.

He comforted her for a while and thought about dropping the
pups in a weighted bag into the bay. Just prior to leaving, he
removed his jacket and rolled up his shirt sleeve, thrust his hand
into the hole in the floor and reached back as far as possible. He felt
a little ball of fur and retrieved it. The last pup was still alive.

He put the pup inside his shirt for warmth, raced to his boat and
to his fishery station base where he fed the pup warm milk and
placed it in a box beside the stove. When it drank milk, it wiggled
and showed signs of clinging to life.

The little black pup had neither littermates nor a mother to
teach him dog behavior, therefore that task fell upon Alex. The man
became Rex's mother, littermates, master and whole world. Rex
started out as a pup. But he didn't know it.

That summer in Yakutat Alex carried the pup with him while
conducting both foot and aerial surveys of the streams.

From an early age Rex disliked the scent of brown bear. His
hackles bristled and a growl rumbled in his throat whenever he
smelled one of the big omnivores. Danger stalks the land in Alaska
where a sow brownie shares the list of man-killers, which includes

avalanche, frigid water and weather, topography and glaciers. Knowing the danger of a man-bear encounter on a bear stream, the ADF&G required stream fisheries biologists to have a sidekick packing a weapon.

On one occasion, while staring panic stricken at a huge brown bear standing erect and gazing down on the two men, Alex's accompanying guard jacked out all but one live round onto the ground. Alex heard the metallic bullet ejector slamming forward several times and turned to see the frantic guard. He told the knee knocking "shooter" to hand him the rifle. With one live round in the chamber, they backed slowly away from the bear. The further away they got, the less agitated the bear became until it slumped to all fours and ghosted into the shoulder-high devil's clubs and taller alder thickets.

Alex's bodyguard fainted and fell into the water.

That first year when Alex left for his ski instructing job in October, he left Rex with friends Larry and Caroline Powell and their two children, 7-year-old Michele and 2-year-old Brandon. His job would not allow him to take his dog.

The following May when Alex drove to the Powell's in his pickup, Rex lunged into the back of the vehicle and refused to leave. He knew his master.

One day during Rex's second summer Alex and Rex rode in a Jeep along the beach of the bay. Suddenly a large brownie came into view in front of the vehicle. Rex lunged from the Jeep and gave chase, catching the bear and biting its behind.

A cloud of dust erupted instantly as the ursine beast screeched to a stop in the sand. Seconds later from the cloud emerged a frantic dog bee-lining to the Jeep, a ferocious brown bear on his heels.

Alex jumped into the fray using the Jeep as a metallic jousting device, pointed toward the bear, its engine revving and horn blaring in an effort to divert the brownie. When the vehicle was close enough, Rex lunged toward the 4-wheel savior, clattering to a stop inside and nearly breaking his neck. Alex immediately spun the wheel and retreated until they were out of reach from an enraged fur clad gladiator chasing toward the Jeep.

Dog does dumb thing. Bad dog. Bear reacts with good reason. Master saves the day. Dog learns lesson about chasing and biting big bears in the behind.

In time Rex became a great companion and guard dog for Alex. If the conditions were good, he could smell a brown bear 200 yards away. Whenever a bear was near, Rex gave his "bear" growl, which Alex came to know. Rex pointed his nose in its direction until he and Alex were safely past the danger point.

By the end of his second summer Rex had attained his full weight of 85 pounds. His blended Siberian and black Labrador heritage manifested itself. From the father came the husky look and markings–pointed ears and wolf-like appearance; heavy neck, deep chest and thick coat; no great love for people in general; and he loved running, sometimes up to 20 miles behind Alex's pickup, seemingly enjoying it best when it was cold. From his mother came his shiny black coat; wagging tail; brown eyes; sense of smell and retrieving; and his desire to please.

The Powells kept Rex the second winter. However when he became very protective of their general store and their children and fought stray dogs, they decided it would be best not to keep the dog in the future.

After Alex returned in the spring, Rex traveled year around with him–riding in his truck, flying aerial surveys, guarding the fishery station, barking from the bow of the Whaler while skittering over the water, walking the streams and sniffing out bears.

Alex had some reticence when it came to taking Rex from the less peopled frontier atmosphere of Alaska into the ski community, but only once did Rex embarrass him. The dog got into a scrap while chasing a St. Bernard through a crowd of Easter revelers.

Alex used a ski pole to discipline Rex. Some of the crowd criticized him for whipping Rex yet others saw the dog's behavior as reason enough to destroy him. After an entire day passed before the dog sought forgiveness from Alex, only a vocal warning was ever necessary to control him.

Rex's loyalty to Alex was total, often planting himself between his master and someone that Rex, for reasons of his own, mistrusted or suspected of possibly posing a threat to the slim 40-ish bachelor.

In time Rex had command of 20-some word combinations and could differentiate between "We'll go in the jeep" or "In the pickup" and "This way."

Each year spawning salmon, like a slimy magnet, attracted the man and his dog as well as the brownies. From 1968-1975 Alex worked the rivers with Rex as his bodyguard. He had a commendable record chasing bears from the fishery station and apprising Alex of their presence in the neighborhood while managing to stay out of their reach.

On August 30, 1975, there was no one to go with him as a guard to Humpy Creek so Alex leashed Rex and took him. For good measure, he strapped a .44 Magnum pistol on his hip as last resort bear protection.

Humpy Creek is a mile-long stream near Yakutat, small and choked with brush and tall grass in the off winter seasons. Fifteen thousand spawning pink salmon jammed the water between the banks, and carcasses lined the shore. The smell of rotting fish gagged the air and flies buzzed over the decaying flesh for their share of the bounty. Bears and birds had come to the stream to gorge themselves on what they could catch or pilfer. Bald eagles were in abundance, and the surveyors flushed half a dozen off the bars. Eagle droppings covered beaches and the bloated birds sat along both banks. A cacophony of squawking and shrieking gulls and crows wheeled overhead.

Man and dog continued along the stream counting salmon, one punch for every 25 swimming fish. They were half-finished when Rex growled *bear* and riveted his nose across the stream.

Alex looked over the water at a large male brownie standing erect on the bank and looking at them. Then it dropped back to all fours and phantomed into the foliage bordering the stream.

Suddenly Alex heard brush breaking and gravel rattling. He spun around to behold a monster brownie closing on him in a full-out gallop within 15-yards.

He dropped the dog leash and pulled for his pistol. At seven yards the bear rose on hind legs, towered over man and dog and stepped toward them. Alex still fumbled for his .44. Rex launched himself at the bear's throat, jumping into the jaws of certain death.

Alex reacted simultaneously with Rex's leap, lunging to the top of a 3-foot bank. Landing atop the bank with the pistol in his hand, Alex whirled to face the bear and saw Rex tattooed to the bear's chest, his teeth bared and snapping for the bruin's throat.

Alex loosed a round over the bear's head in an attempt to scare it and drive it away. Holding the dog in its huge forelegs it bit Rex one time.

Pistol poised in both hands, Alex stood facing the bear and looking over the weapon's sights. The bear dropped the limp form of Rex into the shallow water, and the dog never twitched.

The brownie then lowered itself to the ground and melted into the grass and alder thickets. Moments later Alex saw her and two cubs retreating up a small hill. He surmised that the sow had smelled the boar across the stream, heard him and the dog, and assumed that the boar scent and the man-dog sound were one and the same and charged to defend her cubs. Rex had not smelled her because she was down wind.

The result was one upset sow, one dead dog and a melancholy man.

Alex went to Rex and discovered that his neck was broken. Still adrenaline charged and shaking, he pulled himself together and packed his pal into the forest. There he lay the dog among the ground roots of a tree and looked down on what appeared to be a sleeping dog. They'd shared much together. The dog gave its life for him, repaying Alex for saving his.

Alex returned later to post an inscribed marker to a tree on the bank of Humpy Creek that read, "In Memory of Rex, Who Here Sacrificed His Life to Save His Master. August 30, 1975."

Life from death has long been a familiar theme to man. In this case a man saves a pup; that pup, in adulthood, saves his savior. In this case the dog was a hero, but not all dogs have a demeanor combining bravery and good judgement.

Gene Moe, Ben Kaniut and Brad Risch (author's son and son-in-law) in Gene and Shirley's home with the Buck knife that killed the bear. *(Story page 29)*

5

PROTAGONIST OR ANTAGONIST?

Wondering if Levi tied his dog to avoid duplicating the bear-dog game of chase, Andy interrupted him to ask.

All too often the bear is blamed for being a bear, doing what comes natural. While reading *Grizzly Country* for the zillionth time, I enjoyed Russell's comments about a friend and his common sense.

In some circles the grizzly is labeled a no-good, man-killing beast. Some people like authors Enos Mills, Will Wright and Andy Russell, defend the grizzly. They credit its curiosity and self-defense characteristics as causes for its behavior. Another reason bears are maligned is people's lack of knowledge and, thus, their misunderstanding of the animal.

The defenders offer arguments such as Russell's story of a friend whose dog interfered with a grizzly. After the fray, the old timer placed the blame where the blame was due.

A well-known and experienced British Columbia trapper and good friend, Levi Ashman, once told Andy about an experience he'd had with a grizzly. One hot June afternoon on a mountain slope Levi was cutting a trail. Having developed a raging thirst during the heat of the day, he dropped into the canyon to assuage it. His dog, a husky-German shepherd and a gift from a friend, followed him.

As Levi lay prostrate on the ground next to a stream, quenching his thirst, reveling in the opportunity and enjoying the moment, suddenly the dog set up a clamor and hit the brush on the far side of the creek, obviously on the trail of an animal. Before Levi had time to raise his head, the dog came bouncing back accompanied by a galloping grizzly hot on his heels. As they sliced through the stream, water geysered from the creek and into the sky.

Levi had been around long enough to know that his chances of avoiding harm would be greatly enhanced in a position where the bear couldn't reach him. Although he was no longer a youngster, without further ado he scrambled up a tree. He clung to the branches, hanging above the melee. Levi observed the antagonist and the protagonist mashing down the ground below while completing a 360-degree course around the tree trunk without benefit of a compass or a protractor.

Some would wonder which was the protagonist and which the antagonist, however Levi had no doubt.

Before long the bruin gave up the chase and moseyed off into the woods. At that point Levi left the limbs and climbed to the more comfortable confines of the ground.

Happy to see his master and probably thinking that his actions had saved the man, the mutt tore off in the wake of the departing bruin and commenced the process all over again. Levi took to the tree a second time about the moment the bear and pooch show resumed at the tree trunk.

Around and around the tree ran the dog and the bear. Levi wondered how long this scene would continue before the curtain dropped on the act. As Levi tired of his temporary perch, the bear again wandered away to the sanctuary of more sane activities.

Though the tree was without limbs for forty feet, Levi slowly and carefully descended to safety.

When he finally reached the ground, he confronted the antagonist, his bear retrieving dog.

At that point in the narrative, wondering if Levi tied his dog to avoid duplicating bear-dog game of chase, Andy interrupted him to ask.

Levi answered with a strong suggestion as to the dog's canine heritage and stated as strongly as he could that he did NOT tie the dog up thereafter. He shot him on the spot because a "dog like that can get a man killed. Didn't know how to mind his own business."

Although getting into jams is part of life, some dilemmas are more difficult to escape than others. The following story from the Far North attests to that.

DEATH STALKED
THE ICE

Things happened quicker than they can be described in words.

Over the years Polar bear hunting has swung full circle. Originally done by or with Eskimos and dog team, it evolved into same day airborne hunting. However since the early 1970s aerial spot and land hunting for polar bear has been illegal, reverting back to the utilization of native ground methods.

The story below was originally written by the great outdoor writer Ben East and demonstrates some of the grief faced in the cold climes of the Arctic.

The crème-colored-yellow polar bear shuffled along below the aircraft, eerily casting a long, blue-gray shadow across the pack ice. Hunter and pilot peered from the cockpit of the Aeronca. Although brutal conditions on the northern icepack present some of the greatest challenges known to man–frigid, bleak, unforgiving and windblown land, this was the reason for their presence. This was their dream.

The man who stalks Nanook, is a man who savors the challenge of taking a bite out of life, a man who revels from the adventures lurking at the edge of the envelope. He thrusts into the teeth of the storm to see how he stacks up with his view of himself and his self worth.

The hunter of the northern pack ice must be constantly aware of the dangers that lay in wait for him. Severe cold and blistering winds scour the ice. Sea ice is unstable. The ice bear fears no man–his only natural enemy is the killer whale. Shifting and dangerously thin ice, pockmarked by open leads and pressure ridges, pose colossal obstacles, formed when large fields of ice, pushed by currents and winds, grind together, piling in blocks as high as 300 feet.

Black salt water, 28 degrees at best, grins from the open leads with arms spread wide, the air above so cold that tendrils of rising vapor appear as steam. If man gets wet in sub-zero conditions with no means of accessing heat for re-heating his body and clothes, he is all but doomed to death.

This is what Tony Sulak and Bill Niemi sought, a thrust at life in the Great Beyond. These friends had hunted on many previous occasions and as far back as they could remember. The men had successfully taken such varied big game as black bear, elk, goat and grizzly. They felt that the ice bear was the ultimate North American trophy. This was their trip of a lifetime, a years-in-coming-long-anticipated hunt.

Tony and Bill left Seattle, Washington March 24, 1958 aboard a Pan Am jetliner for Fairbanks, Alaska. Sulak was a 56-year old tool and die plant operator from the Emerald City. Niemi, who enjoyed flying, had a Beechcraft plane dealership at Boeing Field and was partners with Eddie Bauer in the manufacture of down clothing and sleeping bags.

Now they were flying commercially over Alaska. Thirty thousand feet below, the landscape looked like a huge field of pointed marshmallows covered in a thick blanket of white mixed with scattered browns, grays and blacks which were windswept mountain peaks or patches of spruce trees.

The next morning the men hopped a commuter flight for Point Barrow, a three-hour trip. Most of their cabin mates were Eskimos. Tony and Bill were as excited as two kids on Christmas morning.

While descending to Point Barrow the jetliner dropped over the Brooks Range. The world outside the windows looked cold and clear. Beneath the metallic bird were thousands of caribou feeding in the arctic freezer. Before long the men saw polka-dotted village buildings at their destination, Point Barrow.

They were amazed by the sharp contrast in environments–Seattle had sported green lawns and blooming flowers; Barrow wore the winter white of snow and ice. The temperature was minus 18 degrees and a biting 12-mile per hour wind blew across the flat surface out of the northeast.

Since every hunting locale demands adequate preparation, gear and clothing, their first lesson was that of changing from their light clothing to avoid the chill fingers of Jack Frost. Their outer clothing consisted of heavy wool pants and shirts and down-filled parkas lined around the facial area with wolverine fur. Beneath, they wore down-filled underwear. For foot wear they had commercially made mukluks with rubber soles and wolfskin uppers. They later swapped the cold-absorbing rubber bottomed mukluks for Eskimo ones which were much warmer and kept their feet from sweating so much.

In those days polar bear hunting from an airplane called for flying until the trophy was spotted then landing to hunt on foot. The safest method for this type of event involved the use of two airplanes, the second for security reasons–to aid the first should trouble develop.

They would hunt with Frank Gregory, a Point Barrow pilot and guide with vast experience on the polar ice. Their means of travel was two Aeronca Champions. Their "backup" pilot was Jack Hovland with whom Sulak would fly. Neimi would go up with Gregory. Their headquarters would be the Lodge, located on a frozen lagoon from which they would take off.

They awoke the next morning to minus 26 degrees and a gnawing north wind.

Flying in those conditions required warming of the engine oil for the planes. Each night prior to a flight, the oil was drained and placed on top of a stove. While the plane sat overnight, it wore an engine cover. Next morning the warming up process required two hours. Prior to replacing the oil the plane was preheated by placing a gasoline heater below the engine and allowing the heat to rise under the engine cover to heat the entire engine area.

Because their hunting area spanned thousands of square miles of drifting ice, they spared nothing in the way of emergency preparation. Their greatest danger was that of landing on unsafe ice and breaking through or hitting something hidden, like a crack which could snap off a ski. Frank pointed out that the ice's color was a good indicator of its thickness and safety. White indicated thicker ice whereas gray or darker ice denoted thin ice.

Since they could be 400-miles from Barrow, the safest method of hunting was for one plane to set down while the other flew cover above, awaiting the results of the first. Both pilots kept in constant communication by radio. Whenever the planes stopped, the wait was brief to insure proper starting in the frigid weather.

Because airborne hunters spent the day hunting and returned to Barrow each night, they could take comfort in knowing that their failure to return at the end of the day, signaled mishap and initiated a search. Deteriorating weather conditions that could last for days was the only drawback to an emergency search effort. The men were dressed warmly enough to withstand some hardship on the ice for a few hours or overnight if necessary, assuming they stayed warm.

They were not too concerned about the possibility of water immersion since life expectancy in the Arctic waters that time of year was 3 to 8 minutes. It was not uncommon for men to be hauled lifeless from the water within minutes of their dunking. Falling into the water was probably a blessing as it would be a quick death.

Around midmorning on March 26, the Aeroncas were off over the ice with their cargoes of pilots and passengers, heading northeast. The excited eyes of the sportsmen danced around looking for the crème colored king of the icepack. An hour out Jack banked his bird and pointed a hand down to a polar bear beside an open lead. It was the first ice bear Tony had seen outside a zoo, and it thrilled him through and through.

Giving Tony a chance to take pictures, Jack dropped over the bear and followed it along the pressure ridge until the critter took refuge and hid from them among the pickup sized ice blocks.

They spent the day looking and headed back for the evening. The hunters were pretty excited since they'd seen three bears, one a good trophy, and they felt that their bears were "in the bag."

The next day they flew out and spotted a few bears, but they were in the 6-foot and small class. The men were still excited while learning that bears travel miles over the open ice foraging for food. They still felt it was going to be a good hunt and they'd roll with the punches until their tags were filled.

On the third day the men took up where they'd left off–preheated the planes' engines and oil, fueled up, stashed extra fuel aboard for later refueling, loaded up and took off to the northwest. It was minus 18 degrees and the wind continued unabated. They spotted a bear 135 miles out of Barrow and followed the 8-foot animal for pictures until it jumped into open water, his sanctuary from danger.

It was around 11 a.m. and the pilots decided it was a good time to land, stretch, refuel and try for some photos of Nanook from ground level. Leading the way, Frank dropped down, popped his flaps and settled onto the ice, turning sharply to return over his tracks on 3 to 4-foot thick ice to his touch down spot. Hovland observed the situation and followed. He touched the ice and started a slow 90-degree turn to the right toward the open lead. Sulak later thought that Hovland was not satisfied with the bumpy ice and firewalled the plane to go around and land again.

It didn't happen.

As the Aeronca sliced across the ice closer and closer to the open water, suddenly an explosive sound shattered the air. The plane broke through the ice and dropped like a rock until its wings caught on the ice and stopped its descent. Things happened quicker than they can be described in words. Frigid gray-green water filled the cabin, immediately immersing the occupants up to their chests. However they didn't notice it since their full attention was focused on exiting the craft.

Jack yelled to Tony to kick the door open before ice jammed it.

Tony determined to kick the side of the plane away if necessary in order to get out. Thinking that his down clothes would serve to keep him afloat temporarily once outside the plane, he handed Jack the rolled down-filled sleeping bag for use as a life preserver.

When Tony kicked the door away, more water filled the cabin, rising up to their necks. Jack exited the plane ahead of Tony. He reached the aileron in a couple of strokes and hung onto it.

Tony swam past Jack to the engine cowling and hauled himself onto it then fearlessly walked out onto the wing. He reached out to Jack, grabbed his hands and pulled him onto the wing.

Although they'd reached temporary safety out of the water, the ice continued breaking around them as the plane settled into the water, gurgling sounds coming from beneath them. They were drenched and getting cold with 250 feet of unsafe ice between them and the solid ice beyond.

The dilemma facing them was a sinking plane (which would return them to the water) and ice too thin to support them and probably too thick to break through while attempting to swim to solid ice. But they had no alternative.

Tony kept trying to convince himself that this wasn't a dream.

Jack wondered aloud if they should remove their boots, then assented to Tony's head shaking that it was not a good idea.

Jack wore a sheepskin parka and pants, boots and heavy gloves. He was only 27-years old and in top condition. He'd been flying six years in Alaska, two in the Air Force and four for the Territorial government airlines as a bush pilot. He was resourceful and physically tough and the odds favored him. A single man, he was the son of Mr. and Mrs. Gilman Hovland of Fargo, South Dakota.

Tony's wool pants didn't perform as well as they would have under normal conditions because he had washed them prior to the trip, thus removing some of the lanolin and affecting their water proofing and heat keeping characteristics.

While Jack and Tony had struggled to escape their predicament, Gregory and Niemi frantically pulled rescue gear from Gregory's plane and yelled encouragement. Unfortunately their gear was for ice rescue not water. They emptied gas cans and unrolled the engine cover (a rectangular 4x15-foot hunk of canvas).

Things looked pretty grim for the wet men.

Realizing that their salvation required them to forget the unsalvageable rifle, cameras and other gear in the cabin below them and leave the sinking plane, the men tightened their boots, belts and collars to restrict the water's effect and emptied their pockets preparatory to leaving the wing. Tony removed his down coat and rolled it up for use as a life preserver, told Jack to follow him if he was successful and, hoping that the ice would support his weight, stepped off the wingtip.

He instantly broke through, hit the frigid water and began stroking for the solid ice beyond. Half-inch thick ice lay before him, and he broke it with his fists. Since his gloves compounded his efforts, he shucked them aside. The process required breaking ice, clearing it from his path, breaking through again and removing more as he swam forward.

Tony pounded his way through the ice and left a trail of blood where the sharp, rough ice sliced the skin of his hands. He felt neither the cuts nor the salt water assaulting his hands.

Five yards after leaving the plane Tony looked back and observed Jack atop the thin strip of red aircraft above the icy water grave. He hollered for Jack to join him, encouraging him. That was his one and only look back. All his effort from there on was to strike the ice, push it aside and stroke ahead toward safety and his waiting friends. His action became a routine, one that was to save his life.

He didn't know when Jack joined him in the water nor when the Aeronca slipped the bonds of ice and silently sunk from view.

Gregory and Niemi cautiously worked their way toward Tony, tenderly poking the ice with their hunting knives to test its thickness. There was no need for them to join Jack and Tony in baptism! When they reached a point where the ice swayed up and down and their knives poked through, they stopped and waited, yelling encouragement and hoping that there was enough strength in Jack and Tony to make it to safety and enough time to get them to a warm environment. They could do little else.

At one point Gregory ran to his plane, started it and taxied closer to the open water. He grabbed a sleeping bag, boots and socks.

Jack had dog paddled eight yards from his plane when he hollered to them that he didn't think he could make it. Imagine their shock when they understood and then their sadness when they saw him vanish from sight. They saw only the bobbing sleeping bag. Tony never heard Jack and didn't know what had happened to him until much later.

Tony punched his way closer and closer toward Gregory and Niemi over a twenty-minute period, though time was of little concern to him. At that point his determination and his health were his best friends. As long as he could breathe and coordinate his efforts, he would keep going.

When Tony was close enough, the men tossed him an empty 5-gallon gas can, thinking it would facilitate his staying afloat. But he was afraid his hand would freeze to the metal, compounding his efforts. So he ignored it.

He was tiring and slowing down. He thought he could swim slower to conserve his strength but discovered that he could only stay afloat by swimming fast and hard. He finally reached out and tried to climb onto the ice but was unable to accomplish the task.

However he was within reach of Frank and Bill who tossed him the canvas engine cover. He reached out to grab it but realized that his hands were frozen clubs, ice webbing having formed between the fingers and robbing him of any feeling in them.

Tony shoved forward and managed to get his arms onto the canvas and pull it toward him. Then he bit into it long enough for the others to pull him a little. Next he relaxed so that he could get a better grip with his teeth and arms. As he clung to the canvas for all he was worth, they pulled him over the edge of the ice and out of the water. They dragged him until they thought it was safe, then grabbed him by the wrists and pulled for the plane.

As soon as they grabbed his wrists, Tony passed out. The biting wind coupled with the temperature froze his wet clothes stiff. They pulled him to thicker ice closer to the plane and cut his clothes off. Neither man needed to be reminded that every second counted.

Frantically they got him into Frank's overpants. Then they put socks and mukluks on his feet and Bill's parka on him. They dragged him toward the plane, half-hauling and half carrying him until they encountered rough ice halfway. When they lifted him over the 2-foot high shelf, they discovered his pants had come down and they were dragging him on his bare skin, which was sliced to the bone by the ice and frozen white by the temperature and cold ice.

After tugging his pants back on, they continued. They tried to revive him so he could help get himself into the plane, but he was too far gone. They got him into the rear seat, seat belted him and Bill climbed feet first over him into the luggage compartment.

Frank picked up the tail and turned the craft into the wind, jumped into the cabin, warmed up the plane briefly then powered it up for takeoff. At two thousand feet altitude he called Point Barrow on the radio, reported their situation and requested assistance upon arrival. They'd hardly touched down at the lagoon when a visiting hunter and a Wien pilot helped them haul Tony from the Aeronca.

Next thing Tony knew, he was in a warm room where Doctor Clyde Farson and nurses took control. Blankets, hot water bottles and strong tea became the order of the day. Tony wasn't too keen on the tea but drank it anyway because someone said it would save his life. The doctor observed blood, wondered where it was coming from and discovered Tony's laceration. Next nausea and swallowed seawater surfaced.

Tony began shaking violently and a nurse poked him with a needle.

Bill and Frank were there the rest of the afternoon but Tony was oblivious to their presence. They returned at 9 that night to tell him about Jack. Tony remained eight days before returning for skin grafts and more operations to his home in the City of the Space Needle on the great state of Washington's Puget Sound.

In the hospital he had constant reminders of his episode and wondered what else he could have done to save Jack. Logic convinced him that he did the only thing that he could have done—provided Jack with the sleeping bag and broke a path through the ice for him to follow.

Many times he wondered how he survived when Jack, who was nearly 30-years younger, perished. A few possibilities exist: first, Tony had a tremendous will to live; second, his great physical endurance; third, possibly his down underwear gave him more buoyancy; fourth, perhaps his weight and body fat had something to do with his survival. Tony suggested another reason: perhaps

Someone in a higher place with greater authority had something to do with his triumph over the day.

He felt the pain from the frostbite every day and it took some getting used to before it finally disappeared. But in the end, after five weeks in the hospital, he returned home physically no worse for the wear.

Not one to give up easily, Tony returned the following year to the ice pack and killed a 10-foot polar bear.

Sometimes the tables turn and the hunter becomes the hunted. When a grizzly's breathing down your neck, it pays to be prepared and practiced.

7

TWO, CLOSE TO DEATH

One can only guess at the pain and suffering he experienced at the paws and jaws of North America's nastiest customer.

Most of my early moose, caribou and sheep chasing in the late 1960s took place in south central Alaska's Gunsight Mountain area. Gunsight Mountain Lodge was Whitey Faessler's big game guiding base and a favorite place to stop. One of the first bear mauling stories I heard about in those days was the one I encountered at Whitey's lodge.

As I recall, there was a grizzly rug hanging from a wall in the dining area beside which was a newspaper clipping about the bear, its history and demise. Whitey Faessler tracked down the rogue bear from the air, landed and killed it after it fatally injured his friend Lloyd "Penny" Pennington.

Penny flew commercially out of his Snowshoe Lake hunting and fishing lodge, a couple of dozen miles east of Gunsight Mountain Lodge at Mile 147 on the Glenn Highway. A top-notch guy from the old school of guides and outfitters, he made his living hauling people and materials into the bush in his airplane–either to hunt, fish or prospect. (my first book briefly mentions this tale)

Lloyd had a run in with a big grizzly in 1952. It was the kind of event that any outdoorsman could have had. The end result was pretty satisfactory to the men involved, although the outcome could have gone the bear's way under different circumstances.

Penny'd spent the summer hauling fire fighters, fishermen and prospectors all about his neck of the woods in his plane. Activities didn't slow down much as early September witnessed his dropping off and picking up moose and caribou hunters and their game. Most of them were from Anchorage.

One day Penny invited his stepson Chet to ride along as he flew out to check his hunters. Penny spotted a large grizzly protecting its food cache, probably a moose gut pile. He decided to have a crack at the bear and landed on a nearby lake in his float-equipped plane. Penny and Chet's rifles were a .30-06 and a .300 magnum and powerful enough medicine to stop a grizzly. Leaving the aircraft several hundred yards from the bear cache, they split up 5 to 7-yards apart and stealthily crept through the brush toward the bear and its prize.

As they drew nearer the cache, the grizzly suddenly erupted from the brush, surprising the men because it had actually come to meet them. With lips curled back and teeth popping, it charged Chet. He got his rifle to his shoulder but was so rattled that he kept trying to engage his weapon's safety. In the moments that it took the animal to close on his enemy, Penny instantly jumped into the action and calmly dropped the bear within 15-feet of his stepson.

Fortunately Chet was not alone that day...or the score would have been bear 1, man 0.

Four years later Penny had yet another encounter with a grizzly, but this one did not end in favor of the two-leggeds.

The previous fall he had spotted an outsized grizzly preparing to den up for the winter on a hillside near Snowshoe Lake. Penny made a mental note and planned to revisit the site in the spring to hunt the bear when it left the den. Usually a bear hangs around its den a few days just prior to denning in the winter or emerging in the spring. Knowing that it was just a matter of time before the bear left its den, Penny monitored the area from the sky, watching for signs of its activity.

One day Penny flew treetop high and discovered that the bear was out and about, feeding on the soft bark from a nearby aspen patch. Since a hunter from Anchorage had indicated a desire to shoot a bear, Penny got word to him.

A short time later Everett A. Kendall, a barber from a military base in town, showed up. They climbed into Penny's plane, flew out and landed on an ice-covered lake about a mile from the bear den.

In the flying business it's a good idea for the pilot-guide to let his staff know his flight plan. Penny had told his flying partner Rick Houston where they would be hunting, so when they failed to return by the end of the day, Rick boarded his plane to check on them.

Before long he spotted Penny's plane parked on the ice, and he flew over the hill and the bear den and observed a tragic scene. Penny and Everett were lying prone near the mouth of the den but some distance apart. Both men were dead and there was no sign of the bear.

Rick returned to Snowshoe Lake for assistance and backup. Guide Whitey Faessler went back to the site of the mauling with Rick and they inspected it. They discovered that Penny and Kendall had stopped to smoke cigarettes. The frozen snow allowed them to travel on the surface and would simplify their stalk, so they had left their snowshoes leaning against a tree.

When they reached the attack area and examined the evidence, Rick and Whitey surmised that the bear had rushed Penny from behind. The bear bit through the base of his skull killing him instantly. The bolt of his Model 70 .300 H&H Magnum was partly open and it had not been fired. They weren't sure whether Penny tried to chamber a round or the bear's action threw the bolt open.

Not far away from Penny lay the body of his client. Kendall's .375 H&H Magnum was empty. He had shot every round at the charging animal at point blank range, missing it every time but for one shot in the foot. The mangled body of the barber lay near his rifle. One can only guess at the pain and suffering he experienced at the paws and jaws of North America's nastiest customer.

The Good Samaritans observed the bear's tracks leading away from its den for parts unknown. They returned to the plane, took off and followed the animal's tracks in the snow for 30-miles.

Two days later four men went on a mission to end the bear's life and to avenge the deaths of Everett Kendall and Lloyd Pennington. They flew in two airplanes following the bear's tracks, assuming that they'd find the critter wearing the tracks when they got close enough. And they did. One of the planes circled low over the bear at one point, and he reared up and swiped at it with a large paw. The men landed and moved in on the grizzly.

He was not one to await his execution and roared loudly as he launched into his attack mode. If you've never heard a wounded or angry grizzly bear roar, a sound that seems to shake the earth, you've missed one of nature's scariest sounds. And to see an enraged grizzly charging toward you at 40-miles-per-hour, covering 15 to 20-feet per bound and knocking over everything in its path, is a sight to chill the very blood in your veins. No doubt, that's how Kendall had felt when the bear closed the gap between them prior to his death.

The four men facing the bear's charge were Whittey Faessler, Joe Leland, Stanley Frederickson and Glenn Griffin. They did not shirk their duty but stood tall in the face of the attacking brute. They killed it and discovered that it was eight feet from tip of nose to tip of tail.

Whitey said that "Penny was one of the most experienced bear hunters I have ever known but this proved to be the last hunt for him."

This is just one more example of a bear's determination taking precedence over man's experience–such animal's stealth and cunning can bring it within striking distance of his adversary before the man can react, where death may be the result.

Sometimes a cunning animal causes death; sometimes death results from man's cunning plan gone awry.

8

A BAD MISTAKE

*The searchers discovered fragments of bone–skull, pelvic
and thigh bones–and realized that they were Slim's remains.*

Years ago I read a very tragic and sad story in an outdoor
magazine. It involved a man and a set gun. Although I'm not
sure if the story from *Grizzly Country* involved the same man
and gun, I've rewritten it to share with you here.

Trapper Slim Lynch lived roughly thirty miles
west of Yarrow valley on lower Kishaneena Creek and worked
the North Fork of the Flathead River near the International
Boundary.

His Canadian line cabin was right in the middle of beaver
country ten miles up the Kishaneena. As he busily harvested beaver
pelts and tossed the carcasses into the nearby woods, he didn't give
much thought to the fact that he was providing a powerful temptation for a grizzly. The fat-rich flesh of the beaver is "music to the
ears" of a grizzly and Slim's disposing of the carcasses did not require
a second invitation for any silvertip in the neighborhood. Within a
short period of time a grizzly came calling, and quickly became
emboldened and less fearful of the trapper.

Perhaps that's the reason that Slim began packing a pistol. He
was not able to stay at his cabin to secure it while on his trap line
and no doubt he was concerned about the bear. Maybe it would
make short work of his beaver hides in his absence. After a while
Slim decided to take them to his home cabin on the Flathead, so he
bundled them up and hauled them out.

When he reached the home of his foster parents Mr. and Mrs.
Beebe and their three adult sons, Slim told them about the

unwanted grizzly and hinted of his plan to eliminate the problem with a set gun.

The set gun was a reliable means of ridding a pest. The concept was to lash said weapon to a solid position and devise a trip wire or string attached to bait. The bait was positioned in front of the muzzle. The string passed over the trigger, usually to a nail or bolt in the butt of the weapon and then forward to the bait. Another means was to tie the string to the trigger or anchor it to a nail on either side of the butt, run it over the trigger face and back to the nail, then forward to the bait. The weapon's muzzle rested on a crossbar just aft of the bait.

The mechanical action called for the victim to discover and to tug on the bait, triggering the weapon and causing the firing pin to drop on a cap, discharging the weapon.

To increase the effectiveness of the plan, the gun was usually placed at the rear of a "pen" which was built in a V-shape and consisted of a "wall" of logs on either side that directed the victim toward the bait. At the apex of the V the gun was firmly tied, pointing toward the opening through which the critter of destruction made its way.

A twelve-gauge shotgun was a very effective weapon for this purpose, though some men found a pistol adequate for the job. In this case, for whatever reason, Slim chose to use his Luger semi-automatic pistol.

After Slim finished his work on the set and secured the weapon, he attached a piece of beaver meat as bait and cocked the weapon. Then he retired to his cabin for the evening. All that remained was for the trespasser to arrive and shoot itself while yanking on the bait.

During the night the crack of his Luger awakened Slim. Delighted that his plan had worked, he was eager to discover its success. Even though the area before his cabin was bathed in moonlight, Slim saw nothing out of the ordinary. He cautiously slipped outside in his moccasins and discovered that the pistol had been moved somewhat in the triggering. Apparently the shot was high and missed the mark.

Anticipating the bear's return and eager to reset the gun, Slim made a bad mistake. Forgetting to set the gun on safety, he adjusted another bait, triggered the semi-automatic and shot himself. The stabbing yellow-orange flame licked out at him, slamming the cupronickel-jacketed bullet into his abdomen. The bullet passed through him and exited beneath a shoulder blade.

For all intents and purposes he was dead, however death lingered until he reached his cabin and collapsed onto his bunk.

For many years the story of a man-killing grizzly made the rounds of the locals. They thought that the beaver eating grizzly had returned, struck Slim's blood trail, followed it to the cabin, killed and consumed the trapper.

Andy Russell learned the true story forty years after the event.

In 1912 Slim Lynch died, but it wasn't until 1952 that Russell heard his friend Charlie's version of the incident. While engaged in guiding some geologists in British Columbia's headwaters of the Flathead River, Andy met Charlie Wise, who was then 70-years old, still trapping and the epitome of good health.

According to Charlie, at the time of Slim's accident a heavy downpour lasted several days. The Kishaneena and other creeks overflowed their banks as a result of the rain and the melting snow and fed into the Flathead, causing a flood that curtailed navigation.

Slim's failure to return didn't strike much of a note of concern for the Beebes because they understood that travel was out of the question until the waters receded.

When the water finally dropped and Slim failed to show up, concern mounted and friends went to his trapping cabin to check on him. One of the members of the group was Charlie Wise.

Searching from horseback, the party had some difficulty fording streams but eventually reached Slim's cabin. When they saw no smoke coming from his chimney, they knew that something was amiss. The door was ajar and the odor of death hung in the air.

The inside of the cabin was a shambles. Debris cluttered the dwelling's entrance. The searchers discovered fragments of bone–skull, pelvic and thigh bones–and realized that they were Slim's remains. A dark-stained wool undershirt revealed a bullet hole ranging from front to back. Two bullets were missing from the pistol and two empty shell casings lay on the ground near the pistol, indicating that the weapon had been fired twice. The story unfolded as the group pieced together the evidence.

Slim had reported a grizzly near his cabin on his last visit, but all bear signs had been washed away by the rain and high water. They did find some fresh black bear tracks, however and it appeared as though Slim had died and that an opportunistic blackie, not a grizzly, happened onto his body.

As Charlie Wise indicated, the trapper was the victim of his own hand. The grizzly had been falsely accused.

Grizzlies of the Old West were not only falsely accused, but they were also captured with ropes to provide sport for man.

9

BEAR AND BULL
FIGHTS

*As soon as the bull spotted bruin, the horned one zeroed in
on the clawed one, like a heat-seeking Sidewinder missile.*

Whenever I've read about grizzlies doing battle, I've been
amazed at their strength, speed and style. Although the
accounts about bears and bulls have been both incredible
and informative, it's disappointing to learn that people have
made sport of the animal's nature by pitting it against other
creatures.

In the early days of Spanish California bear and bull
fighting was staged. As early as 1816, a fight was held in
Monterey. Later, settlements presented these events, either in an
amphitheater, the town plaza or a fenced arena. Either the townspeople had little other entertainment or the excitement of the
battling brutes was too much to pass up because spectators included
men, women and children. Often people watched the event from
balconies along the town's street. Some arenas housed bleachers
behind the fence from which women and children sat and watched.

"Having given a number of hours to prayer and religious rituals,
the people were ready and eager for the noise and thrills of a holiday.
Nothing satisfied their appetite for excitement better than to
unleash a bear against a bull." The fight became the subject of conversation in the area for months.

No doubt, the fight was enjoyed by the human spectators more
so than by the combatants.

One such event featuring the grizzly General Scott, valued at
$1,500, drew miners clad in red, white and blue, their shiny

revolvers and Bowie knives hanging from their sides. Women wore white dresses and red and blue French bonnets. Brightly colored Mexican blankets were in abundance.

A bear-bull fight in the open, however, was different from one in a public arena. Staging such an event involved vaqueros riding out, killing a beef and dragging it around a meadow (to disperse its scent), where they left it for a bear to find while they retired to a nearby cabin or place of repose. When a scout observed an approaching bruin, he roused his compadres and they rode to the scene, encompassing the meadow and converging on the "trapped" bear. The cowboys then lassoed the bruin and tied it securely to a tree until they could rope and return with a bull. The punchers then led the bull into the meadow, released it and the bear, encircled the "arena" and watched the fight.

Obviously the horsemen had gotten exceedingly bored on the cattle range. Or having become quite adept in their roping skills, perhaps they had found roping a grizzly great sport. On the other hand, selling a live grizzly for a bear-bull fight was a lucrative enterprise, both to the seller and the new owner (who charged an admittance fee at staged settlement fights).

Although the process of acquiring a bull and a bear took some very brave horsemen and involved no little effort or risk, the saddle pounders rode out as if going to fetch a Christmas goose.

Mortal enemies, neither the bull nor the bear held much love for the other.

The bulls were thick necked, lithe and agile Spanish animals, with sharp horns and quick hooves. These bad tempered, range animals were a combination of weight and speed, always fearless and ready for a fight–they'd as soon charge 100 men as one. One man stated that the bull was "the noblest game in America, with possibly the single exception of the...California grizzly."

The bears, too, were wild beasts. The means of acquiring a wild bear that roamed the adjacent country varied. Sometimes riders baited it with a dead beef into an open area from which they could throw their ropes, often at night. At other times the cowboys rode out in daylight and surrounded a bear of their choice, then tossed their ropes–sometimes they found their quarry on beaches where the processing of whales by that industry attracted it.

Some roped bears sought reprisal by grasping the rope in their paws and pulling the rope paw over paw, reeling in the rider. Since the rope was tied off to the saddle horn, the pulling bear dragged the relenting horse and cowpoke toward itself (more than one person witnessed an outsize grizzly simultaneously dragging as many as two horses and riders several yards in spite of the contrary efforts by horses and riders). Vaqueros and horses were often toppled onto their sides or saddles ripped from their mounts. Sometimes the cowboys greased their reatas so a bear had more difficulty gripping them.

One means of transporting the bear was to place him in a cage on wheels, a cart so designed to accommodate a grizzly. Sometimes the bear was lashed to a cart without bars. Some captors gave the animal water to keep it refreshed.

Over time the producers of the event developed a couple of methods for keeping the bear on scene. A bear's hind leg was tethered to a post in the center of the arena, maybe a leather thong 20-30 yards long. Another method involved tethering the hind leg of the bear to a fore-ankle of the bull (this kept the animals closer together and discouraged the bear from climbing the walls to get to the excited crowd).

When the bull was thrust into the arena, it usually looked for something to attack, often attempting to get at the men on horse-back on the opposite side of the fence. Meanwhile the bear normally crouched and watched every move the bull made, awaiting his opportunity to dismantle the range bovine. It was common for the bear to rise on hind legs to face the bull.

Once the event began, clouds of dust filled the air accompanied by the rising shouts and cheers of the excited audience. One thing these sanguine bear-bull fights depict is that the Romans had nothing on us.

However as more Americans settled in the West and their disgust for bear-bull fights rose, the "sport" became an endangered species. The rising disdain resulted in less attendance, and, thus, a loss of revenue. Before long it became more difficult to find fighting bears. Records indicate that fights were staged as late as 1881, however in time they ceased altogether. And it was just a matter of time before the bear-bull fights no longer filled fighting arenas but rather the pages of history.

Major Horace Bell recorded an interesting bear-bull fight and describes the last one of which he was aware. It took place at Pala at a branch of the Mission San Luis Rey in the San Diego County mountains. I've summarized that account below.

A mission lay in the shadow of 6,000-foot Palomar Mountain. On the site of the religious grounds was an adobe-walled quadrangle. At the center a huge, permanently anchored post stuck a yard or so out of the ground. To this post was tethered a grizzly bear which had previously roamed the pine-clad shoulders of the nearby mountain.

On four legs the silvertip stood nearly as tall as a horse. It was the very epitome of fury. The bear's hind feet were secured by a rawhide reata, one leg on each end a yard apart, to allow for movement. A doubled reata ran from the center of that tether to and around the post. Whenever the animal tried to chew on the tether, a man on horseback prodded it in an effort to dissuade the grizzly's chewing.

The bear ambled about the arena, nervously eyeing the crowd. Just about then a long-horned bull was unleashed into the compound. This bull had roamed the surrounding hills since birth–it had acquired strength and the necessary survival training to avoid death by a grizzly or any other critter. It was the essence of great weight and power.

As soon as the bull hit the arena, he dashed about, tossing his head from side to side, up and down, eyes darting about for someone or something to attack. He was as quick and wild as any whitetail deer. The anchored bear and free wheeling bull came from the same region and were old but distant acquaintances–in their wild woodlands the bull never allowed the bear to get close enough to inflict damage.

As soon as the bull spotted bruin, the horned one zeroed in on the clawed one, like a heat-seeking, Sidewinder missile.

With the bull's rush, the bear rose on hind legs and awaited the impact. He raised his paws to either side of the bull's head, and just as the bull rammed its head toward his body, the grizzly swung downward onto the horns until, in the blink of an eye, they went from horizontal to perpendicular and back around to horizontal. Instantly the bear regained his feet, but the bull lay limp on the ground with a broken neck.

Four horsemen rode in, lassoed the bull's legs and dragged it from the arena.

Hardly had they exited one gate when another bull spun into the madness. This big, black bovine pranced in with tail arced aloft and charged around the arena much the same as the first one had. His horns were so long that a spectator might wonder whether the bear would be able to reach the bull's head without being impaled when the animals closed.

A grizzly that has made a living from eating cattle would not likely be concerned about facing a wild range bull such as met his gaze.

This bull launched itself toward the shaggy silvertip. When the bull thrust at the grizzly, the bruin sidestepped and smashed a huge paw onto the bull's neck. The resulting *whack* could be heard throughout the arena–a blow so strong that, coupled with the bull's weight and momentum, a horn snapped when it stabbed into the ground.

The bull quickly rose out of the bear's reach and twisted around with lightning like speed. The bear rushed toward the bull but was yanked off balance when he reached the end of his tether. Before bruin could recover, the bull spun around and charged, ramming its remaining horn into the bear's shoulder.

Its thrust was not sufficient because it lacked the speed and momentum to penetrate the bear's shoulder, the horn merely glancing off the scapula, ripping a gash in the hide and further angering the bear. Bruin then reached for the bull's head but the reata's shortness again kept him from contacting his foe.

Meanwhile the bull turned and charged instantly, aiming his horn at the middle of the bear's chest. Just as the bull reached the grizzly, the bruin grabbed the bull's head with both paws and twisted it halfway around, the bull's nose turning inward. Bruin chomped onto the bull's nose with his teeth and both animals went down in a cloud of dust amidst the roar of the crowd.

Although he rose more slowly this time, the bear rose. The bull didn't. Another victim of a broken neck.

The bear's owners wanted to stop the show. However roars from the crowd of *"Otro! Otro! Otro toro!"* (Another! Another! Another bull!") rang across the arena. The owners protested because of the bear's injury and weakened condition, but it was to no avail. The crowd wanted more.

Before long another bellowing bull shot onto the battlefield. He was larger, thinner, faster and rangier than the first two. At that point the bear was probably more harried than the office worker who'd spent countless hours in overtime and wanted to go home at the end of a very long day. On seeing the bull, he no doubt thought, *That's a fine how-do-you-do!*

Thundering onto the scene in the same manner as his predecessors, tossing his head and tail flagged erect, this bull zeroed in on the bear and lunged toward it.

Slowed from his previous activity, the bear gained an erect posture later than anticipated and not before a sharp horn sliced through his skin at the base of his neck. Simultaneously bruin's powerful paws clasped the bull's neck. An echoing *crack* filled the air and both brutes slumped to the ground, the bull's momentum carrying the bear over backward against the tethering post.

The bear rose more slowly than before and appeared a little more exhausted. Riders removed the third dead bull while the bruin's owners discussed removing him to his cage. But the crowd crowed for yet another bull, knowing that one remained, the largest, most powerful and wildest of the lot.

Wanting to give the bear a better fighting chance, horsemen rode in and lassoed his forepaws to spread him out while two men loosened his tether rope, allowing him more play. The extra time provided bruin some rest and recuperation. Their work on Mr. Griz Lee completed, the men released the final bull into the arena.

He appeared to be another old acquaintance of the bear's and immediately trotted toward the silvertip. In a scant half dozen jumps he'd closed the distance. With head lowered and horn pointed at the chest of the bear the bull came on.

The grizzly met the challenge, though he rose on hind feet much more slowly than all previous times. His right paw slipped when he grabbed the bull's head. He was unable to twist the neck as he had done before. The bull's horn speared him near the base of the neck and both animals rolled over as one.

Cheers of appreciation rose from the crowd. Blood oozed from his neck wound that was near the first one. When the bull reached his hooves still another cheer rose to fill the air, louder than before.

The bull whipped his sides with his tail and lunged toward the bear.

Bruin rolled into a ball and popped up, but one foot caught in the reata and prevented him from gaining his feet and the necessary balance required to meet the bull's challenge. The bear fell forward as the bull's horn plunged dead center of bruin's chest, up to the hilt.

As quickly as he'd pierced the bear's heart, Mr. Range Bull withdrew his horn and thrust at the grizzly again.

While the bear struggled to his feet, blood gushed from his wound. He turned to face the bull. But he never made it. The bull's horn struck just forward of his shoulder bone and plunged its entire length. That final blow released Old Ephraim forever from his pain and his prison.

Although the bulls were too much for this imprisoned grizzly, bears have provided sufficient pain with their weaponry to imprison more than one person.

Tree Climbing

"Many adult grizzlies can climb trees by lunging up a lower limbless trunk, by climbing on strong limbs, or by hugging the tree."

"I continued to scale the tree about 35 feet...Scared half to death in excruciating pain, I watched the griz climb the tree."

"...he climbed at least 20 feet. The bear climbed Mark's tree, grabbed his ankle with its mouth, and pulled Mark from the tree...Adam had climbed over 20 feet and felt he was safe...the next thing Adam knew, the bear was coming up between his ankles."

–Excerpts from: *Bear Attacks, The Deadly Truth*, chapter 7, Gary Shelton

10

HE TALKED
TO THE BEAR

He didn't know where he was, how he got there,
what his circumstance was or remember shooting the bear.

Growing up, I could never get enough adventure. When I was not out on the Snake River swimming, fishing, boating or water skiing...or on the breaks of the river hunting chukar, Hungarian partridge or mule deer...or wandering the aqueduct behind Clarkston, Washington, wearing out the skyways with errant birdshot intended to hit Chinese ring-neck pheasants or those beautiful, rocketing, green headed mallards, I was reading *Alaska Sportsman* or *Outdoor Life* magazines and living the adventure from the armchair.

During those reading stints it was my pleasure to discover Ben East. I never had a clue then that some day I would chronicle similar adventures. Hopefully you will enjoy these tales as much as those penned by the master outdoor writers like East, Jack O'Connor (I grew up across the river from him) and Andy Russell.

I've rewritten a Ben East story that has always fascinated me because a man refused to quit and admitted that he made a mistake.

W hen the ice in the Yukon River went out in the spring of 1950, the Pitka family followed it. Every year they journeyed from their home in Kaltag, Alaska (400 miles upstream from the mouth) to their summer fish camp. Alexie Pitka and his wife and two teen-aged daughters made the 22-mile trip down river to the mouth of the Khotol River, understandably called 22-Mile Camp.

Since the local Athapascan Indians depended on nature for the bulk of their food provisions, the family's annual activities included hunting, fishing, trapping and berry gathering. Moving down river enabled them to fish more effectively. A couple of other families from the village also stayed in the few cabins there and fished. Their main method of fishing was through the use of fish wheels–four paddles with built in "nets" and catch boxes spoked from an axle spun continually by the river's current–which scooped up fish as they swam upstream.

Other wildlife such as moose, bear, ducks, geese and muskrats were abundant in the area and provided table fare.

The Khotol, called Kaiyuh Slough by the Indians, is a sleepy river less than a hundred yards across that winds miles through swampy slough-like flats. Its headwaters are in the Kaiyuh Mountains northeast of 22-Mile Camp. On either side of the Slough numerous shallow lakes drain into it. During the summer the lakes dry up somewhat and form open marshes, which the Indians call grass lakes.

Usually every morning Alexie paddled up the Slough, left the canoe, hiked to a grass lake and hunted small game. A life-long hunter, Alexie was a 65-year-old Indian having killed ten black bears.

He used a .30-30 Savage rifle, powerful enough to stop a black bear and, hopefully, a grizzly should one give him a problem.

Several mornings in a row Alexie had spotted a bear at the same spot about ten miles upstream from camp. He never approached within a half mile of the animal and thought the bear a small grizzly. Interestingly enough, Alexie always felt that the animal knew he was in the vicinity and was wary of him.

The culture of many peoples includes a reverence for nature and its inhabitants and a belief that the animal has a spirit bond with humans. Traditionally Indian people made offerings to the bear's spirit after harvesting it. In some areas of Canada and Alaska people left part of a front leg in a bark box attached to a tree to show their sorrow for killing the animal. Part of that culture and the reverence for the animal includes talking to it.

Since he'd never shot a grizzly and because they could use the meat, Alexie decided to hunt the bear if he saw it again.

The morning of Friday, June 2, 1950 Alexie hunted his way up the Slough. It was suppertime when he reached the bear's locale. Rounding a bend in the waterway Alexie spotted the animal at the far end of the grass lake.

He paddled upstream another mile in order to approach the bear more closely and provide cover for his stalk. Paddling as stealthily as possible, he reached a point where he left his craft on the bank to begin his stalk. Even though the bear had moved and was still a half-mile away, Alexie began crawling through the brush.

He approached within 200 yards of the animal before he ran out of cover. He was surprised to discover that the bear was not a grizzly after all, but rather a large black bear.

He wasn't too keen about shooting that distance without a scope on the old .30-30. However something ate at him, a feeling that if he didn't kill the bear, it would create a problem for him later. He figured he'd not get a better opportunity.

Lying prone in the bushes, he leveled his rifle. The bear stood broadside to him as he took careful aim through the iron sights. Holding his open sights at the top of the bear's shoulder, he fired.

The bear dropped and lay motionless, apparently a one shot kill. Alexie assumed that he'd hit it behind the upper front leg and that the bullet had opened up inside the body, resulting in death from internal bleeding. Even though he believed he had killed the animal in its tracks, he waited a full minute before firing a second shot over the bear's head to assure himself of its demise.

It didn't move and Alexie started for it. For reasons unknown to him he departed from his habit of approaching dead game with his rifle at the ready. Perhaps his eagerness to stick the animal over-powered his good judgement. He leaned his weapon against some brush and approached the bear with only the knife hanging from his belt.

Every time he stopped to listen and watch, the bear lay on its side appearing lifeless. Covering the last twenty steps, he was confident it was dead.

Alexie was within ten feet of the beast when it rolled to its feet and lunged for him. Instantly he turned and fled for his rifle. No man can outrun a bear in such a scenario and within a couple of jumps the bear was on him.

A blow from the bear knocked him senseless and the lights went out for him.

He gradually regained consciousness as though awakening from a sound sleep, unable to completely wake up. He couldn't decide whether the brute hit him in the head, his back or his shoulders.

He knew that something big stood over him. He felt shaggy hair on his arms and smelled something sickeningly foul. He didn't know where he was, how he got there, what his circumstance was or remember shooting the bear. It took some time for his head to clear. Then he remembered what had happened before the bear jumped him.

He lay flat on his back with the bear straddling him, the bear's hind legs on either side of his and its front legs outside his shoulders. They were face to face, no less than a foot apart. The bear stared into what was formerly Alexie's face.

At first Alexie felt no pain. Within moments of regaining consciousness, he blacked out again. He didn't know how long he was unconscious but when he came to the second time, the bear was still staring at him.

Maybe I can crawl from between its legs. But if I do, the movement may trigger another attack.

The bear just stood over him, making no sounds, only breathing its foul breath onto him.

I wonder how bad I'm hurt? Maybe the bear's waiting for me to move so it can pounce on me like a cat would a mouse. Maybe it thinks I'm dead because I'm not moving. How can I get away from it?

At length Alexie remembered his belt knife. The skinning knife had a 4-inch blade. He wasn't sure how badly he was hurt, how much blood he'd lost, how he'd manage to return to his canoe nor how much time he had before his chances of survival vanished. *Maybe I can get my knife and finish off the bear. If I stab it, maybe it will kill me. It's my only chance at the moment.*

He slowly moved his hand toward the knife until he touched the handle. *So far, so good. The bear hasn't moved.* Removing the weapon from its sheath, Alexie pointed the blade upward and thrust it into the bear's belly with all the power he could muster.

The animal made no noticeable sound, movement or facial expression. *It's standing there like a fur-covered, soft statue.* Again and again Alexie thrust the blade into the animal's bloody fur.

Alexie wasn't sure how many times he lost consciousness, but every time he came to, he stabbed the bear more. It never showed signs of pain. Its blood geysered onto him like warm sticky water and he wondered if he'd choke from it.

Recalling his ancestral heritage, Alexie considered talking to the bear. It might be the bear would hear his request. "Go away. I won't hurt you any more if you go away." Then he blacked out again.

When he regained consciousness, the animal was gone. He heard the bear moving off into the alders, bellering an almost human heart-rending cry of suffering mixed with rage. It was the first sound Alexie had heard from the bear.

He spoke to it again, "I know I got you."

Alexie tried to get up. He couldn't see anything out of his right eye and very little from his left. Unable to rise, he reached a hand to his face...*my face is gone...it's just bloody pulp.* Indescribable pain erupted in his head and panic rocked his body.

How can I find my way to the canoe if I can't see? No one expects me to return tonight. No one will miss me until tomorrow night. If someone comes for me and finds the canoe, they won't know which way I went. I'll probably die before they find me.

Alexie was at a loss to know how long the mauling lasted, how long the bear stood over him and how long he lay on the ground lapsing into and out of consciousness. He later guessed it was less than half an hour though it seemed like hours at the time.

With pain increasing in his head he blacked out again. When he came to, he felt somewhat stronger and determined to save himself.

Uncertain that he could maneuver the half mile of grass lake and unable to see, he was concerned that he wouldn't find his way.

My face is a mangled mess, but my arms and legs seem okay. I can see a blur of light through my left eye. Maybe I can find my way. Alexie prayed, then started crawling.

Although he lost track of time, he thought the bear had left him somewhere around 8 p.m. In the month of June darkness at night is rare in the northern climes. There is a smidgen of dusk for half an hour each night for a week or so at the height of the summer solstice. His survival crawl began late that night.

Pushing with his knees, digging in his elbows and pulling with them resulted in little progress, but it was movement toward salvation. Within a short distance he was exhausted and sank into the damp grass. *I won't give up.*

He prayed. Then, wiggling like a snake, he slowly slithered forward. Every few feet he stopped to rest. Sometimes he had enough strength to rise to his hands and knees and travel that way.

He continued to lose consciousness, regain it and move forward.

At length he reached the edge of the grass lake that was bordered by thick brush. Alder and willow bushes covered the distance between him and his canoe. He knew this would be his most difficult obstacle.

He rested. Wiping the blood from his left eye, he waited for it to clear somewhat so that he could discern his pathway. Then he pushed on into the alders.

Stopping often to pray and to encourage himself audibly, he kept moving in what he hoped was the proper direction.

At one point he observed a bit of darkness and felt the chill of the night. *Must be around midnight.* He refused to give up and kept crawling, fighting through the tangles. For hours he struggled on, each move covering less than the length of his body before stopping to rest. *It seems like I'm resting more than moving.*

Hammering pain in his head never ceased.

The crawl was total torture, physically and mentally.

Saturday morning Alexie finally came to an opening and discovered he'd reached the shore of the Slough. It had taken him a dozen hours to cover the half-mile.

Even though he had not found the canoe, he was too exhausted to care. He collapsed onto his belly and slept. The entire day passed while he lay there, more dead than alive.

During the brightest part of the day, he managed to force himself onto his elbows to look around. He could see enough to make out blurred outlines of brush. He looked downstream but failed to see the canoe. Next he looked upstream. He saw the outline of something. *I can't be sure it's the canoe, but it may be.*

At that point he collapsed, too weak to attempt the crawl.

Clouds of mosquitoes swarmed around him and he felt the chill of the evening coming on. He fought the incessantly buzzing insects and tried to determine whether the object he'd seen upstream was the canoe.

He'd not eaten anything or had a drink since leaving camp Friday morning, two full days. In his canoe were a cup, bread, tea, smoked salmon and sugar. These proved powerful motivators for him.

If I'm going to make it, I've got to check out the object.

He rose onto his hands and knees but promptly fell onto his belly, too weak to hold himself up. The second time he tried brought the same results. Grasping grass in both hands, he pulled himself along, legs trailing behind, useless. He covered an inch at a time.

After agonizing hours he reached the blurry object and reached out to touch it. Glory! *It is the canoe.*

Feeling for the food box, Alexie reached over the side. He retrieved a piece of bread and a strip of salmon and pushed them toward his mouth.

But he had no mouth. He found only torn and swollen flesh, splintered bone and teeth hanging off to one side.

Trying desperately to drink, he grasped his cup and dipped it into the water. He placed the full cup to his face, attempting to find his mouth. Water ran down his chin and neck but none reached his throat.

Frustrated, he cried out, "Help me. Someone please come and help me! I haven't much time now."

Immersed in the agony of pain from his injury, hunger and thirst and plagued by the pesky mosquitoes, Alexie slithered into a mud hole seeking protection from the chill air of evening. He pulled his parka over his head to stave off the marauding mosquitoes but it was futile. Sleep escaped him.

Much later he felt the warmth of the sun bathing his body and he knew it was another day.

As he had expected, his wife Pauline and daughters Mary Rose and Edith, were not concerned when he failed to arrive in camp Saturday. They knew of his plans to hunt the bear if he saw it. It wasn't until Sunday morning when he hadn't returned that worry set in. By that Sunday evening Pauline was convinced something bad had befallen Alexie. She organized a search party.

She asked Big George Semaken, a Kaltag neighbor who was at the fish camp, to help. The Pitka family had a skiff and an outboard motor, as did George, however the outboards for both were in need of repairs. The only way to maneuver the skiffs was by manpower. George had a lighter, shorter boat for greater efficiency in the sloughs, aptly called a slough canoe. He chose it and took off up river while Pauline and Mary Rose followed in their skiff.

They left camp at 7 p.m. Sunday, determined to row into every lake along the way to search for Alexie.

Meantime Sunday breezed by for Alexie. He struggled unsuccessfully to get food and water into his throat. Although the pain in his head never diminished, he was able to sleep some. As he lay there feeling he'd been there for weeks, the chill of a third evening crept over him. *More cold; more mosquitoes. Will help come? Will they find me? Will it be too late?*

Alexie had matches for a fire but he lacked the energy to gather firewood so he looked upon the matches as useless. Wanting to alert his rescuers, he crawled up the bank and dangled his feet into the water, planning to splash them should help arrive–although important to him, it was an unnecessary act since they would see the canoe.

Hours later Alexie thought he heard something coming up the Slough. Ratcheting up his hearing, he listened intently but nothing came of it. *My ears are playing tricks on me.* Then he heard it. *Dip. Swish.* A paddle dug into the water and pulled a canoe over the surface.

Alexie raised up but could not see Big George driving himself forward with long strokes. Alexie fell back unconscious.

Then George was beside him, talking. Alexie thought he'd never heard a more wonderful sound. It was Monday morning, June 5 and 55-hours had elapsed since the bear had jumped him.

Following closely behind Big George were Alexie's wife and daughter. Mary Rose had rowed the skiff the ten miles.

Suddenly Alexie heard Pauline's startled cry, "What's wrong? What happened to you?"

Alexie warned, "Stay back. You'll be scared." Next he heard her gasp as she stood over him, looking at his mutilated face.

The right side of his face was torn away from his right eye across the nose and down to his chin. His eye was ripped from its socket and his nose sheared away, with only cartilage sticking out of the raw flesh where it should have been. Both cheeks were gone and his mouth was mangled, revealing only three front teeth in his jaw. All the others hung loose. The flap of flesh that had been his face, hung beneath his chin like a red beard.

No one ever knew how the bear inflicted the damage, but Alexie surmised it did so with a single swipe of the paw, hooking the skin and bone and peeling it like a banana.

Pauline dipped a cup of water and managed to trickle some into his throat. It was the first he'd had in three days and water never tasted so good. With the love of a wife she coddled the facial flesh and placed it where it should have been. Then she tore up a flour sack and secured it in place.

Big George, Pauline and Mary Rose lifted him into the Pitka skiff and the group began downstream. Mary rowed the skiff and Big George paddled his canoe. She drove the skiff with every ounce of energy she possessed, pushing the craft and the clock to get her father to safety.

Alexie remembered little of the voyage.

They reached their camp at 4 o'clock the next morning. Alexie's family did as much as possible to ease his pain and got him into bed. Big George went to work feverishly on his outboard. He was rewarded sooner than he expected with a purring motor.

Just in case Big George had more engine trouble, the group decided that he would run to Kaltag while Alexie waited in camp for help to return.

When George reached Kaltag, a call for help went out over short-wave radio.

Six hours after Big George had departed 22-Mile Camp, Alexie's family heard the deep throated throbbing of an inboard and knew that help was close at hand.

Alexie's son, Albert and a friend from Nulato, a village 37-miles upstream from Kaltag, had come with Big George in separate boats. As they turned into the beach, a small rescue plane arrived a short distance upstream exactly 72-hours after the bear had attacked Pitka.

The men, Pauline and Mary Rose maneuvered Alexie into Albert's boat and delivered him to the waiting plane. From there he was hastened 250 miles upstream to Tanana and the U.S. Public Health Service Hospital.

Doctors were amazed that Alexie had survived long enough to reach the hospital. Though the medical professionals stabilized him, he lay near death's door for days. They planned to send him to Seattle's Alaska Native Health Hospital when he was well enough to make the trip because he needed additional medical attention.

While recuperating, Alexie had a lot of time to think about the bear's reaction to his stabbing. He assumed the bear was dying on its feet—too sick and too weak to realize what Alexie was doing.

While he regained his strength at the hospital preparatory to his Seattle trip, his friends from Kaltag returned to the site of the mauling to retrieve his gear. They were amazed at the feat he had performed both in surviving the attack and in reaching his canoe. One friend said, "They couldn't kill you with an ax."

Near the scene of the attack Alexie's friends found the dead black bear. Another bear had taken over the carcass and moved it a short distance. They surmised it must have been a grizzly as it would have taken a large bear to move Alexie's huge black.

Even though the carcass was bloated and ripe, the Indians skinned it in hopes of learning where Alexie's bullet had gone. Probably due to the condition of the carcass, their efforts were unsuccessful. Three months after Alexie reached the Tanana hospital he was readied for travel to Seattle where he spent seven and a half months undergoing reconstruction of a new face. Six operations later he was finally permitted to step outside the doors of the hospital for the first time.

Alexie's length of time indoors was almost as painful to the outdoorsman as the bear mauling and attendant injuries. He was never so thankful to be outside and for what the doctor had done for him.

Alexie arrived in Kaltag where his entire home village welcomed him April 14, 1951. Although the German plastic surgeon had made him a new face, it was not one that the villagers recognized. However Alexie was so happy to be alive and back in his native land among friends, mountains and the mighty Yukon River that he wasn't much concerned about how he looked.

A couple of years later Alexie traveled by dog team with his son Albert to Unalakleet, a route he carried mail over years earlier. As mail carrier, he crossed Old Woman River, ascended a rough mountain pass, met the Unalakleet carrier, traded mailbags and returned to Kaltag.

On his trip with Albert the bright sun caused snow blindness in Alexie's good eye and he never fully recovered his sight. In his final years Alexie lamented his plight. He was unable to hunt and fish as he had when younger. His activities centered on feeding the dogs and light chores, and he rested often. He said, "I killed the bear, but I do not think I won much of a victory. I shall never get over the things he did to me. It would have been better if I had talked to him the first time I saw him, half a mile away, and said, 'Go away. If you do not hurt me, I will not hunt you.' Then maybe none of it would have happened."

Although bear attacks are not common, a man stands a better chance against bruin if armed—even a pocketknife increases the odds in man's favor.

Charging Brownie

"A charging brownie is one of the most dramatic and chilling spectacles nature has to offer. As often as not, bears start their attacks with no preliminary warning, and invariably at close range…A bear charges on all four feet, in great leaping bounds, very reminiscent of a huge, eager dog chasing a cat…On the several occasions I've faced charging brownies, I have never had time to get in more than one hastily aimed shot, and the only thing I've seen in my sights is blurred hair.

"During the years, I've seen so many bears do so many things that I take nothing for granted when hunting them. It's one of the many reasons my wife is not a widow."

–Ralph W. Young, "Brown Bears *Do* Attack,"
Outdoor Life, August 1959

11

TWO BEARS, TOO CLOSE

Every time the bear ripped into him,
her claws tore clothing, skin and flesh like paper.

For decades people in North America believed that black bears would not attack a human. And even if one did, it was meant as a bluff and would never culminate in an actual mauling. Longtime woodsman Art LeGault shared that belief. However within a five year span he found not one but two exceptions to that rule.

Berry picking usually requires only a picker and a pail. In August 1955 Arthur LeGault went wild raspberry picking. Black bears were common near his home. Only the day before Art's wife Eva observed a fair amount of bear sign while berrying a mile from their place. Their dog was excited enough to convince Eva that she was sharing the patch with a picker whose hair covered its entire body so she stopped picking for the day and returned home.

Probably Eva's experience the previous day in combination with the mood of those in the Upper Peninsula who were upset with recent black bear problems, contributed to Art's decision to take a rifle. He grabbed his Winchester .30-30 carbine, jammed some soft-point bullets into the magazine and tucked it under his arm as an equalizer should an occasion to use it arise.

Arthur was a 66-year-old pulpwood cutter.

He lived three miles northwest of Engadine, just off U.S. 2, and fifteen miles south of Newberry in the eastern end of the Upper Peninsula. He'd lived in the UP his entire life and started hunting when he was old enough to lug a firearm. He had hunted deer every year since adulthood and couldn't recall a season when he hadn't harvested one. Over that period of time he'd taken three black bears. Encountering a bear on this berry trip, much less shooting one, wasn't something he anticipated.

Once he reached the berry patch, he heard a noise that caused the hair on his neck to rise. He heard no other sound and assumed he'd flushed a ruffed grouse or similar large bird.

But the next instant, he heard a bawl and breaking brush. Something was coming his way in high gear. Then he caught a glimpse of a small black bear running into a clearing and making straight for him, bellowing on every jump.

Just then he noticed two big cubs clawing their way up a hemlock within a hundred feet of him. They looked to be about a hundred pounds each and not much smaller than their mother which was closing the distance between her and Art in great leaps.

LeGault assumed the sow would stop her charge when the cubs reached safety, but she never broke stride. As she pressed the attack, bellowing belligerently, he found it hard to believe that she was so intent on the attack. He figured she'd change her mind when she got close enough to see that he wouldn't be bluffed nor back down.

Art had no desire to shoot a bear, especially one with cubs, however to be on the safe side, he shouldered his Winchester and waited as long as he dared. In full charge 5-steps away, mouth open and roaring defiance she came on. Art touched off a round into her mouth that knocked her sprawling. She skidded to a stop, stone dead, just seven feet away.

With rubbery legs he approached the downed bear. He fingered the trigger and with the hammer back, prodded her with the gun's muzzle. She was well fed as evidenced by the fat that layered her body when dressed out later. But she weighed no more than 150-pounds.

Art thought that perhaps she was too young to know better than to attack him. He walked to the tree, observed that the cubs were large enough to fend for themselves and left them there.

One bear charge in a man's lifetime is pretty rare (unless he's a consummate outdoorsman in bear country). Because of that rarity, it seems a second attack would be nearly impossible. However Art was one of a gaggle of people charged more than once.

Five years later he meandered into the woods in search of an ax and hand hook that he and his son Bud had left during a heavy March snowfall. It was June 5, 1960, a warm Sunday afternoon and a nice day for a walk. Recovering the tools gave him an excuse to be out.

He wore a green and black plaid wool shirt over a light flannel one.

Driving his pickup truck down a gravel road a half mile from home, he parked and walked an old brush-choked logging road. Three-quarters of a mile later he crested a sandy ridge rising out of a swamp. The tools were just ahead on the skid road. As it turned out, he was also within 350 yards of the berry patch where he'd killed the bear in1955.

When the road swung to the right, Art looked out across the willow-grown flats below. He saw movement about eighty yards away. Looking more closely, he discovered a black bear sneaking through the willows straight toward him. He concluded it was a sow moving quietly from bush to bush and that she was stalking him.

Flashbacks of his earlier brush with the bawling black bear bounced around his brain. He was scared. He was no spring chicken at 71-years of age. Should this bear be as determined as the other one, what were his chances of surviving the attack?

A number of factors favored the bear. Art was weaponless. His heart condition limited him to minimal physical activity–he could perform only light lifting, work and exertion. Even a half-minute of extended effort caused him to breathe heavily. He knew he couldn't outrun the animal.

He turned immediately and began walking as fast as he could toward his truck. When he looked again, he couldn't see the bear. Hopeful he thought, *Maybe she's not interested in me after all.* But when he looked back, he knew that he was wrong. She hit the road behind him and was in full gallop.

Reminding himself to keep calm, he kept walking.

She let out a roar when she reached him and lunged toward him, clamping her teeth into his left thigh. She tried to pull him off his feet by wrenching on his leg. Knowing that allowing her to get at him in a prone position was a precursor to death, he stood erect and refused to fall.

Screaming, Art turned to face her and slugged her on the nose as hard as he could.

The bear released her grip on his leg and rose on hind legs. Snarling and snapping, she swung a forepaw at him.

Her claws caught the shoulder of his outer shirt and ripped the sleeve half away. LeGault felt claws rake his flesh. He looked at his arm and saw blood running down. Then he punched the bear on the snout again.

It was a real donnybrook, each combatant swinging and roaring at the other–the bear trying to pull the man down and the man trying to stay on his feet.

The bear growled, snorted and woofed in rage, constantly swatting with her paws and snapping her jaws. She was a well conditioned 250-pound bear with a hide that looked like sleek black satin.

Her next strategy was to pull Art toward her, perhaps so that she could reach him with her teeth. She rained several hay maker blows on him, but none was sufficient to break his neck or crush his skull.

Clawing at his face, arms and legs, she managed to reach around him a few times and to rip into his hips, shoulders and back.

Art maintained his balance while backing away, constantly raining blows anywhere he could on the bear's head. He also kept his hands up to protect his face.

On two occasions she got through his guard and clawed him around the face. The first time she ripped loose a flap of skin and flesh at the corner of his right eye, barely missing the socket. Her second effort loosened a couple of teeth and knocked one out.

Even though he'd always known that wild animals were strong, it was hard to conceive this animal's power. Art was amazed by the animal's strength. He wondered why she didn't just smack him with a single blow to end it all. She was definitely capable of it.

Every time the bear ripped into him, her claws tore clothing, skin and flesh like paper. Her blows were like the kick of a mule.

Committed to his demise, the bear never let up.

He failed to remember the final few moments of the battle. They'd fought several minutes and Art was exhausted. He thought he was about finished. His heart-condition and short-windedness had taken their toll. He now fought blacking out.

He refused to give up because he knew that should he fall, the bear would be all over him, finishing him in an instant. Even though he harbored the thought that the bear would win in the end, he determined to fight her as long as he had breath.

Now his vision blurred and he realized his exhaustion was causing visual problems. He could hardly see the bear. Feeling the end was near, he stumbled against a tree and backed behind it for protection. His rest was short lived as the sow reached around it and clawed at him before he had a chance to catch his wind.

Every time she landed a blow, it jolted him, but he never felt any pain throughout the ordeal. By now his shirt hung in ribbons, his pants were ripped and his body–arms, face, buttocks and legs–streamed blood.

Art was about to give up when suddenly he remembered his pocketknife. It was an old, two-bladed tool. The larger 2-inch blade was worn down to a blunt point. It wasn't much of a weapon, but he reached for it.

When his hand went into his pocket, the bear raked his arm, slashing it to the bone, almost as if she had read his mind. But her action more than likely resulted from his momentarily lowering his guard and his arm.

With his knife in his hand, later unable to remember opening it, he jabbed her around the nose until he felt the blade stop against bone. That got her attention, and she didn't like it.

She dropped to all fours for the first time since the fight began. Then she glared up at Art, eyes as red as two hot coals.

The idea of stabbing her in the eye and blinding her was reason to be hopeful. He stabbed at her eye.

Unable to see that well, he didn't know how effective his aim was. However he felt the knife blade sink its full length into something soft. The eyes and nose are the only two places on a bear's head that are soft.

The bear flinched as though poked with a hot branding iron. She swerved away from him sideways and instantly vanished from his sight. He didn't see her leave and didn't know if she ran or walked. And he didn't know where she went.

None of that mattered as he was clinging to his fading strength. His only desire was to reach his pickup and get home *sans* bruin!

He immediately turned and tottered a few steps toward his truck. He looked back over his shoulder but she was nowhere in sight. After a few more faltering steps, he dropped in a heap onto the ground.

He rested a few minutes before he ratcheted up his courage, rose and began his trek. Art walked a little ways before stopping once more. He relaxed only briefly before rising to tackle the task again. He didn't want to sit long in one place because he was beginning to hurt all over. His arms and legs were on fire.

Even though his limbs grew heavier, his vision began clearing up with the frequent rest stops. Before long he'd reached his vehicle. But then he experienced another letdown.

When he reached for the truck keys in his pocket, he discovered that the pocket and his keys were gone. That meant an additional half-mile to cover to his place. The thought of it seemed impossible but he had no choice and pushed on.

Art finally reached home, a tattered man greeting his wife at the door. Blood oozed down his face and his hands. His clothes hung in ribbons. His mouth bled from the missing tooth.

Eva was frantic. Since he was winded from the fight and the hike, he couldn't explain the events of the past two hours. Before too much time passed, however, he was able to gasp that he'd had a run-in with a bear.

Their son Tom rushed him to a hospital at Newberry where a surgeon, Dr. R.P. Hicks, immediately went to work on him. The doctor found no evidence of internal injuries but concluded that Art was in a state of shock and total exhaustion. The deputy sheriff dropped by to interview Art, but he was still too tired to talk coherently.

Acknowledging his injuries, Hicks told LeGault that he was in real danger, not so much from the wounds but from the shock and exhaustion. He told Art that even at his age, his temperament and vigor were in his favor.

Five days later Art went home from the hospital, still in bad shape–his main hurdle now was enduring the stiffness and weakness which lasted for months. In time he was as good as new.

The Michigan Conservation Department's District Supervisor Ernest Ruecker contacted Tom Singleton and Arnold Norman, two experienced bear hunters with the best bear dogs in the area, to hunt down and destroy the troublesome bear.

It was late in the day and unfamiliar territory, so the men took their two best dogs to hunt the few hours till dark. Around 5:30 Singleton, Norman and Ruecker met at LeGault's. Two of Art's sons, Tom and Joe, guided the three others to the battlefield.

They had no trouble finding it as they discovered blood on the grass and ferns where Art had sat to rest after the attack.

Although it was man blood, the leashed dogs followed it, nosing from spot to spot and backtracking to the actual attack area. The men were amazed by the site they saw and marveled that a man, especially one Art's age, could fight off a determined black bear as he had done and survive. The ground was trampled and torn up worse than they'd anticipated. The entire area reeked of bear and the dogs went wild, lunging at their leashes in anticipation of the chase.

Singleton and Norman turned loose one dog. While it ran around sorting out the maze in an effort to find the freshest bear scent, the men inspected the area. They found a large yellow birch tree scarred with fresh claw marks the size that bear cubs would leave. They surmised that the bear had attacked Art at the point where he'd come closest to the treed cubs. They speculated that she had run the cubs up the tree then circled into the swamp in an effort to stalk him.

When they took the second dog to the tree, their theory was confirmed when they released it and it launched like a rocket into the forest. Their reasoning was that the sow had returned to the tree, fetched the cubs and retreated into the protection of the deeper woods.

The dogs ran back and forth across the ridge and through the swamp, never more than a quarter of a mile from the crest. The men theorized that the sow's latest strategy was to send the cubs up a tree for safe keeping while she successfully eluded the dogs in the swamp.

For two hours she crossed and re-crossed the ridge until darkness fell. Then the men's only choice was to gather their dogs and leave.

The next morning Art's sons Joe and Bud returned to the scene with Charles Vanderstar, a Michigan conservation officer from Naubinway. They found additional evidence of what had happened.

Beneath the birch tree where the cubs remained while their mother battled Art, the ferns and grass were broken over and speckled with blood, as if the sow bled from her eye wound while awaiting the cubs to hit the ground. Then the men followed scattered blood spots off the ridge. It was obviously bear blood since Art had never been closer than 100-feet from the birch and he had not left the ridge during the attack.

Although Art's theory was never proven, he always hoped that someone in the neighborhood would bring in a black bear missing one eye. He wanted to make sure that she was out of circulation and to know that he had blinded her.

The twenty-minute fight took place over a 150-200 foot long area, off to one side of the road. In places LeGault's deep footprints in the mud indicated that he had braced himself and shoved the bear away from him. But LeGault doesn't remember that. He recalled that he fought her the way he would fight another man in a brawl.

Even though it was likely that a third bear attack was impossible, to his dying day Art never went into the woods without a firearm.

Author's note:
I wonder if the sow he fought may have been a cub of the sow he shot?

Whether armed with a firearm or a loyal dog, man is wise to enter bear country prepared.

12

BUD'S FAITHFUL KENAI

A dismal snick whispered from the weapon.
His only hope now was to get into a tree and out of reach
of the bear's hay hook claws and mouth full of yellow ivory teeth.

I'm often amazed at the keen hearing of neighbor dogs. When I'm riding my mountain bike or walking out to our mailbox, they start barking at distances up to several hundred yards away when hearing the wheels or my feet on the gravel. If their hearing is that good, I wonder how good a bear's hearing is. A bruin's blinkers aren't so good but his sniffer and his listeners are phenomenal.

It was the first week in December before Bud Branham had time to get his traps out on his trap line. He was concerned by the delay but sometimes those things happen in Alaska when you're busy and it can't be helped. He would just have to work a little harder in hopes of recapturing some of his lost activity.

He kicked along on the sled behind his dog team en route to a trap line cabin where he would spend the night. When he reached his destination, what he discovered boiled his water.

A big brown/grizzly had smashed the windows and ripped off part of the cabin's roof. Mr. Brown Bear broke into the dwelling, destroying his bunk and sleeping bag. It flattened his sheet iron stove, bit into every can of food in the cabin and scattered flour, beans and rice all over the place. Not a can would serve as a pot in which to brew coffee. That was the last straw! Bud was angry enough to chew nails.

It seemed that his long time leader Kenai was as angry as his master. He stood in the trail and looked around as a low growl passed his lips. Kenai was like few dogs. Over the years he'd been the talk of Bud's headquarters at Rainy Pass Lodge. Visitors including hunters, fishermen and summer tourists had smothered the gentle dog with praise and petting. But he'd weathered it all and remained a good, unspoiled and sensible dog.

Kenai had proudly led and tutored the many MacKenzie River huskies in his team. He'd been a masterful leader, strong of will and body, lunging into the tug line when the musher commanded.

But as Kenai had reached older age at the front of the team, Bud was concerned when his favorite dog began ignoring his commands. Because a dog team's success hinges on the leadership of the front dog, Kenai's disobedience troubled Bud for several weeks before he discovered that Kenai was stone deaf.

At that point Bud was forced to make a heart-rending decision. It was obvious that he couldn't leave Kenai in the lead. But he didn't want to leave Kenai behind. Ultimately Bud was left no choice. He'd need to train a new leader. Leaving his favorite dog brought great anguish to both dog and master.

The first night that Bud took his dog team without Kenai, the lodge caretakers took him inside and tried to placate him. He whined and howled into the night, pacing back and forth. The next day at the first opportunity Kenai slipped out the door of the lodge and tore off down the trail after his master.

Several hours later when Kenai rushed up to him, Branham was so glad for the dog's faithfulness that he told him that he'd never leave his pal behind again. Bud decided to allow Kenai to be his loose leader.

And now at the line cabin, they stood side by side. Bud could see that he'd be delayed at least a day repairing his cabin. Considering the way things had gone, Bud wondered if the season would be over before he got started. He didn't like it. And he didn't like thinking about the bear that caused it.

While the team whined and wondered in their traces, Kenai stood with Bud and growled his dislike for the situation.

Even though Bud wanted to take a crack at the brown/grizzly, he could see that the tracks were old and he figured it had long since gone to bed for the winter.

Kenai moved along the old tracks growling then looked back to see if the chief was game to follow him. But Bud had to call Kenai and comfort him, letting him know that it was probably useless as the brownie had little to eat and had probably hibernated. Besides that it was late and darkness was falling.

Even though Kenai couldn't hear his words, he knew his master's meaning. The dog sat down and watched Bud unhitch the team and tether them for the night.

Bud went to work on his cabin and when it was complete, he and his dogs set out on the trap line. After several hours on the trail the dogs picked up speed as if rejuvenated. Bud wondered if they'd scented a moose, lynx or coyote. *Something has their attention.*

Suddenly the dogs slammed to a stop, skidding into a heap on the trail. The new leader had not yet learned how to keep the team strung out to avoid a tangle. Bud yelled and the leader leaped ahead, tightening the tug line and straightening out the team. But there was still a bit of a problem.

As Bud went forward to untangle the dog harnesses, he noticed the huge brown bear tracks that had caused the dogs' abrupt stop. Just then Kenai, who'd been running ahead, came back to the sled and growled deep in his throat. Bud now understood the behavior of the team. The tracks were so fresh that Bud was surprised they weren't smoking. Now he searched his brain to understand the reason that the bear wasn't in its den.

Meanwhile Kenai pointed his nose into the breeze and looked toward a stream. When Bud noticed Kenai's behavior, he recalled that a guide had told him about a moose he'd shot in the vicinity, and Bud guessed that the bear was feasting on the leavings.

Kenai nudged his knee as the other dogs whined in harness. Bud slipped an old .30-30 rifle from his sled boot and looked at it momentarily. He'd taken it in trade for his camp outfit and had never shot it. Expecting bears to be in bed, Bud hadn't considered running into a grizzly on the trap line. He wished he had his good rifle.

Tieing the team to a tree to keep them from engaging in the situation and with rifle in hand, he started on the bear's trail. Kenai leaped past him, taking up the track then looked back. Bud informed him that he'd have to stay with his canine chums. Bud figured the dog's hearing could get him into trouble if the bear got after him, and he didn't want Kenai hurt.

Bud retrieved a piece of light string from his pocket, led Kenai to the front of the team, motioned for the dog to lie down and tied him there. As kindly as he could, he told Kenai that he was tying him for his own protection and that he'd be back shortly. Kenai seemed momentarily satisfied that he had his old job back and was again in charge of the team.

Bud followed the bear's track to the rim of a gully where he stopped above the steep bank. Then he eased cautiously ahead and peered below, spotting the brown/grizzly just as he'd expected.

About that time he felt a nudge at his knee, heard a low whine and looked around.

Kenai stood there with the string dangling from his collar. He'd chewed through it. The high bank prevented the dog from seeing the bear and Bud thought for sure that the dog's whining would reach the bear and give them away.

When Kenai whined again, Bud popped him on the snout with his hand. He hated to discipline the dog that way; but the stakes were high and he did what he had to do.

The bear hadn't heard them. Bud carefully raised the rifle, aimed and pulled the trigger. What should have been an echo, reverberating through the birch trees in the gully bottom and along the sides, was only a sickening *snick*.

Bud knew he didn't have time to waste. He hurriedly considered the problem, *the temperature is below zero maybe the firing pin froze. Maybe it's too short.*

Angry with himself that he hadn't taken time to shoot the weapon beforehand, Bud hastily jacked in another round for a second shot.

By this time the brownie was wise to Bud. It raised its head and stared in his direction. Bud quickly retreated, trying to get back from the rim and hoping that the animal would remain with its food cache.

But the bear wasn't playing by Bud's rules.

Bud had barely moved when the bear boiled up out of the gully in pursuit of the intruders. No one was taking his food from him. He'd teach them a thing or two.

Bud fired again and got the same result. A dismal *click* whispered from the weapon. His only hope now was to get into a tree and out of reach of the bear's hay hook claws and mouth full of yellow ivory teeth. He jumped for the branch of a cottonwood tree ten feet off the ground.

When man races a grizzly, the bear always holds the winning hand–the bear gained on him with every jump. Fortunately, however, Bud's faithful, deaf dog rushed to his master's rescue. With the bear closing in on Bud, Kenai quickly circled behind the grizzly and nipped him in the tail feathers.

The bear spun on his heels after the dog but Kenai was too fast for him. They ran a hundred yards before the bear turned and headed back for Bud. Just before the bear reached the tree, Kenai got another mouthful of bear fur and behind.

This time the bear was not deterred. He was determined to reach the man and plowed on through the snow to the tree. To his credit and health, Bud reached the safety of the limb just before the bear reached his sanctuary. Mr. Brown Bear reared on hind legs to swing at the limb. But Kenai kept snarling and biting the bear's behind. Frustrated and belligerent by the dog's pesky intrusion, the bear turned to deal with the dog.

A swing from its ham-sized paw struck nothing but air and snow as Kenai lurched out of its way. He raced a hundred yards in a circle then came back to the tree with the bear in hot pursuit.

Each time Kenai led the bear away from the tree, the combatants played tag for several minutes. The dog let the bear get dangerously close then eluded it. Fortunately Kenai had a major advantage. The snow was crusted and held him up as he bounded ahead, but the bear floundered in the snow, breaking through the crust. Kenai also had a sense of how close he could let the bear get to him before turning swiftly to outmaneuver him.

Bud watched the action, shivering on the tree limb and castigated himself for smacking his dog...*Kenai should have smacked me.*

For a full hour the bear tried unsuccessfully to catch the dog.

Three times the dog led the bear away from the tree. The first two times the bear reached the tree, Kenai bit into his hindquarters, and the race was on all over again.

The third time they left Bud's perch, Kenai outwitted and outmaneuvered the bear. Then he returned to the foot of the tree and sat waiting to see if the bear would come back. But after a little while, it appeared that the bear had quit the country.

Bud climbed cautiously down the tree and looked all about to be sure that the bear was gone. Then with his big dog licking his face, the man told Kenai that the experience was about as close a call as he ever expected to have. Bud rubbed some tears from the corners of his eyes and fought back others. *How could I have hit my pal? He saved my bacon this trip.* He kneeled over and hugged his loyal dog.

They slowly moved from tree to tree, watching for the grizzly and retracing their steps to the sled and the waiting dogs. When they arrived and the other dogs set up a clamor of barking, Bud told them that they didn't have anything to woof about until they became as good a canine as Kenai.

Bud and Kenai moved off with the team, having no further problems with the winter bear.

When man does not have the nose and ears of canine, the next best thing is woods experience and knowledge of the game you're after.

13

IN SEARCH
OF A MAN-KILLER

But the bear could not locate the hated man

When I discovered *No Room For Bears,* I thought it was an awesome book. Frank Dufrene's story about Hosea Sarber is one of the most hair-raising bear stories I've ever read. With each reading it gets better...Frank captures the brown/grizzly's territorial nature, a terrible mauling and a hunter's crafty stalk for a man-killer. That story appears briefly in my first book, however I've expanded it here including the report written by the sole survivor on that fatal trip into the rainforest.

O n that dreadful day of October 16, 1929, Jack Thayer and his assistant Fred Herring conducted business as usual. But the day held a far different outcome from their planned return. They spent the day conducting a Forest Service timber survey. Jack was a prominent employee of the service and a Forest Examiner.

While returning to the motor vessel at day's end, they encountered a brown bear. Jack and Fred could almost feel the bear's presence, a feeling that both men had come to know in the proximity with the big browns in the rainforest. Most bears flee the presence of man, however they believed that this bear had chosen to take a stand in the face of human interlopers rather than retreat. It lurked nearby in the foliage.

Jack knew that a brown/grizzly could cover thirty feet with two bounds in a shade under two seconds. He knew the impending danger and had decided to shoot fast and accurately should the animal show signs of battle. He would take no chances of endangering himself or Fred, who stood behind him.

Jack pulled his rifle barrel from the crook of his left elbow, slid his finger inside the trigger guard onto the trigger and pushed his thumb against the weapon's safety, all in one single, long practiced movement. He slipped ever so slowly forward. Knowing the speed and power of an aroused brown/grizzly, the one thought that drummed across his mind was *You better be ready; this could be quick.*

But that black October day was a day for the bears.

That's when Fred saw the hulk and hissed a warning to Jack. The big animal had risen off its bed as silently as a silhouette and stood amidst three hemlocks facing the men with its head lowered. Seconds evolved into eternity while the bear's eyes pierced its antagonists; Fred thought its eyes looked like two red marbles. Slowly the black lips parted and curled back over a set of yellow ivories. That's when the bear came.

Fred Henning later wrote up his version of the tragic event (which I've included verbatim):

STATEMENT OF FRED HERRING WITH REGARD TO THE CIRCUMSTNCES OF THE DEATH OF JOHN A. THAYER

On the morning of October sixteenth, 1929, Jack Thayer and I left the launch *Weepoose* to cruise the timber in a creek valley which is located on the westerly shore of Eliza Harbor about 2 miles from the head of the harbor. Eliza Harbor is on the southeastern part of Admiralty Island, Alaska.

Thayer carried as a means of protection a Newton 30-'06 and was using Government steel jacketed ammunition. I was unarmed and carried a light pack containing a compass, increment borer and our lunch.

Leaving the beach at 8:30 a.m. we ascended the mountain side on the north side of the creek until an elevation of nearly one thousand feet was reached, which is the top of the merchantable timber belt on the mountain side. We continued up the valley at this elevation or approximately, depending on the timber. At noon we ate lunch about four miles from the Eliza Harbor beach. It was a cloudy day with some rain.

After lunch the timber in the valley near the creek was investigated, the creek crossed to the south side and we ascended to the muskegs at an elevation of approximately 100 feet above the creek, and began our homeward journey.

We walked about a mile and a half, stopping at a large boulder of conglomerate rock, which we investigated, as was our custom, for mineralization. We continued walking and soon came to another muskeg upon which we noticed a bear tree, where bears stop to rub and claw as an advertisement of their size. We remarked on the size of the bear and the freshness of the chewing and clawing marks. We had seen many bear trees during the summer and so attached no importance to it.

As we left the muskeg and entered the scrub timber I, who was in the rear about three or four feet, heard a snort and saw something move behind a clump of bushes about fifteen feet or twenty feet behind me and to the left of our line of travel. I called Thayer's attention saying: "I think there is a bear or a deer behind that clump of brush, Jack" and I started immediately to run for a tree, as that is man's only refuge–the brown bear being too large to climb small trees. As I passed Jack he shot and almost immediately the bear began to bawl. I ran about twenty five yards and climbed a tree which had limbs close to the ground and would afford speedy ascent. From the tree I heard the noise of a struggle and saw movements through the underbrush and then first realized what had happened.

After a few minutes I saw Jack get to his hands and knees but fall again. I descended the tree and crept close with caution not knowing if the bear had gone far away. This was a short time afterwards, probably less than five minutes after I had climbed the tree.

Jack was conscious and said: "Where did he go, Fred?" I answered I did not know. He then said "Save yourself, Fred" and lapsed into unconsciousness.

Jack was badly scratched and wounded, the worst wound being on the left side of his head. A great chunk from the top of his ear to his shoulder was torn loose. He was bleeding but as far as I could see no artery was severed. There were many other wounds but none of them as serious as on the head. The clothing around the trunk and legs was badly torn.

I removed my pack and shirt and laid his head on the pack with the large wound on his head up and bound my shirt around his head to hold the wound closed. I did what I could to make him comfortable and left for the beach where I met Capt. Carl Collen who was on the flats at the mouth of the creek waiting for us to come out. I informed him of the accident and we rowed to the launch *Weepoose*.

Capt. Collen and I gathered together a first aid outfit consisting of flour, compresses, bandage, blankets, iodine and a piece of canvas for a stretcher. We left the boat about 3:30 p.m. and returned to the scene, which was about two and one-half miles from the beach. Thayer was found only with some difficulty due to the natural condition of the country. When we arrived Thayer was conscious and able to talk a little. We arrived just before dark at approximately five o'clock.

We applied first aid to Jack, built a fire and rigged a stretcher. Jack kept saying: "I am cold, boys, hurry up." He called us by name also. We cut his clothes from his body and bandaged more wounds which were thereby disclosed. He was very restless during the evening and thrashed about, not allowing his wounds to close. We found his broken watch in his pocket, which had stopped and read 2:05 and we supposed that to be the time of the encounter. Some time during the evening Jack passed away. We judge the time as 10 o'clock, neither of us having watches.

During the evening we built a lean-to out of poles and brush for protection from the rain. As it is impossible to travel in the dark due to the heavy brush and wind-falls we were forced to remain till morning. We had intended to remove Jack if he were still alive to the beach in the morning.

At daybreak we attempted to pack the remains to the beach and succeeded in only one-half mile of travel due to our weakened condition from lack of food and exposure. We cached the body and walked to the beach for help.

We arrived at the *Weepoose* at 10:30 a.m. and left immediately for Pybus Bay, the nearest point where help could be obtained. This was October 17.

After a three hour run we entered Pybus Bay and stopped at a fox rancher's island but no men were home, they being fishing. We continued up the bay to the cannery, where the cannery watchmen, Leo R. Christensen, told us of two trollers, George Moreno, a Mexican, and Dave Johnson, a Native. We then moved to the head of Pybus Bay where they were found and their aid solicited. Another fox rancher, Henry Lietro, and a troller, W.E. Logan, were found, making a total of five men to aid us. The hour was then late and the men wishing to place their boats and ranches in order to be left alone, Capt. Colen decided to stay in Pybus Bay till morning.

We left Pybus Bay cannery at 4:30 in the morning October 18, and arrived at the creek mouth in Eliza Harbor at 7 a.m. and started immediately for the body.

No difficulty was experienced in the transporting the remains to the beach. Four men carried the remains and the others selected the trail and removed what obstructions possible. The packers were relieved from time to time by the extra men. (The burden weighed over two hundred pounds due to the rain.) We arrived at the beach at 11:30 a.m. after four and one-half hours of continuous travel.

All of us left immediately on the *Weepoose* for Pybus Bay and returned the men to their homes. At Pybus Bay the body was removed from its crude dressings and placed under better conditions.

We left Pybus Bay at 2:30 p.m. on the *Weepoose* for Juneau. This was October 18. The weather was very doubtful in Frederick Sound and at about 7:00 p.m. a strong northwest breeze and a large sea forced us to seek harbor in Pleasant Bay, Admiralty Island. We laid in harbor for on hour until the wind died and we then proceeded to Juneau. Weather conditions were very unfavorable, having a strong head wind and running against the tide. We arrived in Juneau at 7:30 a.m. on October 19 and reported immediately to the forest Service officials.

The death of Jack Thayer re-ignited and re-opened the age-old clamor to remove protection from the big bears. People preferred living friends to living bears. They suggested re-introducing the use of poison or bounties to rid the territory of bruin.

As Director of Alaska's Game Commission, Frank Dufresne felt the pressure to destroy the man-killer. Fred Herring guided him to the scene of the mauling. An Indian tracker located the tracks of the rogue bear and they followed them to the alpine meadows of the coastal mountains without seeing the brute. Finding no blood and eventually losing the tracks, they had no choice but to give up the search.

A year later the search resumed.

One day Hosea Sarber, told Frank he believed that 1 in 25 grizzlies would just as soon battle man as leave him alone–he joked that it was too bad that bears didn't wear numbers, like a football player, to warn man of the 1 in 25 odds.

Sarber, a savvy woodsman with years' of experience, told Frank that he had a hunch. He figured that enough time had passed so that if the bear had no serious injury from Jack's bullet, it had returned to its old haunts. Sarber wanted to go after it.

Exactly one year to the day after the bear had killed Jack Thayer, Hosea anchored his gas-powered boat in the bay at the mouth of the river in Eliza Harbor. He knew that a wounded, man-killing brownie would harbor a grudge and take no prisoners. And if Jack had injured the bear that Hosea sought, it would be a very dangerous customer indeed.

Before motoring away from the powerboat in his skiff, he instructed his boat mate to expect shooting in the late afternoon followed by three successive shots if he were successful. In the event he hadn't returned the next day, Hosea instructed him to wait until noon before following him up the river.

That said, Hosea climbed into the skiff and rowed to the beach. In moments he'd grabbed his gear and ghosted into the woods. Anyone who's ever been in the rainforest of southeast Alaska, knows that a thick layer of moss blankets the ground. Thick huckleberry bushes, alders and Devil's clubs, with maple leaf shaped leaves and spiny undersides growing a foot-and-a-half across, make up the bulk of the bushy ground cover. Moss hangs from thick branches of spruce, hemlock and cedar, nearly to ground level. It is a veritable jungle of the north.

Normally a silver-gray, smoky mist cloaks the scene, tendrils of fog silently swirling around the trees accompanied by the steady *drip-drip-drip* of falling rain. Winds often lash the forest and a cold chill embraces the land.

Heavy rains had recently flushed spawned out carcasses of pink and calico salmon from the stream's beaches seaward, leaving little for the bears to feed upon. Therefore Hosea encountered nearly no bear sign in the lower regions of the stream. He was encouraged, however, because he knew that the later running coho would be spawning upstream closer to the area where the previous year's tragedy occurred. And he knew that where salmon spawn in Alaska, bears congregate and feed.

At one point he encountered two yearling brown bears and gave them time and room to retreat into the forest before continuing on–he didn't want their woofed warning to alert the target of his mission.

At noon he'd reached the fork of the stream, the physical embodiment of the line Frank Dufresne had drawn on a map for him to follow. Hosea knew that he was getting close to the mauling scene when he encountered a rusty lantern left by the rescue party and pruned blueberry bushes that had been removed to provide better travel for the litter party that had carried Jack Thayer from the forest.

Hosea's approach heightened his senses–he listened more acutely, looked more closely and his sense of smell registered better. He stopped often. He tested the wind and remained motionless for minutes at a time before stealthily stepping forward.

The overhanging branches and typical rainy weather, accompanied by the gray clouds and dampness, added to the spookiness of the scene. The situation was one few men would choose, highlighted by the presence of life-threatening danger and travelling alone.

Because Hosea was within a quarter mile of where the bear struck Thayer down and because he hoped to catch the bear on the river feeding, he had purposely planned to arrive in late afternoon. It would be easier to deal with the animal in the relative openness of the river or the stream bank.

He finally reached the pool known to be the maverick's hangout and discovered partially eaten salmon on the bank. He cautiously eased past fresh bear tracks, wondering if the bear that he sought made them. His nose picked up the all too familiar rank odor of brown bear and he knew that he was very close. He felt the presence of death all around.

Quietly and stealthily, Sarber pushed on until he came to the foot of a windfall, a huge hemlock that had probably been uprooted by a windstorm. There he fixed his gaze on the leaning trunk and measured with his eyes the places where he would step should he need to gain elevation in a hurry.

Hosea was packing a .30-06 sporter rifle, loaded with 220-grain open point-expanding bullets, the kind to deliver a fatal dose of medicine in just such a situation. His rifle had an iron receiver sight and open aperture, which would allow quick use in close quarters.

Rain continued to fall and rain drops accumulated on the rifle barrel and stock. Hosea felt certain that the clock was ticking and that the bear was near. He stopped to evaluate the immediate surroundings. Wanting to be as prepared as possible when the time came, he purposely held the rifle with one hand while alternately reaching beneath his rain slicker to wipe water from each hand on his wool shirt.

Feeling the hair on his neck rise, Hosea broke his long practiced rule of carrying an un-chambered shell in his rifle. He slowly, and as silently as possible, unbolted his .06, eased back on the bolt to activate a cartridge and fed it gently into the chamber. He closed the bolt with a nearly inaudible metallic *shhhnick.*

Immediately the forest erupted in a trumpet-like rage-filled roar. The heart-stopping noise surrounded Hosea, seeming to come from everywhere and echoing throughout the timber, as if magnified from some giant speaker system. Those horrible sounds propelled Hosea up the leaning hemlock where he stopped only after reaching a height of fifteen feet.

Hosea had found his man-killer, and this brute meant business.

It was then that Hosea's apprehension was realized. The bear had been watching for him. No doubt, recalling its previous encounter with a man who sought its demise. With nostrils full of man smell, it had been zeroing in on him. It probably remembered the dreadful click of metal against metal from the previous year, which ignited the beast into a fury of rage.

Finally detecting the source of the bellowing sounds, Hosea looked down into the undergrowth and saw the great beast looking for him. The bear champed its teeth and roared its rage, gyrating about and slavering from its mouth. In all his years in bear country Sarber had never seen a bear so agitated and determined to culminate an attack. But the bear could not locate the hated man–the action of Hosea's moving up the tree trunk had caused his scent to rise on the air currents, taking his scent from the bear.

Because it failed in its efforts to locate him, the bear's chuffing enunciation soon turned to an eager whining.

Within moments it stopped its thrashing leaps almost in mid-air and remained motionless. It had winded Hosea. Slowly it rose on hind legs and for fully ten seconds stared at its foe above. But it was too late for the bear to affect its rage on Hosea.

The man had taken advantage of his position, raised his rifle, taken careful aim and touched off a shot. With the resonating roar on the forest floor the bear sagged to the ground. The bullet blew up a vertebrate and killed instantly. The brute's reign upon earth was finished. The man-killer would harm no one or thing again.

Hosea waited a few moments to assure himself that the bear was incapacitated, then retraced his steps down the tree trunk to the ground. He edged up to the bear and prodded the animal in the back of the neck with the toe of his boot. Then Sarber grabbed an ear and pulled the head around to look for wounds. Near the shoulder was a long scar that may well have been the result of Thayer's bullet.

Hosea raised his rifle in the gathering twilight and fired three successive shots into the night sky, alerting his boat mate of his success. No doubt, Hosea was greatly relieved that he'd chosen the proper time to run up the tree. His woodland expertise paid off handsomely in his personal safety and in the demise of a hell-bent man-killer.

Not all men have had the necessary firepower to stop a charging grizzly and had to rely upon other means for protection.

14

BETWEEN A HARD
PLACE AND A ROCK

When she made her final attack, boys, she approached me
on her hind feet. Her mouth was wide open, and the tone
of her voice was between that of a deep bellow
and a prolonged grunt.

Since 1987 I've maintained an ongoing correspondence
with Charlotte Parent, whom I met through the mail. A couple
of years ago she provided me a list of over 300 bear books that
she was selling from her collection of bear memorabilia.

One of my purchases from her was a 30-page pamphlet
titled *A Fight with a Grizzly* that sold for "10 cents" when published in 1886. The author tells of visiting Boston merchant
Charlie Locksley, who'd gone West during the "49er" days
when the country was little known.

The dècor of the room bespoke the man's adventurous
nature – a long-barreled rifle and a brace of pistols hung from
the fireplace; a powder-horn was suspended by a leather
thong looped over the hilt of a long-bladed bowie knife;
nearby were an Indian bow and quiver of arrows, a buckskin
kilt and moccasins; deer's antlers and longhorns hung over
the entrance.

I left the piece in the words of the author so that the
reader might savor the language of the era. While the group
of men gathered in the great room before the fireplace to
share Christmas Eve with him and gazed at a 5-inch long
grizzly claw, Locksley spoke up.

T hat claw, boys, belonged to a grizzly bear that I slew,
as David slew Goliath, with a stone. We were unequally

matched, yet each rose superior to the occasion. Here, however, the similarity ends; for while David, armed, stood before the foe of his own free will and struck his antagonist on the head, I, without a moment's warning, was required to face a savage brute, far more cruel than Goliath, and in defense hurl my missile into its throat.

Again, boys, David fought his duel, as we are told, in an open plain, surrounded by an army of spectators; mine, on the contrary, was fought on the edge of a precipice, with only one spectator–the ever-present God. In each case the results were the same, differing only in the fact that, while David came out of the conflict without injury, I was badly hurt, and my garments were literally torn to shreds.

To my mind both stones were hurled by the same invisible power and directed by the same unseen hand, while both of us were saved by divine interposition for some good and beneficent purpose.

Well, boys, this bear scrape occurred in '49, some two years before I lost my arm, and while following the trail that led from the Yuba to Feather River, en route for the post office, which was located at Bidwell's Bar. Now the distance between the two rivers was only four miles as the crow flies; but the precipitous hills we had to climb and the craggy cliffs we had to scale increased the distance to twice that number of miles, so the boys decided to fetch the mails by turns.

Accordingly when it fell my lot to pass those dangerous canyons alone, I left our cabin, so to speak, in light marching order, —that is, I wore a sheath-knife in my belt and a tin cup fastened to my girdle.

Although I had started early in the morning, by the time I had reached the ridge the sun was perhaps an hour high; so after a few moments' rest I plunged boldly into the forest, with only some landmarks for guides. After crossing Langley's Gulch in safety, and scaling without trouble the opposite cliff, I halted beneath the spreading branches of a lofty pine, allured to that spot by the advantages it offered, both for rest and observation; and there all alone, in the sleepy calmness of Nature's chamber, lulled by the singing waters below, I fell into a sweet, refreshing slumber.

This point of land, therefore, on which I had stopped to cool and rest, in shape resembled a flat-iron, and was both narrow and rocky. Crested by a group of trees, it was a cool and sightly spot, and sloping as it did to a precipice of frightful dimensions, it commanded a view of almost bewildering grandeur. It was a terminus of a range of mountains extending back for miles, and the *divide*, so called, which separated Feather River from Langley's Gulch. These two streams for centuries had flowed along, deepening their channels year by year, until at that time they were a thousand feet below their original beds. From singing brooks they had become noisy rivers, before whose floods rocks trembled and the earth melted away as snow, and after running for miles in parallel lines, their waters met at the foot of this point on which I sat; then, together, they rolled along through mountains fringed with forests whose summits were covered with eternal snows.

The distance from where I sat to the trail was less than fifty feet, and with the exception of the brambles and briers beyond the trail, there was nothing to obstruct the view until the eye rested upon the heavy belts of timber some distance away; therefore the scene before me was one of dazzling beauty, by far the most magnificent spectacle I ever beheld. There are many wild and picturesque scenes to be found in the Sierra Nevadas; but for a combination of all that is grand and beautiful the view from this point must forever surpass them all.

Well, boys, it was while resting amid these dazzling splendors and dreaming in the centre of one of God's stupendous wonders that I was startled from my slumber by the crackling of the bushes in the rear of where I sat. Alarmed, I instantly sprang to my feet, and, turning my eyes in the direction from whence the noise proceeded, I judged, from the violent agitation of the undergrowth, that some huge monster was breaking cover and coming out in the neighborhood of where I stood.

A moment later a large grizzly bear, followed by her cub, stepped out upon the trail and confronted me. They saw me at once, and both recoiled, —yes, recoiled, from the gaze of a human eye, probably the first they had ever seen. For a while neither retreated a hair's-breadth, nor relaxed a muscle, but stood fixedly in their tracks and gazed upon me in wonder and alarm. Boys, I was struck with horror; I could neither move nor speak. My tongue clove to the roof of my mouth, and my limbs trembled beneath me. Drops of sweat, cold as the ice upon the hills, followed each other down my blanched cheeks, and the roots of my hair stung as if from the sting of a bee. Chilled by fear and gasping for breath, I knew not what to do; so I stood overwhelmed by my situation, and gazed into the eyes of this terrible brute.

My position, therefore, was one of extreme peril, and my reason began to stagger with fright, as I realized that I was hemmed in and cut off from all possibility of reaching the trail, which was the only door of escape. To fall back was but to plunge over the precipice and be dashed to pieces a thousand feet below, while the slightest attempt to flank the monster was but to invite an attack; so my only hope now rested in the brute following her cub, which a moment before had taken to the woods. This she did not do; hence I was lost and my death was inevitable. I could see it staring me in the face as plainly as the soldier sentenced to be shot, who, standing before the concentrated fire, sees his doom in the signal that riddles his body with bullets. I could feel it in the air, in every pulsation of my heart, and there I stood, a living statue, horrified at my impending doom. Look which way I would, not a ray of hope presented itself; there was not a habitation in sight, not a human being to be seen. Alone, unarmed, I looked death in the face. I must meet it, and meet it like a man; it was useless to bemoan my fate; it seemed like folly to resist; better, far better, for me to submit with fortitude, and with Christian resignation meet this wretched death, which could not be otherwise than brief, sharp, and decisive. But how was I to die? that was the question. How should I be destroyed? Would this brute strike and fell me to the ground, deadening the sensibilities, thus relieving me of the pangs and tortures which precede death? Would she rip me open, cutting me through as with a knife, and disembowel me, leaving behind her a mass of quivering flesh? or would she gather me up into her powerful arms, crush out my poor life, and leave my body a mangled corpse?

Wild with emotions and crazed by fear, I watched her poise her body in the air and spring to the attack. It was then and there, in the supremest moment of my life, when the sky grew dark, and the earth swam like a ball in the air, that the first and only cry escaped my lips, —a long, piercing cry that came up from the very depths of my soul, and rolled heavily away over the chasm like the wail of a lost spirit.

During the brief time which elapsed between our meeting and the moment she made the assault, my whole life seemed to pass in review. Every event from my earliest childhood to the hour of leaving our camp upon the Yuba that morning came and went with lightning rapidity.

My recollection of the closing scene is at best but imperfect, — so helpless, indeed, so utterly lost had I become to everything beyond the fact that the savage monster was gradually but surely closing in upon me. But if my memory serves me at all, it recalls a brief, but sincere, prayer, uttered before what seemed an impending death, and addressed to the only Being who has ever responded to the cry of distress in moments of deadly peril. It came up from the bottom of my heart–from a soul standing upon the brink of eternity expecting a speedy dissolution.

When she made her final attack, boys, she approached me on her hind feet. Her mouth was wide open, and the tone of her voice was between that of a deep bellow and a prolonged grunt. Raising herself to her full height, she towered above me as the pine towers above the cedar, her huge body completely shadowing the space between us, and her eyes gleaming like coals of living fire. When she threw up her arms to strike, I stood calmly awaiting my death; and, leaning for support against a large rock with a crumbling surface, my arm rested upon some detached pieces, from which, in the frenzy of the moment, I instinctively grasped a fragment, and as the blow fell, hurled the missile into her throat. I threw it, I know not why; but I threw it as one falling from a staging to his death clutches the air. At the same moment that it lodged in her throat she struck me, cutting away my belt and clothing, and scarifying my body badly; but the effect of the stroke proved less fatal than intended, as the force of the blow was materially lessened by the sudden shock produced by the stone. Instantly and simultaneously she dropped her head and gagged. That gag, which was the first and last effort of the kind that I heard, proved by subsequent events to be the expiring gasp that followed the closing up of the windpipe and the beginning of a struggle fierce and terrible before which all others of a similar nature pale in significance.

Springing upon the bear's back and thence into the air, I caught hold of an overhanging twig and clung to it with the tenacity of death. Lifting my body hand over hand until I firmly grasped the limb hitherto beyond my reach, I threw over my leg, and after twisting my body up and over, I came down firmly seated across it. It was from this limb, this grateful shelf of safety, that I witnessed the tragedy referred to, and became a spectator of one of the most terrible sights on record.

The anguish I experienced when that monster sprang upon me, crazing me by her noise and driving me wild with horror, may be imagined but never described, and to be appreciated must be endured.

The agony that tossed a bear of half a ton weight ten feet into the air, and dashed its body again and again against the rocks till the very ground trembled beneath, can be spoken of, but never understood. To comprehend its fury, to realize its terrors, to feel and be sensible of all the ghastly details, it must be seen, not heard.

From the moment I threw the stone, boys, until I reached my place of safety, I was wholly unconscious of the bear's condition, supposing she had ejected the stone; for I mistook her frantic flights into the air as idle attempts to tear me down from the tree. So when I looked from where I sat and saw this monster plunging wildly among the rocks, her eyes bursting from their sockets, and the blood streaming from her nose and mouth, I was overwhelmed with astonishment, and almost struck dumb with horror, as I learned from her movements that all her efforts to dislodge the stone had proved unavailing. Desperately and wildly did she fight for her life. Slashing her neck with her claws, she cut deep gashes in her throat, from which the blood poured in streams. Leaping and plunging, she beat her head against the rocks, and dashing her body upon the ground, hugged the boulders with a grip which tore them from their beds; then springing up into the air like a rocket, she fell with a crash, driving her head deep into the briars till the ground trembled, and the dust came up in clouds. Boys, this bear was suffocating, actually choking to death.

Just how long it took that grizzly to die I never knew. It may have been five minutes, perhaps less, but to me it seemed an eternity. Wondering how long she would continue to dash her body among the rocks, I watched every movement until she suddenly ceased, and lay so quiet that neither the movement of the muscle nor the tremor of her mangled frame betrayed her existence. Supposing that she had past the great crisis of her life and was dead, I drew a long breath, and began to make preparations for descending the tree, when suddenly her body began to tremble, and then to heave like an inflated balloon. Immediately she went into convulsions; and from that time until she disappeared from view the scene beggared description. Again my fears returned, and once more my life seemed in imminent peril. Clasping the tree with all the strength at my command, I sat there, icy cold, shivering and stupefied at her prodigious powers of endurance. Boys, the sight was shocking; indeed 't was too ghastly to look upon. It was the last scene of that eventful drama, and the curtain rose and fell upon a spectacle such as few men would care to behold; for it was a continuation of the most frantic plunges, interspersed with a variety of violent contortions which followed in quick succession.

The bear's struggles ended when she struck the tree on which I sat; and the division occurred when she stood erect and with her paws blindly sawed the air. But the collapse did not take place until she had made her final plunge, shooting, as she did, straight up into air, passing me in her flight, and falling with a tremendous crash upon a sloping rock which formed the brink of the precipice; after which came the tumult produced by the falling rocks as the bear fell over the precipice and plunged head-first into the abyss below. I heard her body, as it went crashing down through the trees, and the loosened rocks as they plunged furiously after her; then silence, deep and profound as the grave, ensued. The earth and sky came back again to me, and, thanking God for his merciful interposition, I wept like a child.

A moment later, while once more preparing to descend, I was again startled by a slight disturbance in the bushes beyond the trail, which presently revealed itself in the figure of the cub, as she peered through the undergrowth in search of her dam, venturing out as far as the scene of conflict. She smelt each pool of blood, from which she recoiled with dread, and then gazing wistfully around, caught sight of me, which so frightened her that she quickly turned about and fled into the woods, and I saw her no more.

Humbled and awed by the solemnity of the scene and the tragic events which had just transpired, I became deeply impressed by the mysterious power that had so singularly snatched me from the very jaws of death, and with a grateful heart dropped from the tree, and, after arranging my tattered garments as best I could, resumed my journey, which had been so startlingly interrupted.

On arriving at the Bidwell's Bar I found a group of miners lounging about the post office, to whom I told my story, which, being fresh and exciting, culminated when the long scratches on my body were exhibited, showing the deadly peril to which I had but so recently been exposed. The news quickly spread over the flats and throughout the neighboring gulches; and shortly afterwards I found myself surrounded by a large number of anxious sympathizers. Every man present expressing a wish to see the grizzly, a party was soon organized and ready for the start, which was exceedingly gratifying to me, as I had a secret desire to know the fate of my late antagonist, and find out the exact facts which had brought about her death. Desiring very much to know this before returning to the Yuba, I was only too glad to form one of the party to go in search of her remains. Although the distance to the junction of the rivers was scarcely a mile, the route was found both difficult and dangerous. Hence it was high noon ere we had accomplished our purpose; but when found, the remains lay a quivering mass among a pile of rocks, and in a direct line with the precipice over which she had plunged to her death. Her body was still warm, and the blood oozing from the gaping wounds in her side. As the head was flattened and badly disfigured, and the body torn and beaten to a jelly, the sight was ghastly and painful to look upon. To me the scene was impressive, and my heart moved in pity for the noble brute that had made such a heroic struggle for her life; for when viewed from a higher standpoint, with the love of God in my breast, I could not condemn her, but on the contrary I indulged a wish far more pronounced than pity that her death had been more immediate and her struggles less agonizing.

Hence, in attacking me this poor brute did but carry out he true instinct of her nature to shield and protect her cub, or die in the attempt.

Taking out my knife I made an incision in the throat, and found that the stone was wedged in and across the windpipe, as I had supposed, thus effectively stopping the air-passage. So deeply, indeed, had the stone imbedded itself in the muscles that neither the immense weight of the body, nor the great force of the fall, had started it a hair's-breadth from the spot where it had first lodged. Therefore, my investigations proved that the suffocation produced by the stone must have ended life independent of the fall, and that her death was clearly caused by strangulation.

Now, boys, that claw which hangs yonder against the wall was cut from one of her fore paws, which had been severed by the fall from the rest of the foot, and was found hanging by the skin. I carried it back to camp with me, and have kept it ever since, not as a trophy, —for I am no more entitled to it as a pledge of success than was David to Goliath's head, —but in the light of the souvenir to commemorate one of the most tragic events of my life. It is all that is now left of that once powerful brute, and the only reminder of that tremendous struggle for a breath of air that never came.

Author's note:

Were I collecting reminders from my slain bear, I think I'd have retrieved the stone as a souvenir...probably the only rock in history that slew a grizzly.

The choice of weapons used against grizzlies is sometimes limited, however a stone and a .22 rifle are not much of a choice.

Speed and Agility

While John Graybill shared some of his adventures with me, he showed me a picture of a good sized grizzly and a red dog on the tundra while explaining, "Right here is a picture of a long legged Irish setter and a grizzly. The fellow with me thought he'd sic his dog on the bear."

I said, "I don't think I'd do that."

He said, "Oh, no. He can outrun a bear."

I said, "Ohhhhh…maybe," It was all open tundra, just ideal runnin' but it was just as ideal for the bear as it was for the dog.

That grizzly caught that dog so quick. Caught it and ate it.

—John Graybill interview, Tuesday, May 2, 2000

15

SHOOT STRAIGHT

He showed me the correct spot to hit the bear.

In 1956 my junior high buddy, Bob McCauley, invited me to accompany him and his parents on their summer vacation. During that same time I was on a learning curve to gather everything I could about bears and live the adventure from the armchair. We went to Montana's Lake Mary Ronan and spent time fishing and shooting ground squirrels with our .22 rifles. Somewhere in that time frame I read a story from *Outdoor Life* magazine that fueled my imagination about grizzlies.

That story has stuck with me all these years. I was delighted to find it in the pages of *The Outdoor Life Bear Book* in the 1980s. I've quoted a portion of the story as written by Bud Helmericks.

"**Much of my hunting** has been done with Eskimos. I once asked an old Eskimo bear hunter what rifle he generally used. It was an ancient .22, a single-shot Remington of falling-block design. He produced several skulls with a .22 hole drilled neatly through them. Several years ago a mammalogist had paid him $5 for one and he'd been saving skulls ever since. As near as I could tell, he'd killed 13 bears with this tiny rifle.

"On the prairie there are little mounds made by generations of parka squirrels. The old-time Eskimo would find a bear that was hunting squirrels and then slip around into its path. Prone behind a parka squirrel's mound, the Eskimo would thrust up his forearm with fist doubled to imitate a squirrel, at the same time chirping like an alarmed squirrel. The grizzly would come over to investigate, and get shot in the head. The Eskimo I spoke to indicated about a 10-foot distance. He showed me the correct spot to hit the bear—about midway between the ear and the eye and a little either side of center. I examined the skulls closely and found them surprisingly thin, at that point—little thicker than shoe-box cardboard.

"The old fellow finished talking and stared at the teeth of an enormous skull. Then, as if realizing that a little knowledge is dangerous, he cautioned me: 'That brown bear, Oklak, is bad one. You don't hit him right, he come for you!' With this he again indicated the spot where you must hit him."

Although the Eskimo had the opportunity of shooting grizzlies, not all who encounter the horrible bear have any sort of weapon available.

A BEAR
FROM NOWHERE

Next Knut saw the bear's mouth wide open as the beast clamped onto his face, its lower jaw just beneath his and its upper jaw just below his right eye.

Knut Peterson's bear mauling and his powerful hatred for them has always captured my attention. I first read about him in *All About Bears*, which also introduced me to Harry Boyden.

Later Knut published two books of his own, chronicling his Alaskan adventures and other stories from the Great Land – *When Alaska Was Free* and *Old Sourdough*. I acquired these at the time of publication and corresponded with Knut, who was living in Tok at the time. Although his condensed story appears in my first book, I wanted to share this new information.

"Books by the dozen have been written about [bears] and some of them go on to tell you that the grizzly bears are absolutely harmless, but in doing so they only succeed in exposing their own ignorance. If any of you prefer to believe the author of these books that's your business, but if you ever discover that you are in grizzly bear country I would like to advise you to discard the book and carry a powerful rifle and lots of shells."

—Knut Peterson, *All About Bears,* Page 20

She'd taken care of him all his life. Every time he found himself in a pickle she'd bailed him out. Since coming to Alaska he'd been protected by Lady Luck. But the grizzly that rudely interrupted his day in 1949 changed all that. This time

Knut thought the odds were too tough and his ace in the hole, the Lady with the Luck, had turned her back on him.

Nine years after emigrating from Denmark, Knut Peterson made his way by steamship from Seattle to Cordova, Alaska in 1923. Eventually he moved into the area called Slana and Tok Cut-Off, roughly half way between Tok and Glennallen. His base of operations was his cabin in Slana. He had spent the biggest part of his life outdoors in Alaska, prospecting and placer mining.

On the morning of August 30,1949 Knut went to visit his friend Ole Hougland, seven miles north of him and a mile off the road on the banks of the Slana River. He'd covered miles afoot the past twenty-six years in Alaska and had been to Ole's dozens of times without carrying a rifle. He saw no reason to tote one now.

Knut left his car at the gravel highway and walked the well-worn path to his friend's. They spent the night revisiting their oft-discussed desire to find a rich mineral deposit, especially gold and uranium. Knut invited Ole to partner-up with him on a prospecting trip to the Big Tok River. Hoagland was too busy so Knut decided to go alone.

Next morning around 11 Peterson started for home while Ole sharpened tools with a small, power grinder. Following the trail that paralleled the Slana River only a few yards away, Knut had a snap in his gait just thinking about prospecting again.

Less than five hundred yards from Ole's cabin, a roar that sounded like thunder and seemed to shake the very earth startled Knut. Momentarily, he froze in his tracks. Then he looked behind him and saw a 700 to 800-pound grizzly barreling out of a patch of willows towards him–galloping full out, roaring and snarling all the way. The speed of the animal amazed him.

He turned immediately. Fueled by adrenaline, with heart pounding and hoping against hope that the bear wouldn't overtake him, Knut sprinted for the riverbank. He planned to jump in, hold his breath as long as possible under water while the current carried him toward Ole's, then swim the rest of the way to his friend's. But he never made it.

Not even the tennis shoes he wore were up to the task of delivering him to the safety of the river. The bear overtook him and slapped him on the left shoulder with a paw, knocking him onto his stomach on the ground.

Next it grabbed his upper left arm in its jaws and bit to the bone, nearly cutting it in two. When it let go, Knut quickly turned onto his back. The next thing he saw was a mouthful of teeth as it shoved its face toward his.

Hollering "Ole!" as loudly as he could, Knut smacked the bear in the nose with his right hand. The bear snapped its jaws shut on his right hand and wrist, and Knut felt the bones breaking. He was relieved that the bear chomped his hand rather than his face.

He thought that he'd always remember the bear's cold nose and its hot breath.

The bear dropped his hand and tore into his right thigh, biting it to the bone and continuing to chew. With a paw on his stomach just above his pelvis the grizzly held him down. Knut yelled again for Ole.

The bear slapped his left leg at the calf, tearing it wide open. Then it lifted him off the ground and turned him over, its claws ripping into his back and ribs. Knut tried to crawl into an alder thicket on his stomach, but the bear pounced on him, smacked him with a paw to the back of the head and knocked off a patch of his scalp 3 or 4-inches square. Bruin bit him in the neck and Knut saw black disks before his eyes for a few seconds. The inside of his head sounded like a freight train rumbling through a tunnel.

Next Knut saw the bear's mouth wide open as the beast clamped onto his face, its lower jaw just beneath his and its upper jaw just below his right eye. It bit through his face, ripping off part of his nose and upper lip, completely cutting his face in two. Knut felt his upper denture break apart. The action crushed his lower jaw, breaking it in two places, and dislodged four teeth, some of which were found later with pieces of jawbone attached.

The grizzly roared, snorted, foamed at the mouth, bit, hit, chewed and tossed Knut around for less than a minute. Then it abruptly left.

Suddenly it was quite. Not a sound. No more snorting, growling, hitting or biting. Slowly Knut began to think more clearly and to look around. He lay there wondering if he had a chance. He heard

Ole's motor running. He finally maneuvered himself into a sitting position while he listened two or three minutes, trying to collect his thoughts and figure out what to do. He never figured out the reason for the bear's leaving him, but he was glad that it had.

The grizzly inflicted about as much damage as Knut or any man could take and be alive. He was a pathetic mess and didn't care much about anything. All that remained of his clothes was the waist of his pants. His body was covered with blood and cuts. His right arm and wrist were broken. The muscle was torn away from the bone on his right thigh and looked like hamburger. His lower jaw was broken and many lower teeth were missing. His windpipe was exposed and a large piece of his scalp was ripped off. Knut's left biceps was torn away from the bone and rolled away from his arm.

He figured that he was beyond repair. It was somewhat paradoxical because he knew he could try to reach Ole's but wondered if it wasn't a futile plan–either because his injuries would keep him from making it to Ole's or after reaching Ole's, he'd die before he could be rescued. Nevertheless he knew his only hope of survival was to get to Ole's place so that he could get help for him.

First he tried crawling on all fours, but that was problematic because of his broken wrist. Brush also poked at his ripped thigh. He managed to get to his feet and started staggering toward his friend's. He wanted to run, but had to settle for hopping along on his left leg, dragging the right.

He had to stop every few yards to rest and try to get air into his lungs. Breathing was very difficult as blood from his mangled face ran down his throat. Several times he thought he'd choke on his own blood. When he bent over to allow blood to run out of his mouth and from his face, blood from his head injury ran into his eyes, blinding him.

After he'd gone a hundred yards, his fear of the bear's return nearly paralyzed him. But he continued on.

He was afraid to look back.

He will always wonder how he made the 500 yards and decided that, even though he'd made a lot of tough treks as a miner, this was his toughest trip.

After some time, Knut stumbled up the trail to Ole's where his friend was still at the air-cooled engine, sharpening tools. Imagining that he looked like he had been pulled from a barrel of blood, Knut approached Ole from the rear. Peterson feared that Ole would be severely startled when he saw him, and because he was unable to speak, Knut grunted. Ole was hard of hearing and didn't turn around so Knut grunted louder the second time.

Hougland heard him and turned. When he saw the grotesque form of his friend trying to talk to him, he nearly fainted. (Ole told Knut later that he recognized only his eyes)

Knut had not considered his inability to speak. Nor had he taken into account the fact that his lip was torn in half and his face sluffed off to one side. He never forgot the sadness he felt when he realized that he couldn't tell Ole what had happened.

After a long silence, Ole gasped, "Oh, C———! Knut, what happened? A bear?"

Knut shook his head up and down to affirm Ole's premise.

Extremely tired, Knut pointed to the cabin, hoping Ole would understand that he wanted to go in and lie down.

Ole stopped the engine, assisted Knut into his cabin and prepared a place for him on a mattress on the floor. At that point Knut didn't care if he got any further.

Although Ole said he'd go for help, Knut thought his time was about up. He tried to say goodbye to his friend and that he was about done in, but Ole sensed his effort and reminded Knut that he wasn't going to die.

Just before Ole left, Knut made a throaty noise and pointed at Ole's gun hanging near the doorway. Ole agreed with Knut's suggestion and grabbed it on his way out the door. Knut grunted again to get Ole's attention and to remind him to close the door before he left.

Ole closed the door and ran the mile up the trail to his pickup then drove four miles to the Alaska Road Commission camp at Porcupine Creek in an elapsed time of seventeen minutes. Considering the condition of the gravel road and the fact that Ole was more than 60-years old, he'd made record time.

He pulled into camp at dinnertime and the road foreman Clayton Hoy knew that something was wrong when he saw Ole almost roll his pickup. Ole stated his emergency mission and the cook, Lillian Hoy, got on the telephone and alerted officials. Word spread rapidly and men along the route joined in the effort to save Knut.

Using the neighborhood helicopter was out because it was down for repairs.

The Army's Tenth Rescue Squadron scrambled to reach Knut. The Highway Patrol (State Troopers) prepared to stop all traffic on the thirty-mile stretch of roadway between Knut's pickup spot and Chistochina as soon as he reached the road. A fleet of gravel trucks was ordered off the road until Knut passed. In addition, a road grader was sent ahead to smooth the roadway in order to facilitate Knut's transportation.

Meanwhile Knut lay on the mattress feeling very lonesome. In order to breathe more easily he lay with his face down. The pain was heightened as he lay on his raw wounds, however the position allowed the blood to exit his mouth rather than going down his throat.

After resting a little he stood up shakily. He looked at himself in the wall mirror and immediately realized his mistake. He nearly fainted and understood Ole's reaction when he'd first seen him. What he saw staring back at him from the mirror was a faceless man. He looked anything but human.

Although he didn't panic, that glimpse into the looking glass convinced Knut that his injuries were beyond repair. He couldn't understand Ole's reason for leaving him in such bad shape since it didn't appear that he would survive anyway. Knut contented himself in the knowledge that people would understand that he died at the paws and teeth of a grizzly and that he wasn't lying out in the woods for the animals to drag away.

He felt like smashing the mirror but knew that would solve nothing. He thought (and said later), "I guessed my romance with Lady Luck was over. I remembered all the times in the past she had rescued me." Twenty-some years later he still felt like vomiting when he recalled that faceless man staring at him from the mirror.

He wondered how much he could take, how much any man could stand. Then he lay down again.

After a while Knut felt chilled on the mattress and decided to build a fire to warm up. He had to use his left hand. He put shavings and kindling into the stove then lit one match after another, but the blood dripping from his wounds extinguished the flame.

He placed a cigarette between his lips on the left side of his face and managed to light it. He held his face together with his broken hand and tried to smoke the cigarette. But his efforts were in vain.

Even though he'd failed, his actions gave him something to do and occupied his time while help was on the way.

He thought about his four dogs and his cabin and figured that he'd not see them again. Then he decided he'd better leave some kind of will.

He tore a page from an old calendar on the wall and found a pencil on the table. Writing with his left hand proved difficult, but even worse, there was so much blood that he couldn't complete his task. He washed off the blood and took another calendar from the wall and scribbled on the back, "Give my dogs and cabins and whatever I had to my brother, Ole, in Cordova."

Then he took to the mattress again. He discovered that the pain was greatly reduced as long as he didn't move. Even though he was lonesome, he figured it would probably be better not to be around people anyway because he didn't think he'd ever look normal if he did survive. He wanted a drink but didn't want go get up again.

Before he knew it, or even expected it, he heard voices outside. Ole had arrived with two husky road crewmen. They carried him on the mattress down the bank and loaded him into Ole's boat. They went down river about four miles to where the road and river were closest together. Despite the blanket's covering him, Knut was cold. Periodically he dipped his hand into the muddy Slana and poured water down his throat.

When they reached the road, some held the boat steady at the bank while others helped him to his feet and supported him as he stepped ashore. He lay down on a waiting mattress, they picked him up mattress and all, carried him to a brand new panel truck and placed him inside.

Several people encouraged Knut, telling him he'd soon be in the hospital and on his road to recovery. All Knut wanted was to go to his cabin and his own bed, but they raced off to Chistochina. Clayton Hoy drove the truck as fast as possible, knowing he'd face no oncoming traffic because a truck was sent ahead to warn other traffic off the roadway.

An engineer and an A.R.C. surveyor, H.A. Steffen (or Stephan), was the other passenger until they stopped a few miles below Slana. There Mrs. Gailord Cluff of Sinona Lodge, a trained nurse, joined them. Unable to do much for Knut, she held his bloody hand.

Somehow Knut held his mouth together and mumbled to his rescuers, asking them if they thought their efforts were worth it. They assured him that he would be okay. He was having a hard time believing them because weakness was overpowering him.

Even though Knut appreciated the encouragement, he thought the folks were wasting their breath. He kept thinking about the mess the bear had made of him and vowed to return to seek vengeance on the bear clan. His hatred boiled into a rage and strengthened him.

The rescue wagon with Knut aboard arrived only five minutes after the Tenth Rescue plane had landed. They carried him to the plane and set him on the ground near it. The Army doctor gave Knut a shot of morphine in his right arm and told him he'd soon feel better. The doc asked the group if they had Knut's scalp and if not, instructed them to find it and bring it to the hospital as soon as possible. (Later Knut learned that they had returned to the attack site, found the scalp and delivered it to the hospital too late to be replaced.)

The doctor told the soldiers and others to get Knut aboard. They had to take him from the mattress in order to load him into the plane. When they tried to seat him, pain rocked his body and he groaned.

Knut observed the look of utter hopelessness on the pilot's face as he turned his head away from him and shook his head in disbelief.

Thirst plagued Knut and he gestured to the doctor next to him that he'd like a drink of water. The doctor told him that he'd soon be in the hospital where he'd feel better and get some liquid.

Before long the painkiller took effect and Knut felt so good that he considered the whole ordeal rather insignificant. He thought he'd be back in the woods in a few days chasing bears.

Since Knut was a WWI vet, his rescuers took him to the hospital at Elmendorf Air Force Base in Anchorage. They arrived around 5 p.m. and a number of soldiers were there to help him from the plane into the ambulance. He heard many people commenting on his condition and wondering what could have happened to him.

He learned later that he reached the hospital in the nick of time as he probably would have died had he arrived an hour later.

Colonel Browning was in charge of the hospital and Knut knew him. When Knut tried to communicate with him, the colonel went to the safe and extracted Knut's wallet. He saw Knut's ID and said, "Yes, Knut, you know me. Don't worry, we'll soon have you fixed up."

Colonel Browning summoned all available surgeons and doctors. Two soldiers donated blood to Knut before the doctors began working on him. Knut was tired and sleepy when they wheeled him into the operating room where an army of people met him. His last memory was of being wheeled into the emergency room.

They worked on him for hours. Giving him ether was guesswork. All the medical personnel pitched in and did their best, telling him later that he was the most torn up person they'd ever seen who lived to talk about it.

Part of Knut's right thigh was discarded because it couldn't be put back together. When they cleaned his wounds, nurses removed dirt, spruce needles, pieces of underwear, leaves and moss. Surgeons took turns suturing his wounds, losing count of the total number. (Later they removed 418 stitches)

When Knut regained consciousness, it took him some time to realize where he was and to understand his situation. Colonel Browning asked him how he felt. He nodded his head to indicate that he was okay. Then he communicated by writing with his left hand. His head felt encased in cement.

The bone specialist thought that Knut's right wrist would never be any good, and the other doctors felt the same about his left arm.

Miraculously both wrist and arm regained their function. After three or four years his right leg also regained its strength.

He remained in the hospital seventy days, constantly encouraged by the staff who treated him like a long-lost brother. Knut never got over the wonderful support he received from the hospital staff. He often wondered how many people were involved in saving his life. He was treated so well that he wanted to thank everyone by living.

He suffered four months of headaches–they were so extreme that the doctor prescribed two painkillers every four hours. Those painkillers lasted but two hours, so he suffered 12 hours of pain every 24. Twenty years later the thought of those headaches still frightened him.

Knut had nothing but praise for the folks around Slana who had catered to him. Women sent him a robe and other gifts such as a $100 Gruen wristwatch while he was in the hospital until November 10. When he attended a Thanksgiving meal in Slana, the good people presented him with a $125 Smith & Wesson .357 Magnum pistol and a check in the amount of $195. Friends had cut five cords of wood and hauled it to his cabin where his neighbor Fred Bronnichee used his power saw and help from Al Joudain and Don Duffy to cut the wood into stove-length pieces. Knut was eternally grateful to those who took to helping an old, single guy.

Fred's wife bandaged his scalp every day, and two and a half years later he had the semblance of skin on his head which was covered with a thin layer of scar tissue. The scar tissue broke easily and healed slowly.

A couple of decades later when Knut remembered the event, he said he'd just as soon pull a curtain back to block the scene from his memory or look the other way. Some nights Knut awakened from sleep, jumping from bed in terror while sweating and shaking. Even though he did not dream about bears, these episodes still plagued him.

Considering all the efforts taken to move him from Ole's cabin and on to the hospital in Anchorage, he often wondered about his importance to the world.

After a while he began gaining back some of the weight he'd lost. Even though it was a year before Knut was somewhat normal, he felt that he'd never be as strong and healthy as he had been before the grizzly tackled him.

Knut never learned the reason for the bear's attacking him. He believed that a grizzly might not bother a person for years but all of a sudden it could attack with mayhem in mind.

Alaska Department of Fish and Game regulations allow a person to shoot a grizzly any time the person's life is in danger, and, often, when his property is in jeopardy. But Knut proclaimed, "Don't wait till he attacks. If he is bold enough to show up at or near your home do away with him before he decides to take over, expecially [sic] if you have children around."

Knut talked about book authors and their theory that grizzlies are harmless and equated grizzlies to the safety of bullets, unless you happen to be in their pathway! And he went to his grave telling people to "look out for grizzlies." He died preaching self-preservation. He felt it was better for people to read and learn from his experience and to prepare for an eventual defense of your life from a run-in with a grizzly than to be his victim.

Knut wasn't armed, but Dan Ludington was...fortunately.

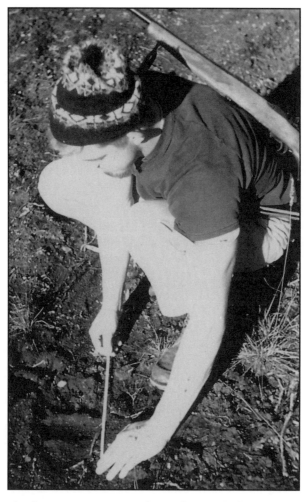

Author measuring grizzly track near Lake Louise
Road, August 1967.
Photo from author's personal collection

ALMOST TOO MUCH GRIZZLY

In the stillness it finally came to him. I'm alive!

I can't remember where I first read about Dan Ludington, but it was an incredible story that stuck with me and became one of my favorite bear tales.

Dan and Maxine Ludington owned Mooch-igan Lodge at Summit Lake on Alaska's Richardson Highway. That day in October 1949 they eagerly welcomed Jerry Luebke, their friend and neighbor. The gentle giant, whom they hadn't seen for weeks, wore a winning smile and a size 44 wolf skin parka. Their lodge was nine miles north of his homestead. He and Dan had shared many a good memory around the campfire. He was a foreman on the Alaska Road Commission camp at Paxson, a few miles south of Summit Lake and about halfway between Glennallen and the Alaska Highway. He kind of took it upon himself to be the local town crier in a less vocal manner.

He dropped by to tell Dan that he should be expecting visitors soon. Because Dan and the twenty or so lodge owners along the highway depended upon visitors for their income, Dan almost visibly rubbed his palms together in anticipation of a ringing cash register. But then Jerry informed Dan that the visitors were not of the cash and carry customers but rather the 4-legged, pointy-toothed-and-razor-sharp-clawed variety, wearing shaggy, brown coats. A sow grizzly and her cub were on the prowl for some free grub.

When Jerry spoke of the bears, Dan wasn't much impressed. He assumed it was probably the one that had been creating a stir in the vicinity of late. But they weren't the only bears looking for food. Bears had been moseying into old fish camps, raiding garbage cans, and breaking into food caches. There had been a berry shortage beginning in August after an early frost.

Dan knew that there were very few bear maulings in Alaska, usually a couple a year. During a season when bear maulings are abnormally high, the cause is often attributed to a failed berry crop.

Dan wasn't too concerned until Jerry related a personal tale from the previous evening. The grizzly and cub had showed up at his place on the edge of a road commission camp. While they were grubbing around for something to eat, Jerry was working in a clearing behind his cabin near dusk and knew nothing of the bruins. Without warning the sow announced herself in a full out charge, barreling from a brush patch straight for him.

His wife screamed a warning to Jerry from the family porch, and he immediately looked up and recognized the situation. Cut off from the safety of his house, he ran to a nearby camp bunkhouse, barely beating the bear.

The area has long been noted for its big game that includes the long-legged moose, the constantly moving caribou, the wily wolf and the take-no-prisoner grizzly bear. Each hunting season men fanned out in the forested hills and tundra country hoping to fill their freezers and larders with their winter's meat supply.

The Paxson-Summit Lake locale harbored some of the best grizzly hunting in the state. A good number of hunters and sportsmen regularly visited Luddington's lodge. They knew about bears and had no qualms about liquidating one.

Maxine reminded Dan that the caribou he'd downed the previous week hung outside next to the kitchen door, resembling a dinner invitation. Just a few years before Maxine had learned about hunting. She now waxed eloquent about the wind direction and the bear's nose–the wind had been blowing from the caribou to the bear, sending a message equating to "the table's set, come and get it." Maxine predicted that the old she-rip would show up around dark, looking to exploit Dan's hunting success by bellying up to the hanging caribou carcass.

Dan downplayed the significance of the danger but failed to fool Maxine. This situation was a little irregular. Take grizzly bears, add man, mix in a bad berry season and you've got trouble. In Dan's case he didn't wait for trouble, he tracked it down.

He suggested the fresh snow would make for good tracking. With his comment Maxine crossed the room and took his .401 Winchester autoloader from its gun pegs. Even though the model had been discontinued in 1936, he'd owned it since 1932 and had it rebuilt a few years later. When Maxine handed him the weapon, she showed no sign of worry or concern. She had confidence in Dan's hunting ability as he had killed more than a few bears during his 22 years in Alaska.

Dan and Jerry left the lodge in Jerry's pickup. When Dan turned to look over his shoulder, he spotted Maxine waving good-bye from the porch. Traveling south on the Richardson Highway Jerry mentioned that the buffalo colored sow had last been poking around near Fish Creek and suggested that as a good starting point. He also noted that the bear would go around 800-pounds and was a nasty customer. Thinking a backup gun and an extra pair of eyes would be good medicine, he suggested taking the next day off work to help Dan find her. Although Dan appreciated the offer, he shrugged it off.

He had a hunch that part of the chip on the she-rip's shoulder was a dislike for man because of an old wound. He told Jerry that he figured someone had winged the bear with a small caliber weapon, the wound had festered and her temperament correlated with her pain—as it increased so did her fury and her dislike for man. Dan thought the situation demanded urgency and he wanted to deal with the bear sooner than later.

Dan's experience told him that bears aren't interested in man unless, of course, the animal's panhandling, injured or protecting something. He wasn't particularly fearful of the big omnivores, having scared off more than one with sticks or stones, or even with a rebel yell. He knew the bear to be an opportunist but not one to take on man unless properly provoked. In fact, his guiding convinced him that bears were pretty sociable with regard to people and he'd never heard of a healthy one attacking a person. The bear normally avoids contact with man, constantly traveling with its nose into the wind.

They'd gone less than a mile when Dan signaled for Jerry to stop. There were tracks near a small culvert. Jerry thought perhaps a trucker had stopped, but further examination revealed the obvious—the tracks of the sow and her cub. The fresh tracks showed small tracks off to one side of the larger ones that meandered up a small ridge paralleling the highway.

Excitement coursed through Dan as he climbed atop the pickup with his binoculars. He scanned the slope through the snow flurries. Recalling past hunts in the area, he knew the locale like the back of his hand. The binoculars produced only snow and a field of vision devoid of a living critter. The bears were beyond the ridge.

As Dan hopped to the ground, he was puzzled when Jerry backed his rig off the highway. Dan asked his pal what he was doing and Jerry replied that he'd accompany him to the top of the ridge to see what was stirring, maybe they'd see something on the back side of the ridge.

They pushed along following the broad trail of footprints. Climbing the ridge in 10-degree temperature was almost effortless.

The surrounding 3000-foot valleys rose from rolling hills to 5,000 and 6,000-foot peaks in the foothills of the Alaska Range that housed the giant Mt. McKinley, a 20,230 foot hunk of rock near the center of the state.

Dan marveled at the first snowfall blanketing the environs. Only the day before the land looked brown and bare. He was reminded that each year frost hastened the traditional panorama of fall. The golden leaves of the birch, aspen and cottonwoods spanning valleys and hills contrasted with the black-green of the spruce cloistered in hillside patches. Above timberline the reds and violets fired the ground, carpeting the country. Pockets of mountain willows dotted the landscape, inviting the big ungulates with the beards, brown eyes and paddle shaped horns to sample their leaves as a prelude to winter.

But that was yesterday. The evolution from fall to winter was as regular as water flowing downhill. But the locals never knew exactly when winter would arrive with its snow and freezing, raw winds.

Thinking about the change in appearance that snow brings, Dan and Jerry rimmed out and discovered bear scat. It appeared that the animals had passed about three hours earlier. The tracks dropped off the ridge into the valley below and up the next ridge a half mile distant.

Because Jerry's road crew awaited his direction for a tough day of snow removal, he departed for his pickup, leaving Dan with a parting warning to be careful. Jerry waved good-bye and Dan continued his mission.

Dan's pace increased with the snowfall. Even though he knew that he and the falling snow raced time, he was motivated more by the fact that the bear-pair ahead of him was on an unwavering bruin-olfactory-compass course for his lodge. By nightfall they'd be at his kitchen door sampling the caribou intended for his family during the winter months ahead.

Dan reached the crest of the second knoll as the snow thickened, all but obliterating the line of brush where the bear tracks disappeared a mere ten yards below.

He pondered his plan. Should he push on or should he backtrack? The snow filled the bears' tracks, making it increasingly more difficult to follow them. Perhaps it would be better to return to the highway and his home to see if the bears showed that evening. The bear knew man's ways and she was mean. He knew that either she plodded on ahead in the thickening soup or, perhaps, she had winded him and was even now stalking him.

When one hunts alone in the wilderness, danger stalks the huntsman. Clothed in confusion, injury, changing weather, unfriendly environs, unexpected accident or failed equipment or gear, danger plagues the outdoorsman: singular thinking clouds the mind–a misinterpreted landmark or lack of a compass misdirects, and misdirection panics; a twisted ankle slows travel; a sudden drop in temperature handcuffs; snow bridges disguise glacial crevasses; an accidental fall immobilizes; a faulty firing pin disarms.

Dan's situation was a powder keg wrapped in a fur coat. The fuse was short. Once lit, explosion was swift and certain. Armed with a mouthful of ivory and razor sharp claws, a grizzly nearly always wins a duel with an unarmed man.

Still undecided, Dan stood on the crest of the knoll, his rifle in one hand his binoculars in the other. That's when the old gal made the decision for him.

Roaring and bounding uphill over the thirty feet that separated them took less than two seconds. In that time span Dan instinctively dropped the binoculars on the neck strap and swung his rifle to meet the grizzly's charge. With her red eyes boring a hole in him and her hackles rigid the beast lunged. Both of them heard the same sound as he jerked the trigger...a sickening, hollow, metallic *plink*.

Normally the Winchester .401 belched death with a resonating roar. But this time the rifle whimpered.

Dan jacked another shell into the rifle's chamber, stepped backward and smacked her on the snout with the rifle's butt just as her sledgehammer blow knocked him reeling to the ground. Her right paw had connected with the binoculars, reducing the damage to him. Yet, even the binoculars and his four layers of clothes did not stop her claws from slicing into his chest as neatly as a surgeon's scalpel. But he never felt a thing.

He clung to the weapon–his life's hope–as she snarled and bit savagely at it.

She pounced on Dan and munched on his left arm. When he screamed in pain, she went for his head. He clasped the rifle as though it were life itself. His plan was to use his hands and feet until he could bring it into play. Unsure whether it would even fire, he kept kicking the bear.

With every kick Dan thought about his dependent family–a wife, two kids and one on the way–and an unpaid mortgage on his property. Dan had been on the ground mere seconds but it seemed like an eternity. He kept slamming his size 12 boots into the sow's belly and thinking *what a lousy way to die*.

Her next bite across his face sent her canine teeth through his nose and spanned to his right temple. She crunched down. Her teeth clamping onto his face was the last thing Dan saw through his right eye. The pain was indescribable. He fought blacking out and clung to the rifle rather than reaching for his head.

Evidently annoyed that the man-thing kept striking back or that he was so hard to dispatch, she stopped chewing on his head and left leg and attacked his right leg just above his boot. That action gave him the opportunity he needed to swivel his rifle into the fray. In a nano-second Dan swung the muzzle into her chest and the rifle bellowed death.

Through his left eye he saw displaced hair blow off her back as the 250-grain bullet rocketed out of her body. It was almost as if the muzzle blast drove her upward onto her hind legs. Her roar blended with the dying echo of the rifle blast; both bullet and bear lost their energy and fell to earth.

With a final shudder, she dropped onto the snow at Dan's feet and never twitched.

Dan fell back onto the silent snow. Ringing filled his ears. The air and falling snow wrapped him in silence. In the stillness it finally came to him. *I'm alive! The bear's dead.* He couldn't believe his good fortune. Half dozen times he reminded himself that he tossed the final punch; he sidestepped a knockout blow and lay on the canvas, the victor.

Now it fell upon him to crawl out of the ring and negotiate safely to the locker room—to rise from the snow covered ground and to get to the gravel road.

A wave of pain shot through him. After it passed, he struggled to his feet. Running his right hand over his scalp, he discovered it was shredded and part of it hung over his left eye. He gently laid it back over his head, but it fell again releasing more blood from his head wounds.

Three deep claw marks crossed his chest. He marveled that they'd have ended his life had they been a half-foot higher.

Then he managed to use his right arm to wrap what was left of his undershirt around his head. He was impartial as he examined himself and assumed, from the condition of his left arm, that he would lose it. His greatest concern, however, was his left leg.

It felt like it was on fire. Blood poured from a wound just above his ankle. The pain was almost unbearable, but his leg supported him. He regretted the pain as well as the thought of the distance between him and the highway.

When a fit of shaking overcame him, he forced himself to calm down. He reminded himself that he was a long way from help and then challenged himself, *You've got to settle down and save yourself because nobody's here to do it.*

He reached over to pick up his rifle and passed out. Moments later he came to and gained his feet.

Knowing that he had some distance to go to reach the road, and from there, medical attention, he began his trek. During that pain-wracked, dreadful journey four things came to mind. The first was a self-debate on the advantages and disadvantages of taking a shortcut to the highway. If he detoured from his original path and didn't make it, no one knew where to look immediately for him. On the other hand, Jerry knew which way he had traveled, so if he retraced his tracks and failed to make it, at least they would be able to search, and, more than likely, find him easier.

Second, he noticed the brush move at one point and assumed it was the orphaned bear cub. Without its mother's protection and direction, he knew that the bear was as good as dead...*Too bad, Little Fella. Mr. Jack Frost will gobble you up before too long.*

Third, when he realized that he clutched his rifle in his right hand, he tossed it aside and chastised himself for his stupidity in packing the extra weight.

And the fourth thing that he became aware of was that something was banging against his left cheek. He tried to brush it away by reaching across his chest with his right hand. He discovered that it was his torn left ear. Figuring the doctors could save it, he gently pushed it beneath his undershirt head covering.

An hour and a half after starting his hike Dan miraculously stumbled onto the roadway then slumped to the ground, just as a trucker friend braked to a stop at the culvert that Dan had left earlier.

After Lewis Clarke loaded him into his rig and headed north, Dan related the battle. He didn't want his wife and kids to see him as he was and asked Lewis to go to the nearest hospital in Delta Junction, 70 miles north where the Richardson and the Alaska highways intersect near the site of an U.S. Air Force base.

Lewis stopped part way and called to inform Maxine that Dan had been hurt and to suggest she go to Fairbanks where he would ultimately be taken. Lewis also passed on the word to the Army Alaska Arctic Training Center that occupied the base and ran the hospital.

Several miles south of Delta an army ambulance met the pair. Once at the base Ludington was given sedatives and first aid, loaded into another ambulance and hustled off to Fairbanks in a blinding snowstorm. It seemed as though even the snow drifts conspired against Dan as the mercy vehicle got stuck four times in the fifty miles before reaching Fairbanks and Dr. William Smith's operating table.

For several hours the doc sutured leg, arm, face, scalp and chest, administering over 200 stitches. He saved Dan's arm and leg, but his right eye was beyond repair.

Ten days later Dan was on his way to Seattle where he underwent a series of operations over the next half-year.

While recuperating in the hospital Dan had time to review his mauling. He believed that his stop on the ridge to determine whether to proceed or to return saved his life. His rationale was that had he turned to leave, the bear would have attacked him from behind. Had he continued into the brush, he would not have had time to react to her charge.

One of the changes he experienced was being fitted with a plastic eye to which he tried to adjust for more than ten years. He regained complete use of his left arm and leg. One of his pleasures was rising daily, walking across his bedroom and kicking the head of the offending bear which Jerry Luebke had had made into a rug for him.

Jerry had returned the day after Dan's battle and skinned out the bear and retrieved his rifle. He discovered that the bruin had been previously injured by the slug of a .25/20.

A year after the battle Dan returned to the scene and found the bullet that had misfired. The primer was dented. He theorized that the cold affected the firing pin–perhaps taking the rifle from the warm interior of his home into a colder environment had frozen the oil and prevented the rifle's firing. He thought it also possible that snow entered the mechanism and froze. Either case would have been cause enough to keep the firing pin from moving forward and striking the primer hard enough to elicit a discharge.

As years went by, Dan kicked himself awake in a cold sweat over a thousand times when dreaming about the sound of the sow's teeth scraping across his skull as her jaws closed.

Her attack effectively ended Dan's hunting days. He was unable to shoot right-handed without his right eye and didn't particularly want to learn to shoot left-handed. After his recovery Dan's hunting was confined to occasional bird hunting. Nevertheless he was mighty glad to be alive.

Dan was able to dispatch his swarming grizzly and make his way to succor. Field Johnson eventually reached safety also, however only after crawling from the debris where his mauler left him.

18

BURIED ALIVE...TWICE

The grizzly then tossed her to the ground and
bit the back of her neck repeatedly.

When researching bear stories for *Alaska Bear Tales*, I had the good fortune of meeting John Graybill, a long time Alaskan and big game guide. He told me about a boat skipper whom a grizzly buried alive near a fresh water stream in Prince William Sound, and I included his story in that book. Some time later I read about Field Johnson, another man buried by a grizzly. In the annals of recorded history there are few such tales–less than half dozen that I've heard of–where the person crawled out from under the foliage and toiled to safety.

Another was Mattie Jack, whose story Mike Cramond and Kathy Etling recorded in their books. Mattie's story follows this one.

Hopefully you'll enjoy both these unbelievable tales and marvel at Field's and Mattie's determination as much as I have.

ield Johnson needed meat for the table in the spring of 1950. He took his faithful .30-30 rifle and headed into the hills, hunting moose. Moving quietly through the woods in the predawn darkness, he knew that daylight would open a world of vision and possibilities for him. Field's long experience as an Indian big game hunting guide gave him the knowledge and preparation that he needed for procuring moose. He hailed from Champagne, Yukon Territory, Canada, a very long day's walk from White-horse...or if you prefer, around 50 miles.

While Field crept through the woods as silently as a shadow, without warning, a blow knocked him flying end over end and flattened him. When he realized a grizzly was the antagonist, he knew his only chance of surviving the situation was to play dead. In hopes that the critter would leave, he called upon his outdoor knowledge and did not move nor make a sound.

The bear knocked him around and bit him a little before mounding vegetation around him in a cache, normal behavior for grizzlies intending to return at a later time to utilize its prey for food.

A big grizzly had been making a nuisance of itself in the neighborhood for some time and Field wondered if it was the same one that beat him up.

Sniffing and grunting, the animal padded around the fallen man, possibly for an hour.

While Field lay in the pile of dirt and debris, blood oozed from his wounds. It was very difficult to be quiet while enduring the pain that wracked his body.

When the bear's movement ceased and the man heard it no more, he decided it must have departed and he decided it was safe to crawl from under the debris. Freeing himself from the cache, Field tottered to his feet.

Unbeknownst to him, the grizzly had been waiting and watching from the bushes nearby. In a flash the roaring bear jumped him. It knocked him down and began the beating all over again–cuffing and chewing him until he lost consciousness. The bear dragged Field by the legs somewhere between a half-mile and a mile as he banged along over the ground, oblivious to the activity. Then the bear buried him again.

When the tough Indian regained consciousness, it was late afternoon. By now his loss of blood had given him a driving thirst for water. His injuries hurt to beat the devil.

Aware that he'd not survive a night in the woods or another mauling, and that he needed to get help soon or die, Field had little choice but to rise and seek his own rescue. He dug himself from the dirt pile, stumbled to his feet and made his way toward the Alaska Highway.

The bear probably assumed the man was dead because it had left the vicinity.

In due time Field reached the Highway. Despite the fact that he was covered from head to foot in grime in the form of blood, dirt and vegetation, a passing driver of a pickup truck stopped and gave him a lift into Whitehorse and the hospital.

Field learned that both his arms and several ribs were broken. His scalp hung from his head. His feet were chewed and his thighs gashed. He was in the hospital two months before he was released.

The first thing he did after leaving the medical facility was to return to the scene of his mauling and find his .30-30. Then he went grizzly bear hunting...for the same animal that inflicted his injuries!

He told Thomas Hardin, "Him a bad bear. Someday I findum and shootum. Maybe I don't shootum, he killum other people."

A year later Field was a mere shadow of his former self and never did fully recover from the bear's damage.

Both he and Alexie Pitka wasted away after their maulings, providing a strong message about safety in bear country if the outdoorsman wants to live a normal and productive life.

As a side note, I've included an interesting story written by Ran Lake.

Because of Field's last name, Lake asked if his father were Swedish. Field told the hunter that his family was Indian as far back as his grandparents. Field was a man in his early forties, slender and wiry. He'd spent his life guiding, trapping, fishing and hunting in the bush.

Some years previous Field had stopped to visit a prospector-friend while returning to his home place in Champagne. While walking up the trail from the creek to the friend's cabin, Field discovered an overturned bucket. Paying little attention to the container, he walked on to the cabin.

When he discovered the cabin's owner absent, Field brewed himself some tea as was customary in the country.

After completing his cup of tea, he went outside where he strolled about the cabin for a bit, anticipating the return of the prospector any minute. Abruptly he came upon the torso of his friend lying in the nearby foliage. His friend's body was mangled and his legs were missing.

Struck with the need to protect his friend's remains and to contact the authorities, Field carried the prospector's body into the cabin, barricaded the door so that the offending bear could not enter and hastened to notify the Royal Canadian Mounted Police.

Field and the Mounties returned to discover that the bear had arrived first, torn the door off and absconded with the prospector's corpse. They theorized that the bear had initially taken the prospector by surprise as he carried the water bucket to his cabin.

The men spent several days searching for the dead man but never found him.

Although Field Johnson was buried alive and survived, he is not alone. Another person buried and left by a grizzly was Mattie Jack. She was a British Columbia Alkatcho Indian from the Anahim Indian Reserve at Anahim Lake.

In 1963 Mattie and her husband John were working out of a cabin at the Mud Lake ranch. Some of their horses had strayed and the couple rode out in separate directions looking for them. When she came to a brushy, marshy area that was too dense for her saddle horse, she dismounted, tied him and continued up the hillside on foot.

She proceeded absent-mindedly and before long she surprised herself and a grizzly sow with two cubs when she looked up to discover them within seventy yards of her. The first thought jumping into her head was the repeated advice she'd been given over the years from old timers…that someone encountering a grizzly close up, should remain still and silent. Her grandfather had always told her that the worst thing to do in such a situation was to run.

As the bear approached her, walking briskly, Mattie initiated the advice and remained still. When the animal walked behind her, Mattie closed her eyes and held her breath.

By now the bear was growling. Mattie forced herself to stay calm and to make no sound. She heard the bear popping its teeth just before it stood up and clamped her head in its jaws. She felt the bear's teeth scrape over the top of her head and rip her scalp away.

The grizzly then tossed her to the ground and bit the back of her neck repeatedly. Next it bit behind her shoulder and all over her right leg. After the bear had all but torn her arm off, it picked her up in its jaws. Mattie was overwhelmed at the pain she felt as the bear shook her until she passed out.

Some time later when she regained consciousness, she discovered that the bear had buried her under dirt and leaves.

Her next thought was about God. Her Catholic grandmother had always told her that God would save her.

Dirt and vegetation mixed with the blood from her wounds. As she crawled from beneath the pile, she discovered her torn clothing and noticed that the bleeding continued. She struggled to her feet and started the trek to her horse, anticipating that John would be there.

She fought the pain and waves of nausea, hoping she wouldn't pass out again.

Her boots filled with blood as she neared her mount. With shock and fear she saw her husband pointing his rifle at her. In the darkness he was unable to determine what kind of critter she was. He was scared because he didn't know that she was human. Her clothes were in tatters and her scalp hung from her head. He continued covering her with his rifle until she shouted, "Don't shoot me, John. It's Mattie."

John hastily attended her wounds then lifted her onto her horse. He took off immediately, leading the horse four miles to the cabin where he left her and rode his horse 15-miles further to call for an emergency airlift.

The lake was too small for a light plane to safely land, however local pilot Dick Poet risked his life and blasted onto the lake on floats. He and John carried Mattie to the plane and gently eased her inside. She was so weak from blood loss that she scarcely knew what was happening. Dick whisked her away to the Bella Coola hospital. His piloting skills and the risk of his rescue no doubt saved Mattie's life. (He later died in another rescue attempt)

The grizzly had bitten the back of her neck, the area around her right breast, her right underarm and right leg, requiring over 200 sutures. She remained in the hospital four months, going back periodically during the next four years for treatment.

Although Mattie became an attractive grandmother with no noticeable scars, she developed a lasting fear of grizzlies. She avoided entering grizzly country for the rest of her life.

The will to live is an overwhelming characteristic in people. Field and Mattie demonstrated that trait as did Hugh Glass, the legendary mountain man who lived one of the greatest survival stories in history.

19

DETERMINED TO LIVE

Although his campmates marveled at Hugh's plucky spirit,
they were certain that it would not stave off the Grim Reaper.

Decades ago when I learned about Hugh Glass, I marveled at the story. It became one of my favorites because of his spirit, injury, healing and will to live–he clung to life's flickering flame like a man striking his last match in winter's 60-below death grip. The hatred that motivated him gave him a shot at life, which he grabbed by the throat and clung to, eking out each day's full measure, one sunrise at a time.

I lived with the half dozen versions of Glass until I attempted to "get to the bottom" of his legend. Even though I wanted to know the facts, they are illusive because of the disparity of accounts. John Myers suggests that some historians purposely misrepresented the Glass legend for purposes of their own (I suggest you read his very interesting book).

Some of the diverse information includes:

The party:
One account names the leader of the trapping party as Sublette, a well-known captain of the West.

The attack:
Glass was either looking for berries or trapping.

One mentions that he traveled with a partner, though other sources suggest that he had at least three companions traveling ahead of the main party and hunting for meat.

Glass was alone and surprised the bear.

Glass and a companion sighted and shot simultaneously, both hitting the animal.

According to one, Hugh fired his pistol whereas another mentioned his firing two pistols.

The rescue:
Glass fought the bear with his knife after stumbling, and his friend watched.

Glass's two companions came to his rescue, each shooting a charging cub.

While Glass knifed the bear, the rest of the party shot the bear off him.

The abandonment:
One says that those who abandoned Glass took all of his weapons while another states that he was left with his knife and flint, enabling him to cut and to cook meat.

The bulk of the accounts suggest that the main trapping party left him the day after the attack, yet one mentions that the same party carried him for up to six days on a stretcher before leaving him beside a spring and near berries.

His recovery:
One account indicated that he lay beneath berry bushes at the water's edge, facilitating access to food and water; another refers to the fruit as wild cherries.

One suggests that he traveled with a band of Sioux Indians or the French Company.

Glass covered between 100 and 350 miles, depending upon the version that you read.

Some accounts suggest that Glass had an Indian wife, but Myers–who thoroughly studied all versions–fails to mention such an arrangement.

At least one account says Glass lived his final years in Taos, New Mexico; however a couple mention his travel to Indian country where the red-skins killed him and lifted his hair.

Regardless of the confusion, at least three elements prevail...he was mauled; he was abandoned and he survived. John Myers examined all the accounts and reasons for the most probable development of Hugh's epic. Since Myers put the legend to bed, it would be superfluous to ressurect it. My purpose here is NOT to tell the historical account in all its accuracy–if it's even known–but to incorporate enough details from the several accounts and hope to provide a readable and reasonable story.

H ugh Glass is the subject of one of the most incredible survival episodes in all of recorded history. Before he was a mountain man, he was the captain of an American ship, that is, before Pirate Jean Lafitte captured him and another man, the two being given the choice of joining the pirates or walking the plank—some choice.

Glass was tall, in his mid-30s, physically well built and full of spirit. He and his buddy awaited a chance to slip over the side of the boat one night then swam two miles through waters frequented by sharks to the beach near present day Galveston. For the trip each took a knife, flint and steel, some food and minimum essentials. Their survival necessitated their turning inland to avoid cannibalistic Karankawa Indians.

They succeeded until some time later when Wolf Pawnees captured them. Hugh's partner was burned at the stake. While Hugh awaited his turn, he gave the chief a packet of cinnabar (red war paint material). Evidently the chief viewed Hugh as a gift bringer and allowed him to live, adopting him as a son. Glass lived with the Pawnees for several years before traveling with the chief to St. Louis to discuss the benefits of Indian trapping and fur trading. At that point Hugh exchanged the Indian way of life to become a mountain man. On March 7, 1823 Hugh joined the Major Andrew Henry trapping group, ascending the Missouri with Bill Sublette, Black Harris and others.

Eager to return to the Yellowstone country and beaver trapping in the Rocky Mountains, Major Andrew Henry led a company of less than a dozen rugged mountain men-free trappers through unexplored Montana country. They crossed the scrubby, barren country near the modern day borders of Wyoming, Montana and South Dakota. Their journey took them up the Grand River, a stream with headwaters in the Black Hills, a range north of the Platte.

These men kept their hair by outsmarting their wily red-skinned foe by reading sign, reacting accordingly and fighting in self-defense when necessary. Hugh Glass was independent and strong willed. Though fellow trappers attested to his honor, fidelity and integrity, some say he was reckless and insubordinate. By then he was in his mid-40s and the most experienced of the band, his age and graying hair earning him the moniker Old Glass.

On the morning of August 23rd Major Henry handpicked two men to hunt for camp meat. Meanwhile Hugh and Moses (Black) Harris had wandered away from the group in search of fruit. While leading through a cherry thicket along the stream, Glass surprised a yellow she-rip grizzly bear.

She immediately charged the two-legged who managed to get off a shot before she reached him. His bullet wound did not immediately deter the bear, though it had a long-term effect on her.

Hugh had time to unsheathe his knife and bring it into play. He plunged it repeatedly into the thoroughly aroused sow while she bit and slashed his body. As she ripped into him with her claws, the two fell to the ground in mortal combat. While she bit and clawed, Glass stabbed her time and again.

In the meantime, Black Harris rushed onto the scene where he was confronted by one of the sow's grown yearling cubs. He blasted the charging bear, killing it.

As the snarling silvertip ripped the flesh from Hugh's ribs, exposing bones, his blood poured into his eyes and complicated his gallant self-defense. Weak from the beating he'd absorbed and the loss of blood, Glass finally dropped his weapon to the ground. Within that brief time the bear succumbed to the many wounds that Hugh had inflicted and collapsed on top of him.

By now the party of trappers, hearing the clamor and suspecting Indian trouble, reached the scene of the desperate fight. They discovered a mixture of man-bear blood splattered over the area. Some of them, doubtless, felt that Old Glass had gotten his come-uppance for his freewheeling spirit and absence from the party.

When the men rolled the carcass of the dead silvertip from him, they were astonished to find him still breathing. They observed grave injuries–scalp hanging from his head, crushed ribs, a gaping hole in his neck that bubbled with blood and other body fluids every time he breathed, intestines exposed and his body mangled with deep, bleeding wounds. Any of the fifteen major wounds inflicted upon him could have sped him on his way to another world.

One ball and multiple stab wounds punctured the bear—more than twenty gashes to the bruin's chest and belly.

Although his campmates marveled at Hugh's plucky spirit, they were certain that it would not stave off the Grim Reaper. They believed that Old Glass had bought the farm this time—his hourglass was about empty.

Initially, his party expected Glass to die within minutes. The only "medical help" available on the plains was a stiff shot of brandy and strips of cloth to bandage wounds. Even if they thought he'd live, his neck injury prevented him from drinking. All they could do was bind his wounds and make camp preparatory to burying him. Glass was the favorite of the camp and talk of him was a major subject of conversation that night around the campfire.

The next morning, however, Hugh was still alive. Now, that was a shock and produced a dilemma. Hostile Indians roamed the neighborhood. In fact only two days previous Indians had attacked the party and killed two men. Because of the danger of lingering in the area for the sake of burying a companion, Major Henry elected to move on out of harm's way.

Still expecting him to die any minute, Hugh's comrades constructed a litter from tree boughs in order to move him. Then they shouldered their burden and continued on their journey, always alert for Indians intent on terminating their activities. Shrubs, dwarf-plum trees and brushwood forced the litter bearers to pick their way along. The group periodically stopped to switch positions, to rest or to give Hugh a breather from the jolting movement.

They moved steadily, though slowly, onward, possibly for six days, before Major Henry called for a halt. Although ethics demanded they provide their friend a decent burial, common sense told Major Henry that prudence required getting the party to safety. The men set the litter on the ground in a grove of trees in the center of which was a freshwater spring. Rather than jeopardize the group, Henry called for two volunteers to stay with Glass a few hours until he died, to bury him and then to catch up to the party.

Jim Bridger, a 19-year-old kid, quickly volunteered. Major Henry waited for a second volunteer until John Fitzgerald finally spoke up.

John acknowledged the danger, stating that anyone staying behind might miss the fall hunt and that it might be a good idea to pay the volunteers. Henry allowed that he'd provide a monetary reward to anyone who stayed to bury the irascible mountain man. Knowing the amount was equivalent to three months' pay, Fitzgerald volunteered.

The eight remaining trappers moved on toward their objective.

Next morning Glass was still alive. Fitzgerald and Bridger wondered how things would go if Hugh hung on for two weeks. Their only activity revolved around looking for enemies, checking Glass' condition or giving him water to try to drink.

How many times did they raise the question of Old Glass' chances of recovering or of a war party of Indians coming across their camp? If savages discovered them, would their chances of escape and survival be as good as those Hugh experienced with Old Ephraim? How much longer would Glass hold out? What should they do?

The air about camp hung like a dreaded shroud. Both men knew that their only friends at the moment were their wilderness skills and concealment. They also knew that their campmate was unable to provide any form of assistance should Indians discover them.

Glass lay on his litter showing no signs of getting better, though from time to time his throat worked well enough to take on a little water administered by Fitzgerald or Bridger. The red bandages covering him resembled a winding sheet. He could not talk and his breathing was so feeble that he seemed dead.

The following morning Bridger couldn't tell whether Glass was alive. Hugh had gone into a deep sleep and appeared near death. Later in the day Fitzgerald hinted that he and Bridger had been good companions to stay with Glass as long as they had. That risk earned them the money Henry offered. Fitzgerald suggested that maybe it was time for them to clear out.

When the sliver of silver sliced the eastern sky the next morning, Fitzgerald was packing to leave. Bridger told him that Old Glass's eyes were opened and glazed and he wasn't sure if Hugh could see. Fitzgerald told the youngster that they'd stayed longer than Henry had expected–staying on wasn't reasonable and he was moving out. Part of his rationale was that Hugh had lapsed into a coma-like state, the implication being that death was very near.

Glass had experienced several "death sweats" or periods of feverish sweating. Bridger wasn't sure if the old man was delirious, however he thought Glass could both see and understand what he and Fitzgerald were saying.

Fitzgerald told Bridger that he was leaving and asked it he were going along.

Bridger said that he couldn't go. He held fast until Fitzgerald suggested what the Indians would do to him if they caught him and emphasized that a corpse wasn't worth risking his life for. He suggested that there was no reason to stay and fend off hostiles. Then he commanded the younger man to grab Glass's gun, knife and possibles, implying there was no need to leave them for a dead man. And he emphasized that "we buried Old Glass."

In order for their claim of Hugh's death to be believed, removal of his "possibles" was necessary (since a dead and buried trapper would no longer have need of them). These items included his tomahawk, flint and steel, knife, sidearm, powder, shot and percussion caps and his rifle. The frontiersman lived and died by his rifle. To remove it was to sentence him to almost certain death, though it appeared likely Glass was at death's doorstep and unable to use it.

They mounted their horses and rode off to rejoin their party. Surely each must have considered his decision of leaving a living comrade. Each must have expected Old Glass to die from his wounds, yet each must have wondered about his chances of surviving. And if he survived, how would he manage?

The two finally reached their companions, within a few days of the party's reaching the fort. Fitzgerald and Bridger reported that Hugh had died and that they had buried him as promised and as paid.

Meanwhile Glass' body continued to heal and gradually to gain strength. When he regained consciousness, he was uncertain of his predicament. He had dropped into and out of consciousness numerous times before he was able to evaluate his situation. Since he didn't hear harps or smell smoke, it eventually dawned on him that he was still on the planet. And he realized that he was alone, his body was a wreck and his gear and weapons were gone.

His greatest need besides medical treatment was for food and water. Because Fitzgerald and Bridger had moved his pallet close to the spring before leaving him, Glass was able to reach out with a cupped hand and transport water from the spring to his parched lips. Water provided hydration, which quelled his fever, lubricated his internal machinations and cleaned his stomach injuries. He was also able to reach buffalo berries on overhanging bushes nearby. He managed to crush and mix them with water to force them down his throat to stave off starvation.

Gradually a growing rage and determination to avenge himself on those who'd abandoned him enabled him to overcome much of his pain and fever. Revenge burned like an unquenchable fire, *I'll get those two if it's the last thing I do.*

Awakening from a nap, possibly as the result of the weight of something on his arm, he discovered a thick rattlesnake, in a state of torpor from having swallowed a small rodent, slithering over his arm, oblivious to the prostate man on the ground.

Most Americans have never missed meals or been without food for any period; therefore hunger is a stranger to them. It's hard for them to visualize eating only what they could stumble onto or catch for food. They've never considered nor been forced to eat raw meat, bugs, insects, frogs or snakes. A lot of people have never even eaten improperly prepared food. So what must it have been like for a man in Hugh's condition to eat whatever he could acquire. Or was he so far gone that he wouldn't notice the things he thrust into his mouth?

Glass reached a sharp stone and smashed the reptile's head. By sawing through its skin, severing the head and shredding the meat in the same manner he had made pulp of the berries, Hugh provided himself with the first of many snake meals. He used a couple of stones to smash the meat then combined it with water to assist his swallowing.

Because he thought that all his possibles had been taken, it was with great joy that he discovered his wallet, which contained a razor.

Blow flies laid their eggs around his back wounds. As they hatched, the maggots fed on his putrid flesh, partially cleaning the wounds though the infection stayed with him.

In all likelihood Glass ate cherries and berries, and later, as he gained strength, insects, roots, rose haws, frogs, snakes and other small critters.

Although Major Henry's trapping party was bound to Fort Henry, Fort Kiowa was closer, some 350 miles away and near present day Chamberlain in southeast South Dakota. It was also generally downhill so Glass ultimately chose to strive for Fort Kiowa.

Perhaps you've played games as a child, like leapfrog, where you walked on all fours for a few minutes. How would that compare to crawling on hands and knees through broken country, polka-dotted with cacti, sagebrush and tumbleweed? Not for a few minutes, but for days. Not for play, but for life!

Glass was not strong enough to rise and walk, but he could crawl. And that he did. He was a pathetic figure, groveling along the ground on all fours, able to cover only a few rods by day's end. When he'd exhausted his last effort, he collapsed.

Repetitious thoughts filled the screen of his mind's eye–using caution to avoid those hostiles who would kill him on sight, procuring food and, the ever present motivator, killing the two varmints who left him to die.

He remained where he'd dropped, nothing protecting him from the night's cold save his ripped buckskin garb and dirty rags, by now black with dried blood and grime. Only his deerskin clothes and his iron will protected him from the elements, be they heat, cold or wet. His only means of defense against hostile Indians, grizzlies or wolves was his razor, which he was too weak to wield.

Even though his chances of surviving would improve if he could acquire some meat, it was not likely that he'd catch live food any time soon.

In the days ahead he managed to add more distance to each trek until he was covering two miles a day.

During those days he used sharp stones to dig up roots. Throughout his ordeal he called upon his Indian training for sustenance and sanctuary. One day he happened across a dead bison and smashed the bones with rocks to get at their marrow, which he mixed with berries for nourishment.

About that time Hugh was alerted to the chase of predator and prey. A pack of wolves was hot on the heels of a bison calf and dropped it within yards of the hapless human. No doubt the calf was born in April, five months previous, and represented substantial food if he could commandeer it from the wolves.

He was still unable to stand and would be forced to make the most of his efforts on all fours, the same level as the wolves. Somehow he managed to take possession of the partially devoured calf (one account suggested he lit a grass fire and another stated that he rose onto his legs and screeched to scare the wolves), his reward being fresh meat which the wolves had rough skinned. Hugh's former Pawnee captors considered the raw entrails of a freshly killed bison a treat, so whatever he could salvage, would be fine by him. Here, at last was enough bounty to strengthen and fortify him for the journey ahead, literally elevating him in a few short days above the four-leggeds of the environs to two legs and enabling him to walk.

He ripped the flesh away from the calf and ate it in great quantities. In all likelihood the thought racing across his mind was *I'm going to live! I'm going to live!*

Even though his wounds healed and were much better, the one on his back was still festering because he was unable to clean it.

After gorging on the flesh for a few days, Hugh left the carcass and moved on. He left in an upright manner, giving him confidence and enabling him to see over the grasses and watch through trees for Indian parties. Stronger now, he thought he might even be able to procure birds, frogs or snakes. He could now swing or toss a stick. He might even bag a rabbit or the sharp clawed, desert digging badger.

He found that he could cover a mile in an hour and felt he might soon be covering ten miles a day. His new found strength gave him hope, and that coupled with his hatred for being left behind propelled him onward toward the Grand River at its confluence with the Missouri and ever southward toward Fort Kiowa.

About this time Hugh came upon a deserted Indian village which harbored a few dogs. He coaxed one within his reach and sliced its throat with his razor before using the same tool to butcher it. He fed on what many considered the prime meat of the Plains.

That's about when a band of Sioux Indians in transit stumbled onto Glass. They showed him favor, marveling at his conquest of Old Ephraim. Indians looked upon the yellow bear as the number one foe on the plains and they revered anyone who killed one in a hand to paw fight with more respect than killing a rival brave.

Finally someone could clean Hugh's maggot plagued back wound and give him hope for its healing. They carefully washed it and applied a vegetable liquid. They helped him reach Fort Kiowa before the second week of October. It had been seven weeks since his merciless mauling.

He'd made it, living alone, crawling and walking nearly 350 miles through hostile Indian territory. Those at Fort Kiowa who thought him dead were astounded when they saw Old Glass. He was disappointed to learn that he'd missed Ashley by less than two weeks.

Glass gained information about the two men who had abandoned him and within a couple of days of his arrival, he started off with five others aboard a dugout canoe toward the Missouri and Yellowstone rivers. Unfriendly Indians interrupted their journey and Glass managed to escape, thinking until later that he was the sole survivor.

On the last night of 1823, December 31, he caught up with Jim Bridger at Fort Henry where Major Henry's band celebrated the new year.

To the amazement of all present, especially Bridger who had "buried" him, Glass strode into their midst. The astonished revelers stared at him. Though they recognized him, his voice had been considerably altered. Then he spoke directly to the youngster, "It's Glass, Bridger–the one you left to die–and robbed of them things as might have helped him survive, alone and crippled, on them plains...I came back because I swore I'd put you under."

He told the party that he'd heard the palaver between Fitzgerald and Bridger before they abandoned him. Told how he'd been left without even a knife and that he'd scrounged enough food for several days until regaining strength enough to crawl, packing some with him. He suffered from his pain, the cold and hunger while eating roots, berries and whatever he could find.

When he saw the look of remorse on Bridger's face and realized that he was just a kid and under the command of the older Fitzgerald when he had left him, Glass told Bridger that he would let him go and that he forgave him.

The release of weeks of pent up anger took a load off Hugh's mind. But the words and the memory of leaving Glass behind were hard on Bridger. His shame was such he'd rather that Glass had finished him.

After four adventure-packed months involving more Indian trouble and a thousand miles of travel Glass met up with Fitzgerald at Fort Atkinson in Council Bluffs on April 19, 1824. A slight problem had developed, however. Eliminating his foe would be a hanging offense–Fitzgerald was now an U.S. Army soldier. Captain Riley had Fitzgerald come in, and Glass dressed him down for leaving him and taking his possibles and his rifle.

The Captain acquired Hugh's favorite rifle from Fitzgerald, dismissed him and offered Glass his possessions and a grubstake in exchange for leaving the fort and forgetting about Fitzgerald. Old Glass accepted.

For the next nine years he immersed himself in the Yellowstone country and the profession that he loved. But then in 1833, Glass again met with some unfriendly Indians who finished what the old she-rip grizzly had started. They killed and scalped him. But that did not end his reputation. If anything it added to the tale of an old mountain man, beloved and highly respected by his companions for his outdoor skills. His legend was reinvigorated and lives on even now.

Over the years since "heading West" a handful of men have fought a grizzly hand to paw or knife to claw. One such man was James Moore. I'm including his condensed story, which originally appeared in *Notorious Grizzly Bears*.

James A. Moore and his partner were professional hunters providing deer meat for soldiers at Ft. Bayard. He and his partner left camp one morning hunting in different directions near the headwaters of the Gila River in New Mexico in1893.

Later that morning Moore spotted a mahogany-chocolate colored grizzly of large proportions on the opposite side of a large log. Able to see only the bear's back above the log, Moore shot and the bear disappeared from sight. Thinking that he'd hit it in the spine, Moore proceeded to investigate.

As he rounded the log to examine his kill, he was met by the angry, pain-racked bruin that sought the cause of its injury. The unhappy bear lunged for him.

His partner found Moore that night grievously injured. Moore's heart was exposed and still beating. The dead bear lay nearby, its intestines strung out over the ground. Between the dead bear and the man lay Moore's skinning knife.

He was taken to Hermosa, New Mexico, where he received medical treatment. Later he was moved to St. Louis for additional surgery. Although he lived, half his face was missing and his neck was terribly scarred.

Moore later returned to New Mexico where he lived at the Charles Rathburn Ranch. In an effort to hide his disfigurement and scars he allowed his hair and beard to grow. In his later years he moved to the mountains where he lived as a recluse, panning for gold and trapping in the Turkey Creek vicinity.

In the same sense that Hugh Glass utilized his scanty resources to survive, Harry Boyden called upon his only weapons when confronted by a grizzly—his cap and his fists.

Miscellaneous Bear Information

A brown/grizzly has a running stride of nearly 20 feet.

A brown/grizzly runs close to 40 miles an hour which equates to 20 yards a second and 100 yards in 5 seconds.

Predatory animals usually do not make a sound, stalk or sneak and lower their bodies close to the ground or utilize ground cover, bushes or trees. Their intent is to surprise and kill the victim.

One brown/grizzly bear ran 200-yards with its heart shot out and mangled a man (*Alaska Bear Tales*, page 13)

Bud Branham told me about a brown bear that carried a 900-pound carcass in its jaws 200-yards before putting it down.

–The author

20

A MAN'S MAN

Harry's escape depended upon his determination
to face down the bear and to utilize whatever was at hand
in order to placate or turn it.

All About Bears is among my first few bear book purchases. DeHart's book was my introduction to Harry Boyden and his stocking cap. Don attests to the story's authenticity because he heard it from his friend Harry in the 1950s.

Not long after I read the book, I purchased and read Clyde Ormond's *Bear!* He adds additional information about Harry.

Below you will read a truly amazing story which I re-wrote using these gentlemen's accounts.

Harry was born as Henry in England on November 13, 1884 and had come to the Yukon – Alaska bush country circa 1906. He mushed dogs in the winter and used a pack string of horses to freight miners' supplies during the remainder of the year, living in the McCarthy-Nabesna-Slana area until his death. After the gold fever died down, Harry took to big game guiding and outfitting as a profession. He guided many famous sportsmen including Sam Webb of the Boone and Crockett Club and Wily Post, the famous aviator.

Harry also received fame as a hunter and outdoorsman and used dog teams and pack strings to cross some major glaciers including the Russell where he once cut footholds for seven hours for horses' hoof placement. For a long time he was known as Alaska's king of the dog mushers.

Harry feared nothing and possessed a wealth of bear knowledge.

Because his freighting business had tapered off, Harry fell back on trapping to provide income. He planned to trap the winter of

1943 in the Chitina River country of Alaska on the fringe of the Wrangell-St. Elias Mountains. A neighbor told Harry that he'd lost a horse in the vicinity of his trapping cabin and that "if you can find him and will get him, he's yours." Horses were worth $500 so Harry decided to take a shot at finding the critter to add to his pack string.

The day after Harry's birthday on November 14th he and his friend, Joe Malloy, started up the Chitina River with a packhorse in tow. The horse carried enough supplies to last a couple of weeks should the search for the hay burner take that long. The water was low and snow was deeper along the river.

Neither man felt the need to carry a firearm. They weren't hunting, they wanted to go light and grizzlies were in their dens in the high country beyond.

Daylight was fading as is normal that time of the year in the mid-to-late afternoon. They'd traveled quite a stretch and the horse was playing out. Because Harry maintained a pretty stiff pace and wanted to get to the cabin, start a fire and fetch some meat from his cache to thaw for dinner, he suggested that Joe take his time with the horse and he'd go on ahead.

Harry grabbed a small camp ax from the packhorse gear to use for separating the sheep ribs and started out ahead of Joe and the horse.

Near dark Harry saw his cabin nestled on the flat on the top of a rise.

When he approached his cabin, Harry discovered a dark object close by. Instantly thinking it was the lost horse grazing there conveniently, he was pretty happy. In the same chain of thought he realized that it was a monster silvertip. A 500-pound grizzly on the Chitina was considered big, but Harry estimated this one at an extremely unusual 800-pounds.

The bear was tearing at an old mattress that Harry had discarded. Boyden knew enough about grizzlies that he didn't want to surprise one. When a silvertip is given enough warning or scents man, he normally vanishes without a fuss. Harry figured he was far enough away from this one to shout for its attention so that it would leave in a dignified manner.

He hollered at the bear, commented on its ancestry and waved his ax.

The animal immediately stopped his activity but, surprisingly, did not flee. Rather it came straight for him.

Although a bear's charge was usually enough to scare away any intruder, Harry knew false charges for what they were–a grizzly bluffs toward the trespasser and the foreigner flees. This bear, however, meant business and this was no false charge. It was the real deal.

Some people feel that man's confidence is a deterrent in a bear charge. Some theorize that a man afraid gives off an odor similar to other animals, a smell that the bear recognizes and often investigates. That hypothesis also postulates that bears do not bother a man in whom they recognize the lack of fear, either because he is confident or because he masks his fear.

Because of his experience with bears, his lack of fear of them and his knowledge that a man can't outrun one, Harry chose to put that theory into practice and stood his ground.

Under normal circumstances when armed, Harry would have protected his personal space by picking a spot and allowing the animal to come no closer before dropping it. But these were not normal circumstances. Harry's escape depended upon his determination to face down the bear and to utilize whatever was at hand in order to placate or turn it. He might be able to stall it long enough for Joe to arrive to assist him.

Harry wanted to dissuade the animal without igniting further anger or belligerence and thought a tap with the ax might send the message that he wasn't going to back down and that he was not to be trifled with. When the bear was almost on him, he swung the ax. The animal reacted in the blink of an eye, effortlessly swatting the ax from his hand. It landed ten yards away in the snow.

With its lips curled back and fangs showing, the bear was in Harry's lap. It stayed on all fours, popping its jaws repeatedly and snarling at the man, its eyes piercing his.

Knowing about the effect noise has on bears, Harry yelled into the brute's face. Simultaneously he jerked off his wool stocking cap and struck the bear in the face with it. Harry kept up a constant holler and swatted the bear in the face and on the head with his stocking cap while backing slowly toward the ax.

The next two things Harry did were almost unbelievable. They garnered high praise for him as a giant among men.

First, he had the presence of mind to notice that the bear had four long, diagonal scars on its face and surmised that they were the result of a fight with another grizzly.

Second, because Harry's yelling and hat swatting failed to achieve the results he desired, he returned the hat to his head and began pummeling the beast around the head and neck with his fists. He hit the bear so hard and for so long that his fists and arms were black and blue to his elbows for weeks afterwards. His hands swelled to the size of small hams, and because of the stress upon his vocal chords, he was only able to whisper for two weeks following his experience.

Anyone who knows wild grizzlies would consider this story a fabrication for a number of reasons. A blow from a grizzly can break the neck of a barnyard bull. The movement of its swatting paw is so fast that it is difficult to see–it's just a flash. Once engaged in battle the animal knows no fear and fights to the death. But this was a most unusual event.

Harry was amazed that the bear hadn't knocked him down or finished him off. He knew that his puny 2-legged presence was nothing to a grizzly–it could kill him in a heartbeat. The bear allowed Harry to hit it in the face with his fists yet never once laid a paw on him. He couldn't understand that none of his clothes had been torn and he hadn't even been scratched.

Fully expecting the grizzly to end the fight and his existence on earth any second, Harry kept fighting. As he screamed and pummeled the bear, he continued to back down the slope in the direction from which he had come. At one point Harry tripped on a snow-covered chunk of cottonwood and fell backward into the snow, thinking that was the end. When he fell, his cap came off and the bear bit it.

The cap momentarily distracted the bear, allowing Harry to regain his feet. When his hand touched the ground, it contacted a 3-foot chunk of cottonwood, the same wood he'd tripped on. Harry picked it up while rising and poked it at the bear. The animal swatted at and bit it.

The beast never once rose to its hind legs. It merely curled its lips over its yellowed teeth, snarled and roared and snapped its jaws while coughing a *ho, ho, ho* the entire time.

Was the bear merely playing with him? Did it intentionally miss him when it struck? Had the bear injured itself when slapping away the ax? Was the terrain unsuited to the bear's fighting style? Harry never found out the reason for the bear's failure to press home the attack.

Boyden remembered some horse bells hanging from the cabin. Thinking he could bring them into play, he made for the cabin. Because bears hear so well and bells on pack animals alert bruins of man's presence, Harry had brought the bells to the cabin years before. Each fall he had rung them periodically to deter migrating bears from the area.

Slowly backpedaling until he reached the cabin, Harry grabbed the bells and began shaking them.

The noise was no greater than all of Harry's screaming, but it was enough to cause bruin to back off a little.

This proved another paradox to Harry. Whereas other grizzlies on the Chitina had been sufficiently moved to flee the clanging of the horse bells, this beast, nearly twice the size of its kin, stood its ground amidst the bedlam of the bells.

At that moment Joe and the packhorse came onto the scene. Malloy had heard the commotion and urged the tired horse onward. Wondering if Harry was mixed up with a wolverine, Joe shouted to him. Boyden hollered back that it was a bear and that he could use some help.

Joe dropped the lead rope, scooped up the ax and ran to help Harry.

Even though the bear faced an additional foe and the horse stood nearby, it continued to slap at the men and to bawl its displeasure.

Harry told Joe that they should try to maneuver the bear behind the cabin. Once there, Harry exchanged the cottonwood for the larger ax on the cabin wall. They renewed their assault on the bear and managed to beat it back to the edge of the cabin's clearing.

Seeing that the bear had called a temporary truce, one grabbed the lead line on the horse while the other opened the cabin door.

Dark was upon them when Malloy tied the horse beside the broken cabin window.

They discovered that the bear had tried to gain entrance to the dwelling before their arrival–it had scratched the door and broken the panes of the small window. Preparing for the bear's return, they hung a dish towel in front of the broken window and set the glowing lantern next to it, planning to leave it on all night.

Meanwhile Harry built a fire in the sheet iron stove. While Malloy stood guard with an ax, Boyden climbed his pole ladder to retrieve sheep meat from the cache to be thawed for supper. After dinner, Malloy washed the dishes and went to the door to toss out the dishwater.

To his surprise, the bear was there to greet him and eager to enter the dwelling, almost as if responding to an RSVP dinner invitation. The grizzly sat on the doorstep blocking the doorway as if it were the bottom of a Dutch door.

Joe dropped the dishwater and hollered for Harry.

Since both axes were in the cabin, Harry thought they could split the bear's skull if it came through the door. However, visualizing two men frenetically swinging axes inside the 10-foot cabin, he immediately saw the danger of such action and the likelihood of their braining each other while the bruin watched.

Harry slammed the door in the bear's face and the two men shoved the door back into place and latched it.

Exhausted from the hike and ready for a good night's sleep, Harry took to bed. Joe, however, spent the night stoking the stove with wood.

Finishing breakfast the next morning at daybreak, Malloy opened the door and was again surprised to discover Mr. Bear camped on the doorstep. Joe grabbed stove wood from the floor near the stove and pelted the bear in the head with them. Later Harry jokingly commented that Joe's aim was good as he connected seven of nine times.

The bear retreated to the edge of the clearing again and the men hurriedly readied the packhorse and departed the cabin. They were amazed that the horse had remained at its post during the night.

One wonders what mental anguish the steed experienced in its proximity to bruin while the men remained safely inside. Merely forty feet from the cabin they discovered a bear bed melted in the snow, where it had spent the night.

After traveling some time the men stopped to rest and discussed the bear's reason for staying at the cabin all night. Harry explained to his partner that it was because of the sheep ribs left on the woodpile just inside the door. That revelation gave new meaning to rule of not having food in your tent!

As a postscript, two years after Harry's adventure with the outsized bear, it invaded other trappers' cabins, leaving the interiors in a state of utter disarray. Inside one cabin the bear punctured a motor oil container and drank a gallon of it that went to work immediately. The animal's digestive system quickly passed the petroleum along with the stomach's other contents...all over the cabin from floor to ceiling.

The returning trapper encountered the bear dismantling his cabin and quickly dispatched it. Harry later learned of the tale and was reminded again of his encounter when the trapper told him the bear was twice the size of any local bears and that it had four diagonal scars across its face.

Harry was, indeed, a man's man.

How many __real__ men inhabited the North country? At least two, considering the fact that Frank Kibbee was cut from the same cloth as Harry Boyden.

Power and Maulings

"Once I witnessed a bear attacking a deer. It leaped out of the forest like a huge cat, seized the deer in its jaws and tore the animal's head off! As often as not, these bears start their attacks with no warning and at close range. If the man isn't ready to shoot—and shoot straight—he's a goner."

–Ralph W. Young, *Grizzlies Don't Come Easy!* Page 82

Most bear maulings last no more than 30 seconds.

–The author

21

ONE TOUGH COOKIE

The bear was furious to the bone and wanted some pay back.

One of the first books I read about Alaska was *The Alaska Book*, a wonderful anthology. I would have used it as a textbook for literature of the North, a great class at Dimond High School that I inherited from Marie Lundstrom, but the tome was out of print. The effort to find a publisher to edit a book of Alaskan adventures featuring the pioneers, prospectors and pilots was the impetus that led to my first book. The following story was originally in that great book by Ferguson Publishing Company (which, interestingly, the publisher of my first book had co-produced).

S ome time ago Thomas Martindale and some like-minded men booked a hunting trip in northern British Columbia. Their head guide was an experienced woodsman and a good trapper named Frank Kibbee. The group enjoyed his colorful disposition and found him to be a natural for the country. He possessed the qualities necessary to face the rigors of the far North–strength, endurance, agility and nerve. They agreed that Frank was the rare type of individual of whom the world could use more.

He'd come north to Bear Lake from Montana some years before. Frank felt that the trapping life suited him just fine and that his occasional guiding activities were also reasonably satisfying and prosperous.

Although he loved the country and his situation, there was one thing he desired with the passing days. He wanted a wife. In that era the North was inhabited mostly by men–there just weren't a whole lot of marriageable women around. There really weren't even enough women around for him to develop a courting relationship, so Frank fell to the temptation of taking drastic measures.

He'd heard about the possibility of advertising for a wife and that if a person followed the proper procedures, good results were to be expected. Kibbee decided to give it a go. He was witty and had an interesting way of stringing words and phrases together, so he drafted his plea and sent it to the nearest local newspaper in Ashcroft. Many readers were taken by the humor of the ad's phraseology and enjoyed it from the human-interest angle. And, as it turned out, some magazines picked up the ad and published it for the same reasons.

Before long Frank had a heap of work on his hands. He had received sixty-five answers that necessitated reading each one, determining the plausibility of the prospective spouse and eliminating those that did not meet his expectations. In time he narrowed the prospects down to two for whom he was willing to "pay the freight."

After some correspondence and time had elapsed, an English lady accepted his offer. She traveled several thousand miles to meet him, and so far as is known neither marital candidate was disappointed.

After the Martindale party returned to the states, they heard by letter about a couple of Frank's latest adventures–one involved a bear and one, a pistol.

Having decided to trap a grizzly, Kibbee set a bear trap about a quarter of a mile from his house. When he returned a week later to check the trap, he discovered it missing. He wasn't worried about retrieving it, however, because the culprit that absconded with it left a trail of churned up earth and broken brush that was easy for Frank to follow.

He followed the trail three-fourths of a mile and found the trap on a steep hill. The biggest problem that he faced was the trap's prisoner, a highly upset grizzly bear. The trap's toggle–the log tied to the opposite end of the trap–had hung up several times. Each time the bear had chewed enough of the log to free itself, and the toggle was now a very short piece of wood.

The bear was furious to the bone and wanted some pay back.

It did not help that the grizzly was uphill, because bear shooting strategy calls for the shooter to be above the intended victim. Even worse, the grizzly was close.

Without taking a whole lot of time to maneuver, Kibbee opened fire. The bear came for him in that classic grizzly bear ground-eating gallop. Even though Kibbee pumped shells into it and wounded it, that didn't stop the animal. He crashed down the hill until he reached his nemesis.

What followed was a battle to the end. It was Frank's bare hands against the grizzly's claws and teeth. Kibbee's strategy was to keep the bear from chewing his throat until he got in a finishing round from his rifle. In addition to the bear's paws and jaws, Frank had to avoid the flying trap fastened to the animal's foreleg. In the melee Frank kept trying to ward off the bear's bites and his hands and arms took a shellacking–they were covered with tooth marks and became badly mutilated.

In spite of his efforts, however, Frank's head got the worst of the punishment. The right half of his face, including his teeth, was torn aside. The bear shredded his scalp. In the end Kibbee got in a final shot and the bear stumbled away and died.

Frank started for his home place, and when he reached it, a man from a nearby survey party who was camped on the lake shore, started immediately to fetch a doctor, who lived twenty-two miles away.

The sawbones arrived at 4:30 a.m. Because of his dismembered jaw, Kibbee was in no condition to speak. But as soon as his face was stitched together, he regaled the medical professional with his bear tale. Kibbee described the battle in great detail, round by round. He told the story in such an entertaining manner that he kept the doctor in stitches laughing until he'd finished suturing, which was the better part of the day.

The doctor had grave doubts about Kibbee's chances of survival, let alone recovery. One of Kibbee's injuries was from a blow or blows to his ribs, which was probably the result of the trap slamming into him. Worse yet, the most serious problem was the threat of blood poisoning.

Five weeks later, however, Kibbee was ready to have some bone splinters removed from his jaw.

Although his condition was not the best, Kibbee was determined to acquire a big catch of furs during the winter, which meant that he'd have to get out on the trail and set some traps. He rounded up a partner to go with him and found a woman to stay with his wife at Bear Lake while he was away. They hauled their last load of supplies to Sandy Lake and began their trapping activities the following day.

Frank ran a five-mile trap line in one direction while his partner worked the line that went to Little Lake. Nearly a week later Kibbee was returning from his line. He reached a beaver pond a little over a mile from camp and began crossing it. Either he did not realize that the water under the ice had receded or he thought the ice was thick enough to support his weight. Whatever the reason, Kibbee broke through the thin ice.

He wore a single-action, .38 Special Smith and Wesson revolver, tied to his belt without a holster. Amidst the splashing of water, breaking of ice and trying to escape his dilemma, the pistol discharged. That would not have been a problem in and of itself, but the bullet traveled down and into his leg.

Kibbee escaped the water and tried to stanch the flow of blood before heading for his cabin. Although weak from blood loss and suffering untold pain from the wound and wet, cold clothes, Frank crawled the last mile.

When he reached his cabin, his partner was still on his portion of the trap line and Kibbee didn't know when he'd return. Frank crawled into his bunk wondering how long he'd last until he could get proper medical attention.

That night his partner showed up and found Kibbee in bed. Frank's knee was discolored and badly swollen, and he was in great pain. Since immediate medical aid was unavailable and the situation was dire, they operated on the spot.

Using a jackknife, Frank made an incision over the entry point of the bullet. His partner then dug down, located the lead and loosened it. Using a piece of wire, they hooked the lead and maneuvered it outward until it was accessible by hand. One side of the bullet was flattened from sliding along the leg bone.

Kibbee remained in the cabin while his partner went for help. Two days later he arrived with three other trappers. They got him onto a stretcher and started toward home at Bear Lake. Part of the journey was by sled and part by canoe. They encountered obstacles and the trip was not an easy one for them–they broke through the ice several times while crossing frozen streams and ponds. The struggle they faced was monumental, but they were accustomed to it. The cold, the wet and the food preparation all had to be planned for and endured. They were men of the North, a truly tough breed. They had to spend the night in the open three nights. They were on the trail for five days.

When the doctor saw Frank this time, he knew Kibbee's stamina. He was more optimistic and he promised him full use of his leg after a few months. The doc was right. Kibbee was scarred but mended and before the next hunting season rolled around, he was ready for work.

There's more to bears than the "bad" side that is all too often sensational-ized. With a better understanding of this magnificent animal we can appreciate some interesting things about its nature.

Polar Bear

Excerpts from Charles T. Feazel's *White Bear*

"...a polar bear's fur is not white but *transparent*. Second, the hairs of his coat aren't solid but rather *hollow*. Third...the bear's skin is *black*. Fourth, living in and on the ice-choked waters of the Arctic Ocean, Nanook has the problem not so much of keeping warm in his frigid world but of *overheating*."   Page 29

"Polar bears do attack people...rarely...over the past fifteen years more people have been killed by polar bears in zoos than have been killed by wild polar bears throughout the North American Arctic."   Page 144

EVER THE WOMAN

She would pretend to be leaving in a huff,
but would coyly look back to see if he was following.

In John Eddy's *Hunting the Alaska Brown Bear*, he describes a brown bear sow's wily mating tactics and the hunter's admiration for the hunted. On a hunt with master guide Andy Simon, they located two bears, and realized that they were a sow and a boar. Because I found his comments humorous and enlightening and hope that the reader will also, I've condensed the several pages of the story in the author's own words.

The fact that this did not at all coincide with the usual procedure of mother and cub was what had first aroused Andy's suspicions.

The smaller one, leading the way in such a persuasive manner, was a female of the usual size, about an eight footer! After studying the situation we both realized that here was a really big fellow.

All idea of a noon day rest vanished, as we slid off the ridge into a ravine by following which we could lessen the distance between us by half a mile, without taking any chances of betraying our presence. When again we crawled up to the brink of the gully and could once more see them, they staged a love scene that was the most perfect travesty on human emotions possible. Picture, if you can, an eight hundred pound she bear, acting coy and shy, flirting and encouraging a bashful swain of twice her size. There on the mountainside under the smoking, towering Pavlof they flirted, quarrelled, made up and loved while Andy and I took advantage of their passions to work our way just a little bit nearer under cover of every fresh outburst.

She would pretend to be leaving in a huff, but would coyly look back to see if he was following. If not she would return, or if he was following, she would wait until he came near. Her great, lumbering lover would waddle up, kiss her, and they would rub their faces and shoulders together. When he became too rough, she would slap him smartly, a love tap that would drop an ox and then scamper away with short bouncing jumps. Then she would coquettishly peep from behind a rock or a clump of alders to make sure that he was following.

As is ever the case, he tired first and lay down on a big boulder, while she crawled into a small bunch of alders. This was evidently for their usual siesta. Andy and I sought shelter out of the wind as much as possible and nibbled at our lunch, all the time keeping our eyes on the resting bears.

It was not a perfect rest for the big fellow, however. Every few minutes his head would come up and he would look down the hill to the little clump of alders, where reclined his lady-love. She did not move, just slept the noon hour through. Several times he pulled himself up on his forelegs and gazed down at her, and then, evidently satisfied that she had not left him, would drop back at ease. We took advantage of each of their rest periods to crawl up a bit closer, trying to get into a position that would command the spot where we had figured they would leave the hillside when they started down to the meadows below for their evening meal. These maneuvers of ours were carried on partly in the deep little gully and partly in creeping from boulder to boulder. All this time the wind was fairly strong, a factor that had to be kept in mind constantly. As a matter of fact, every move we made had to be carefully thought out in advance in order that the bears would neither see us, nor that a treacherous eddy of wind would carry a trace of our scent up to them.

We were now convinced that the male was a trophy worthwhile. Careful study had shown us that he was of good size, well furred, in a rich brown color. The hump on his back was almost black and glistened in the infrequent flashes of sunlight with the sheen of a carefully curried horse. He had especially long forelegs, and carried himself like a monarch of the snows–truly a splendid beast.

And what a coy, scheming, shameless wench she was. I suppose there are women with many of her traits and characteristics. Delilah must have toyed thus with Samson, or Cleopatra with Mark Antony.

All that day she had been leading him on, gently, provocatively but steadily, she had dangled the lure of herself before him, until it seemed to us that, as man to man, we should warn him to beware. All day she had been coaxing him up and down the mountainside, teasing and enticing him along with subtle gestures; and all day he had faithfully followed her, the handsome, masterful devil.

But finally it looked as if a let-up could be detected in his interest. Obviously this long-drawn-out amour was losing, to him at least, its first zestfulness. We could see that when she strolled too far in advance he would often turn his splendid head, pause, gaze across the valley and momentarily seem to be lost in dreams, possibly of other conquests.

Womanlike, she seemed to sense this. As soon as he paused, she would turn in her tracks and come back to him, dispelling any ideas he might be harboring of leaving her with a rub of her shoulder and a voluptuous kiss. That was all he needed. Resistance melted and he followed her on with renewed interest. I got quite a chuckle out of the performance and remarked to Andy, that no matter where you go in all the world, among the palms at the Ritz, on the veldt of Africa or the tundra of Alaska, the game of love is played in just about the same old way.

Once my boot heel rasped on a rock and the wind picked up the sound and carried it to him. With ears cocked and eyes showing annoyance, he raised his great head and looked straight at the boulder that sheltered us. What interloper, he seemed to ask, dared interfere at this critical time in his personal affairs?

At last the pair came off the hillside about two hundred yards from us. He lay down in a depression, leaving only his head visible.

The female was slowly walking in a direction where it was just possible she might pick up our scent. I suggested we crawl to a nearer patch of alders where I thought I would have a better shot. Andy vetoed that idea at once, fortunately, as it proved later, and motioned me to crawl toward the male bear in line with a tuft of grass some thirty feet distant. I started, but had not completed the crawl, when the big fellow rose to his feet, and walking slowly after the female, strolled along in the same hollow in which he had been lying and all I could see was his hump.

Just as he reached the female, he came into full view. She turned to meet him, and together they posed, nose to nose. In this position I could shoot without fear of harming his sweetheart.

Slowly I sighted my rifle, and drawing a fine bead on his shoulder, squeezed the trigger. With the roar of the gun he lurched forward, then jumped back from his friend and reared to his full height, ready to run or attack whoever or whatever was the cause of this disturbance.

I was lying prone when I made that first shot and I fired a second time from the same position. This shot also staggered him. With almost incredible speed and on only three legs at that, he ran, making straight across my front and headed for that patch of alders I had just expressed a desire to shoot from. What a different bear story might have been told if Andy had not warned me to shoot from the open! The bear had no idea where his enemy was concealed. Panic-stricken, he dashed for the friendly cover of the nearest thicket.

I now took a fleeting glance at the other bear; every experienced hunter fears the anger of the female under circumstances such as these; she is liable to charge as though she were defending her cubs. As she made no hostile movement, I swung my gun to finish the wounded male, and had just brought the sights to his hind quarters when Andy's gun rang out, close to me, and the "Sheik of Pavlof Volcano" as I immediately named him, pitched headlong stone dead.

Thus man, as is his wont, brought disaster into yet another Eden. Only the exultation of conquest kept me from dwelling with regret upon having been the fatal instrument of destruction. Should a sportsman regret the slaughter? No! He must take his game when and where he finds it. The "lady" in the case quickly vanished. The last we saw of her she was an ascending spot of brown, climbing over a snow-field in the gathering gloom of evening.

We started immediately to skin the bear out as we wanted to get the pelt to our camp that night. The head was enormous, weighing over one hundred pounds, with great quantities of tough meat covering the skull.

With the big skin on the pack-board we arrived at camp after midnight, tired, hungry, but satisfied and happy.

These men harvested a trophy of a lifetime, however the animal that James Christie sought nearly harvested him!

Bad Bears

"The two types of bears most likely to step out of character are immature boars, and sows with cubs.

"A young brownie of either sex is usually unstable, but the boar particularly is likely to consider himself a tough guy. He loves to strut and swagger, and has the instincts of a hoodlum. He's also a great bluffer, but you can never be sure when he's bluffing and when he isn't. Whenever I meet one at close range, I treat him with deference and respect, always keeping my rifle at the ready."

–Ralph W. Young, "The Bear Nobody Knows,"
Outdoor Life, August 1957

TOE TO TOE
WITH A GRIZZLY

He was weakened to the point of death from blood loss.

Always hungering for adventure, and particularly of the bear variety, I purchased another Outdoor Life book. I was not disappointed as I read the following story of a man pitting his puny weapons against those of Mr. Grizzly. When you consider that a bear can decapitate a deer, what are a man's odds when going toe to toe with bruin?

The time was circa 1908 to 1909. The place was the headwaters of the Stewart River, Yukon Territory, Canada. The man was James M. Christie. The bear was one of the genus *ursus horribilis*. The event was billed as the survival of the fittest.

It was not a tag team match but a one man versus one bear winner-take-all affair. The bear was interested in the moose the hunter had killed. The man wanted to reclaim what was rightfully his. It was a Mexican standoff...momentarily.

Then the ball opened.

In the summer of 1898 Christie left Carman and prospected the Stewart River for a time. He spent his winters trapping. Sometimes he guided government parties and conducted a geological survey across the wilderness between Edmonton, Alberta and Dawson Creek, British Columbia. It was during this time that James met George Chrisfield after which they grubstaked and started north for the Rogue River. They established camp about 350 miles east of Dawson in the heart of the wilderness.

Inhabitants have long known that survival in the harsh climate and rugged terrain of the North depends upon reading its pages, committing them to memory and preparing for every day, incorporating experience as a teacher. Christie survived. He learned the North as if life depended upon it because it did!

He became a sourdough. He learned enough to consider himself king of his domain. He had no fear of its inhabitants. Respect, yes. Fear, no.

In mid-October he struck out over the light snow to reconnoiter trapping possibilities along the Rogue. He told Chrisfield prior to his departure not to expect his early return as he planned to be gone several days

His first day out James shot a moose and gutted it. In order to keep birds away from it, he covered it with branches in a ground cache. He expected no trouble and planned to return within a few days. The next day he discovered a good trapping area for marten and other furbearers. James decided to move his camp to the locale and while returning to camp, he detoured to check his moose kill.

When he found the kill site, he discovered that the brush had been removed. But worse, the moose was gone. He first noted wolf tracks, and then he saw a huge grizzly track that led straight across the river.

Knowing that it would be in the vicinity, he started after the grizzly. The trail was pockmarked with wolf tracks, and before long Christie spotted a wolf. For a trapper to stumble onto old yellow eyes in the open was cause for great joy. The hide would fetch a handsome price and probably keep the critter from interfering with his trapped animals in the future. He hastily took aim and fired at the wolf but missed.

Disappointed and a little perplexed, James checked his rifle sights. They were out of alignment so he re-set them and continued on the grizzly's track.

He crossed the river and climbed the bank, traveling another 200 yards. At that point he entered thick brush, slowing his progress considerably. Within 20 feet he heard a grunt. Instantly looking up, he spotted the grizzly only ten yards away and coming hell-bent for him—its ears pinned back, jowls slavering, teeth bared.

A split second is all that it took for James to swing his .303 rifle up and pop a cap. The soft nosed bullet slammed into the beast's shoulder and ranged the entire length of its body without slowing the animal. Somehow James got off another shot which smashed into the animal's forehead just as the man jumped aside, entangling his feet in the brush where he fell. The bear, spouting blood and ripping into him, landed on top of James.

The brute clamped its jaws onto his head. Although he miracu-lously forced an arm between its jaws and managed to free his head, the bear crushed the appendage. In that brief exchange the bear also broke his jaw in two places and nearly ripped off his scalp. Next the bear bit into his legs.

With his arms free Christie fought desperately, all the while the two bullet wounds taking their effect on bruin. Before long the animal dropped dead three feet from him.

Although Christie won the bout, it was a hollow victory–it took less than a minute for the animal to severely injure him. His face was a fright. The bear had torn his cheeks from ear to mouth, fracturing the right cheekbone and his lower jaw in two places. His scalp was ripped and thrown back like a cap on his head.

He knew that he was in bad shape. His right arm was broken in several places and covered with gaping, raw wounds. It hung loose and useless at his side. He could see only from one eye that constantly filled with blood. Christie fastened his handkerchief about his torn scalp and placed his coat over his head to stop the flow of blood. Loss of blood weakened him to the point of death.

Even though James knew that his injuries would limit his travel, that he needed to re-hydrate himself and that his blood level were critically important in affecting his survival, yet another factor played on his mind…wolves.

Old Yellow Eyes was always lurking about, eager to drop any prey as food. If wolves saw any sign of vulnerability in a prey, they would take him on.

Eight miles on injured legs, suffering excruciating pain, could he make it?

His camp represented safety and succor. In order to avoid wolves and to get the most mileage from his body before total exhaustion and blood loss incapacitated him, James hitched up his will to live and started the 8-mile long journey for his cabin.

Hanging on his chest, his jaw was an impediment to travel. Knowing that his partner was not expecting him for days, he realized all too well that his rescue was in his hands. Although the intense pain from his several wounds swept over his body and compounded his walking, the twin demons of pain and agony prodded James.

For hours he trudged on like a drunken man, reeling, staggering and forcing himself ever onward. At one point he chose to detour to a prospector's cabin a half mile off the trail. He reached the empty shelter and lay down inside, anticipating death yet hoping that his partner would come looking for him.

After a while, however, he regained some strength and decided to try to make his home cabin before his wounds stiffened. Before leaving he wrote a note with his left hand.

Near blind, weak, dragging his legs, which had stiffened, and bleeding from his wounds, he finally reached his cabin and staggered through the doorway. Amazed that he had made it, James, who was totally exhausted, weak, thirsty and on fire with pain, crashed, unconscious onto a bed.

When he regained consciousness, Chrisfield was working on him. James learned later that Chrisfield followed his blood trail to their cabin door. Even though James' body had stiffened by the next morning, his partner made him as comfortable as possible before departing for help.

Chrisfield secured two dog teams and some Indian mushers and returned to James with the intent of hauling him 50 miles to the nearest trading post. They made a toboggan as comfortable as possible, placed him on it and dashed off toward the post. Bouncing over rough and unbroken country caused excruciating pain with every jar.

Deep snow hindered their travel and the jarring impact of the bouncing opened some wounds, causing bleeding anew. Hour after hour they trudged on. Christie was conscious the entire time, which did nothing to dull his pain. Sometimes he prayed for painlessness; sometimes he prayed for death to end his suffering.

At length the group reached Lansing, nothing more than a stockade and a few buildings kept by his friend Ferrell. Mrs. Ferrell washed his wounds with antiseptic solutions, stitched them up and set the broken bones as well as possible. For two months he lay between life and death. When it appeared that he was going to make it and he'd regained some strength, he began the 250-mile trip to Dawson then on to Victoria where Dr. O.M. Jones received him at the hospital. There he underwent several operations to fix his jaw so that he could masticate food.

Christie's survival and recovery are a testament to his vitality and complement his rugged outdoor regimen.

Although Christie survived his bout with the bear, the Johnstone brothers had their hands full with the odd bear that they faced.

Territorial

Bears by nature are territorial–they must fight to protect their turf, their offspring, their food. That trait coupled with its curious nature gets it into most, if not all, its conflicts with man. It is a trait that all who enter bear country must know and consider carefully in order that both man and beast may safely utilize the same territory.

–The author

OLD GROANER

Laboring to control his emotions and moving only his eyes,
Jack followed the black outline as it materialized next to his side,
towering over him.

This is THE classic Alaska bear story–probably the most well-known bear yarn in Alaska's annals of storied man-bear encounters.

In April 2000 my wife and I flew to Ketchikan where I conducted some workshops in the writing process. One of the ladies who attended was Ms. Mary Ida Henrikson of Ward Cove's Danger Island Studios. She asked if we'd like to meet her friend and fellow gold seeker Bruce Johnstone, an octogenarian. Would we? I'll say!

Mary introduced us to Bruce at his home overlooking the Tongass Narrows and he regaled us with some of his amazing tales.

He began hunting bear at the age of eleven, getting $45 for black bears and $75 for browns. He started trapping a year later and guiding at age 13. His rifle, an old Herrington & Richardson single-shot, had a broken ejector which required dropping a piece of lead down the barrel from the muzzle to eject the empty shell. Later after a close call with a mama brownie he acquired a .30-30 carbine.

Over the next twenty years he guided and became a prominent southeast Alaska big-game guide, helping many other guides acquire their licenses and advising the Alaska Department of Fish and Game, U.S. Bureau of Land Management and U.S. Forest Service.

My wife wanted to bring Bruce home with us, but I jokingly reminded her that her commitment to me was "till death, do us part." At any rate, we fell in love with Bruce, a kind, sweet man whose gold fever is still alive and well.

Somewhere over the years he had lost his copy of my first book *Alaska Bear Tales*. I told him I'd send him a copy of the original covered book when I returned to Anchorage.

I've re-written this story from W.H. "Handlogger" Jackson's account.

C omfortable around the campfire's red-orange flames, Bruce and Jack Johnstone settled in for the night, anticipating a hot dinner as the mulligan stew simmered in the pot. Jack's big police dog Slasher lay next to the glowing coals, his head on outstretched paws, gathering in the welcome heat and tantalizing food aroma and absorbing the friendly chatter of companions. Darkness beyond the campfire ring was total.

Suddenly Slasher's ears pricked up and pointed into the blackness. His nose quivered and a low growl parted his lips. The brothers caught a sound beyond the firelight. Bruce straightened from spreading his bedroll and Jack froze with a spoon in hand in mid-air. All three strained their ears for some recognition of what was "out there."

The only sounds they heard came from the crackling campfire and the river nearby, tumbling boulders on its journey to the sea. The earlier sound was gone. Did they really hear it? Or was it imagined? They both knew they'd heard it. And so had Slasher. He quickly looked at his master and Jack's brother.

They wondered. *What was the noise?* It was a distant and indistinct sound. Expert woodsmen, they knew it was not a normal wilderness sound. *Could it be wolverines or wolves? Maybe moose? Perhaps a wild man? Possibly a bear?*

As they wondered, knowing it was like no sound they'd ever heard, a long, deep agonized groan came to them. Slasher lurched to his feet with a growl. Both men hastily glanced at their rifles, leaning against a tree. The groan was more audible and closer. Maybe that was merely due to their finely tuned senses or a combination of that and their nerves.

Whatever its identity, it appeared to be in excruciating pain… beginning in a loud, agonized moan and ending in a low sob, similar to the final breath of a dying animal. It was a sound to cause the most experienced woodsman to grab his firearm while hoping for daylight.

While contemplating its origin, they remembered trapper Jess Sethington who had disappeared some nine years previous on this same stream in Southeast Alaska. Jess was a Canadian from Stewart, British Columbia, who had gone up the river on a short trapping trip. He'd ignored the sage advice given him by old timers and had gone into the wilderness alone. When he failed to return, four experienced woodsmen took up his trail, finding his camps along the way to the very spot where the Johnstone's were now camped on the Unuk River. His trail beyond this point had never been found.

Knowing that no one could survive the cold of Alaska's winters without proper shelter and food, the Johnstones rejected the idea that the sound came from a man. They willed the noise maker into the firelight for a better look and understanding. However it was not to be.

The sound appeared closer but the brothers tried to convince themselves that it was in the distance and not really coming in their direction. However it came a third time, louder and nearer, a spine tingling, bone chilling moan that raised the hair on the backs of their necks and started their hearts racing. The men grabbed their rifles, quickly checked their working mechanisms and added more wood to their fire.

The lack of the animal's moaning merely added to the tension. And it heightened the other sounds, the crackling fire and the rumbling river.

They were familiar with the bawling of injured bears and the loud roar of battling bruins, but this sound was much different. And they knew there was no human within miles. They concluded that it must be a bear. They knew the Unuk's reputation for its huge ursine inhabitants, but the brothers had gotten along with bears in the past. This experience certainly unnerved them. Based on the respect and caution they'd learned in association with bears, they decided that if the sound originated from a bear, it was definitely a dangerous animal. They were confined to their campsite until daylight because any attempt to escape by water in the dark was certain suicide. They'd have to either wait for the intruder to make itself known or for the distant dawn.

Periodically Slasher jumped to his feet and emitted a fierce growl. He knew what creature made the sound but he could not communicate that to his master. Even though Slasher was determined to protect Jack at all costs, he was more interested in the pot on the fire than the noise beyond.

After several minutes the noise went away and they relaxed somewhat. Overcome with fatigue and sated by the hot meal, they crawled into their sleeping bags, dependent upon Slasher for any warning of danger.

Before they knew it, morning had dawned. A brighter day was never more welcomed. Quitting their blankets, they ate breakfast before scouting the area. They'd camped in an excellent salmon spawning area as evidenced by countless salmon carcasses and interwoven bear trails.

All of this excitement took place during the summer of 1933 and their first prospecting trip up the Unuk. At that time they were not privy to the fact that they'd make this run again and again and encounter the mysterious moaning in the future. It was inconceivable that the strange sound would haunt them for three successive summers. And in the end the animal's presence would prove nearly fatal for one of the brothers.

Their plan was to reach the headwaters of the Unuk River, a roily, muddy torrent spawned by the glaciers beyond and boiling through its canyon. They'd covered seventy miles across salt water by way of motor launch from Ketchikan, Alaska. Then they'd transferred their gear to the riverboat, which drew three inches of water when loaded. They would ascend the stream towards its source in Canada, a wilderness and little known country few men had seen. One certainty about the area was that it fiercely protected the yellow metal that all gold miners seek.

Other gold seekers who had preceded them were Rod Elliot, Sam Gowan, Ed Kerr, Harry Ketchum and partners McTaggert, Mitchell and Gingrass and Jake LeBrant.

Jack and Bruce were about to discover, like their predecessors, that their journey would be fraught with dangers from pounding waters, steep walled canyons and the ever present, storied big grizzlies of the Unuk. The brothers would have to fight for every foot of progress on the river, battling the power of the water's hydraulics and pressing their way through the same rapids that others had traveled–a boiling froth that had claimed more human lives than the infamous bears inhabiting her forests.

In the early going it seemed a nearly insurmountable task to move the boat upriver against the current of the silt-laden waters. They lined or poled the vessle by hand. Obstacles included sweepers, cut banks, drift piles, quicksand and treacherous whirlpools where one misstep spelled disaster. Regardless how deeply the towline cut into the shoulder, they could never let down their guard on the river. Each yard gained upriver was a genuine achievement.

Two hours from their genesis at the mouth they were prepared to turn back, but neither would admit defeat. After five days of blistering toil and heart throbbing tension they arrived at Blue River canyon, a narrow gulch between sheer rock walls created by a buildup of lava from an ancient lava flow. Water gouged its way through this canyon, stacking up from wall to wall and threatened to suck anything in its path to the bottom of the streambed. Oars were of no use nor were the poles that found no bottom. The slick walls could not be climbed.

Before attempting to move their empty boat up the canyon, they portaged their gear around the gorge. For a campsite they chose a gravel bar at the foot of Dickinson Peak where Cripple Creek, a freshwater stream, provided ample drinking and cooking water for them. Cottonwood trees bordered the creek and large spruce trees provided shelter under their branches.

Then they returned for their empty boat and found that moving it against the current was nearly impossible.

After an all day effort on the river they were exhausted at sunset but happy to find a safe place to camp where they beached the boat, 19 miles upriver from the Unuk's mouth. That night began their experiences with the strange creature that made the moaning sounds in the forest.

Now, on the morning after they'd heard the sounds, they prepared to leave the campsite. After a thorough examination of the nearby area they discovered nothing unusual—just numerous fresh bear tracks and no injured animal and no blood on any of the trails bordering the murmuring Cripple Creek.

Gold was the focus of their present desires, therefore they put aside their curiosity for the moment. Their objective, Sulphide Creek, a six-mile stretch of roiling water roaring through slab sided walls a thousand feet high, lay beyond. High water witnessed the roar of boulders rolling and bouncing down through the canyon as if tossed by some ancient Greek Olympian, the current of the river more powerful than one could imagine.

The brothers had their work cut out for them because the impassable water demanded leaving their boat and packing their gear around it to prospect above the canyon.

A bear trail high up on the face of a steep mountain, a mere tunnel through thick tangles of vine alder for miles, was the only route past the canyon. This game trail was heavily trafficked by grizzlies. Men carried their heavy packs on their backs over this trail, often hunched over and unable to see more than a few feet ahead, the unmistakable paw prints of huge brown/grizzly bears visible in the mud at their feet.

Jack had shortened the barrel of his .45-70 rifle to fourteen inches so that it was more manageable in the brush. Some men might struggle with the weapon's legality, however it was a great alternative to the mauling mayhem that an aroused bear could deliver without warning and in a moment's notice.

When they emerged above the canyon, they witnessed evidence of previous prospecting forays including Harry Ketchum's cabin. It nestled between 8000-foot Twin John Peak and Knipple Peak above the canyon. A plaque on the door bore the names and date of 1902. Placer working posts bearing location inscriptions as far back as 1867 caused the brothers to wonder at the sagacity of those few men who'd ever come this far through the tumultuous waters and rugged terrain, and especially at such an early date. They wondered about the close calls, the danger filled days those pioneers faced, and, of course, the men's success in their gold prospecting efforts.

All about them the world was in creation. Jagged peaks towered overhead, snowfields covered the slopes and glaciers continued to grind at the valley floor and sides, plowing up any sign of plant life in its path and depositing chewed up earth.

Day turned to day and days to weeks as the brothers mucked away at the ground, digging all about the area of the three glaciers that rested at the head of the valley. The lack of vegetation around the bone-bare rock necessitated that the brothers return to lower elevation for miles down the valley for firewood.

One day on Sulfide Creek Bruce and Jack noticed a huge grizzly on the opposite side of the river. Upon seeing the men, the animal instantly charged into the stream, swimming a straight course for them in spite of the power of the water. No man could have accomplished that feat. Jack emptied his rifle into the animal, slowing it, however it reached the bank below them and hoisted itself up, even with a broken back. Jack unholstered his Luger pistol and emptied its full magazine of ammunition into the beast before it slipped into the water with a final ferocious growl and the current swept it away.

They wondered how the experience might have differed had they been on the narrow bear trail above the canyon.

With guarded apprehension at the culmination of their weeks of digging, they returned down the canyon to their boat, planning to float back to civilization. Jack and Bruce dropped their heavy packs and flopped onto the ground to rest. At length Jack arose and walked to the boat to discover a gaping hole in its side and the seats ripped out.

Bruce was equally shocked when he observed the carnage–the poles were in short pieces and the oars splintered.

Teeth and claw marks indicated a grizzly was the culprit. Now their departure would be delayed until they could improvise repairs to their boat. They wielded their axes and hewed lumber from the forest to rough out oars and poles; then they loaded their gear and set out for the mouth of the river.

The following summer witnessed their return to the Blue River Canyon campsite of the previous year. While preparing camp for the night's stay, they discussed the possibility of some day finding the remains of the moaning critter. Then they heard the baleful moaning coming from the distance across the creek. The noise approached for a time then, as before, trailed off into silence. They wondered if the animal might be harmless after all.

They found a level area under the spruce trees and prepared to spend the night in their sleeping bags. During the night Jack came instantly awake when he sensed something near. With eyes wide open he neither saw nor heard a thing. But he gradually realized that an area which had previously been a spot of light between the trees was now bare of any semblance of light, filled with solid black. Laboring to control his emotions and moving only his eyes, Jack followed the black outline as it materialized next to his side, towering over him. With absolute determination and adeptness he slowly stretched his arm toward his rifle nearby.

Instant pandemonium erupted. A blood-curdling bellow blasted into Jack's face. Barking loudly, Slasher sprang into action. Heavy feet pounded the surrounding brush, crashing away in haste. Ferocious growls, snapping teeth, popping jaws and yapping barks filled the air.

Jack and Bruce yelled as they scrambled from their sleeping bags. While adding fuel to the fire, they fired up the coffeepot. But the excitement was over for the night.

By fall they were back at the campsite wondering if their "hairy friend," the moaning critter they'd named "Old Groaner," would make his appearance.

By midnight the brothers were awakened by the familiar moaning noises approaching their camp. Periods of silence punctuated by periodic moaning reached their ears as the animal appeared to be feasting on salmon. In time the noise moved away and before they knew it, morning met the men.

They determined to search the area and found tons of salmon carcasses and bear sign. But the only unusual discovery was a stretch of dug up ground that exposed quartz. They hurried to camp to gather digging tools.

On their return to the site Slasher raced into the thick under-brush and met a grizzly head on. The tree tops swayed, brush popped and both bear and dog growled and snapped. But even though the bear was within feet of them, they neither saw hide nor hair of it. In the midst of the mayhem the dreadful groans began.

When peace finally returned, the brothers wondered what the bear had been doing and how close it had been when they were there earlier. Had he waited for them in ambush? It was a sobering thought.

The following summer Bruce and Jack encountered their hairy friend again at Cripple Creek. Their partner George Lemmons was along. He and Jack had taken Slasher and gone to examine the quartz showing while Bruce went up the other side of the stream. Expecting to be gone a short time, Bruce left his rifle in the boat.

Plowing through the thick brush along the creek, he suddenly heard a loud snort close to the trail in the foliage. Instantly recall-ing their last visits to the area, visions of the unseen Old Groaner jumped onto the screen of his mind. The large animal's approach shook the branches. Its next snort was followed by the unmistakable groan of the moaning critter.

Unable to see the charging animal through the swaying salmonberry patch, Bruce called upon his only available weapon, a .410 single shot shotgun pistol which would scarcely kill a bird at more than ten yards. Aiming strategically above the moving brush, Bruce fired a round. He backed quickly down the bear trail while the animal came to a stop. Bruce reloaded. Still the critter advanced. Bruce fired again. After each shot Bruce repeated the shooting and reloading process while backing toward the river. With every shot the animal hesitated, coughed, snorted, groaned and came on faster than the time before, always remaining out of sight and mere feet away in the tall brush. The man's supply of ammo was getting dan-gerously low.

When Bruce felt the gravel of the shore beneath his feet, he hastily turned and raced to the boat and his rifle. He grabbed the trusty weapon and spun around expecting to get off a round at the charging beast. But Old Groaner did not follow him out of the brush. The animal had stopped short of the place where Bruce could see him. For a full half-hour the critter paced and groaned back and forth, always craftily hidden from Bruce's view.

Now the brothers knew the brute was dangerous. They recognized that he had intentionally ambushed them at the quartz site and had now followed an armed man. They still wondered why he moved about mostly under cover of darkness. And they wondered why the critter kept out of sight. They were unable to answer their questions though the brothers spent hours discussing them.

Later that year while coming out of Sulphide Creek, they stopped at Cripple Creek to renew their mining interests in the area. Jack Frost followed them all the way nipping at their heels and chasing them with cold winds and snow to the Unuk. When they landed their boat at their old area, they discovered a fresh run of silver salmon and evidence that the area was crawling with bears.

Since they planned to be there a few days, they immediately decided against using their tent as a shelter. Bruce and Jack carried their gear to a cottonwood grove and commenced dropping trees for a cabin of sorts. By nightfall they'd gotten a good start on the lower portion of the cabin, and they crawled into their tent with thoughts of completing the cabin later. In anticipation of Old Groaner's appearance, they had collected a large quantity of wood.

True to form, that night the bear showed up. With each visit he seemed to get bolder and approach them more closely. The brothers were sound asleep when the bear began groaning. This time, even with the fire roaring, their hairy friend came right into camp. Each time Slasher drove the bear away and each time Jack called his faithful dog back from the attack.

With rifles at the ready the men took turns heaping firewood on the blaze. Old Groaner came right to the edge of the firelight. Although they were tempted to fire a few rounds at the animal, they feared not hitting a vital spot at such close range. They didn't want to deal with an injured beast. Sometime during the night the critter left. Later neither Bruce nor Jack could say with certainty that he had seen the animal.

No sleep for the men. They welcomed daybreak and began moving logs to complete their cabin. Before dark they'd achieved their goal. The door on their hastily built shelter was a gunnysack that fully covered the opening. The small hole admitted them but was too small to provide Old Groaner passage. They reasoned they could sleep in the limited quarters and stave off any assault from the moaning marauder.

A day or so later with their work completed and winter fast approaching, Bruce called Slasher, grabbed his .38-72 rifle and made a final trip to stake their claim. The brothers felt it necessary to protect themselves from any newcomers to the country who might be unfamiliar with them and their claims.

Bruce cut off a small tree four feet above the ground and proceeded to hew a square stake of it. With the tree trunk smooth enough Bruce kneeled and penciled onto the surface. His rifle leaned against a nearby tree and Slasher lay beside him watching the bear trail.

Without warning Slasher ripped a growl, bared his teeth and with hair standing on end leapt past Bruce. Jerking his head around to grasp the situation, Bruce noticed a huge, one-eyed bear storming toward him not five yards away with teeth bared.

With a swat of a huge front paw the brute slammed the airborne dog into the brush twenty feet away. The distraction provided Bruce just enough time to spring to his feet, snatch his rifle in one smooth movement, swing and fire from the hip. The muzzle of the weapon was mere inches from the shoulder of the rage filled bear.

Simultaneously with the report and recoil of the rifle Bruce jumped back just as the hulk hurtled past and piled up ten feet away. Hitting the ground the beast emitted the mournful moan that Bruce recognized so well.

In an instant the bear, bellowing hate and bedevilment, gained its feet and spun around to face him. At the same instant Bruce sent a slug into the bear's neck, which he hoped would stop the animal in its tracks. A second time the brute hit the ground.

But instantaneously it scrambled to its feet, steadily spitting out its hatred for man with a spine tingling blast of defiance.

With only one bullet remaining and Slasher incapacitated, Bruce knew this final shot must do the job. Pointing behind the bear's ear he squeezed the trigger. In that instant a blur flew past Bruce, landing on Old Groaner's back. Slasher had returned to the battle just as the black brute moaned its final displeasure with man.

The bear lay dead at Bruce's feet, a picture of grotesque ugliness to give one chills even in death. Covered with a thick leathery skin the beast appeared as hairless as a hog. The hideous creature lay before him, one eye was missing and the right eye socket was grown over with scar tissue. Both jaws were twisted with some teeth missing, others worn, ulcerated or broken.

Since Bruce was out of ammunition in an area with an active bear population, he chose prudence over curiosity, made his examination brief, called Slasher and headed for camp. The dog gave Old Groaner a departing challenge growl and followed.

When Bruce returned with Jack and George, the men were taken with the gigantic size of the bear. But they were far more impressed and disturbed by the scarred, distorted head and twisted teeth. When they realized that the bear had stalked Bruce so quietly that even Slasher was unaware of its presence, they were roundly amazed at the possibilities that could have occurred. Yet Bruce escaped injury.

It took all three men to turn the bear over. They saw the powder burned right shoulder entry point of Bruce's first bullet that ranged through the body and into the left ham. The second shot penetrated the neck.

Because the hide was of no value, they chose to leave it. They would take only the deformed head and a front paw–10-inches across–to illustrate its outsize proportions.

Jack was unable to remove the head with his hunting knife, the tough hide requiring the use of the double-bitted ax. Only when they skinned the skull and examined it did they begin to understand the reasons for the brute's disdain for man, reasons that created a monster with a bad disposition and mournful moan. They discovered that Bruce's final salvo struck the bear dead center in the brain, the bullet lodging in the left cheekbone. Their efforts also explained the unsolved twelve-year mystery of Jess Sethington's disappearance.

Cutting away the meat and gristle from the skull revealed life altering injuries. Part of the right eye socket's bone structure had been shot away, the result of an old, head-on shot. Another bullet from the side penetrated the skull over the right eye, the bullet hole nearly grown over. One bullet had nicked the base of the skull. The most surprising injury of all however, was the damage done to the jaw.

The hinge on the jaw's right side was destroyed. Even though the wound had healed outside, the internal tissue was still infected and the bones did not meet. The other wounds were healed.

Behind the jaw hinge were two .33 caliber bullets, and beneath the jaw's gristle lay three .38 caliber revolver bullets. Because Jess Sethington had been tracked to this very locale before his trail vanished and because he owned both a .33 caliber rifle and a .38 revolver, it is almost a certainty that Old Groaner was the cause of Jess Sethington's disappearance 12 years previously.

A ghastly thought must have run across their minds when considering the position Jess would have had to be in to fire those shots to the animal's head.

Jack returned to the carcass the following summer and discovered a piece of backbone that was quite unusual. Indications were that Old Groaner had his back broken some years before and four vertebrae and two smashed ribs had grown together to form a single piece of bone. The vertebra was eight and three-fourths inches long and the ribs were grown together three and a half inches from the spine.

In Alaska serious man-bear encounters are not the norm. Unfortunately on occasion when man and bear meet, one or both suffers. This is such a case.

I was pleased to discover an SASE in our mailbox on January 24, 2001. It was postmarked Ketchikan and realizing that it was a response to some questions I'd sent Bruce, I excitedly opened it. His friend Louise Harrington wrote that the enclosed was their joint effort. Bruce's answers provide information about his background and include a bear mauling he experienced. I'm including the entire piece below:

We came to the country in September of 1919–my mother and father, two brothers, two sisters and me. I was ten years old. We spent that first winter at Loring where I went to school. The next spring we moved to Rudyerd Bay and started hand logging.

For the next several years we logged in the summer, trapped in the winter and did whatever was needed to survive. It wasn't too easy back then.

But there were houses all the way around the island in those years. At the farthest apart they were twenty miles, some only three or four miles. So when you rowed around the island you'd just stop at some place for dinner and have breakfast the next morning and then take off again. Everybody was glad for company in those days.

Over the years we lived in probably thirty different places between the Canadian boundary and Wrangell. None of them were permanent homes and most were in the area around Behm Canal.

My brother Jack and I went up the Unuk River for the first time in 1933. We went just to be doing something. Back in Depression days there was not much else to do but prospect. And everybody who'd been up there told us about the gold in the area, so we went up to look.

I was about 22 years old that year and weighed 165 pounds. I was 6-foot-1. Jack was six years older, 6-foot-3 and weighed about 180 pounds. We didn't take in much stuff. I always carried a liver can of rice and Jack carried a liver can of cornmeal. Each can held 32 pounds of rice or cornmeal. We each cooked our own.

We also carried a gun and ammunition, an ax, a pick and shovel and gold pans and sleeping bags and tarp. Altogether we each carried about 90 pounds. Back in those days your sleeping bag alone weighed 14 or 15 pounds. The tarp was the same way.

Coming out that first year we only made two miles going downhill while two other guys made five miles going uphill. We'd got so weak from lack of food we were almost starving to death! But you got weak so slow you didn't realize it; we didn't even know how weak we were.

Each year for three years we'd leave around the first of April, some years we'd wait till the fifteenth. We'd get home around the 20th of October, along in there.

We had outboards in those days but they were not dependable so we had to row most of the time. And it would take thirty days from town to our camp. We camped in one of the old timer's cabins, fellow by the name of Ketchum. That's where our headquarters were, just at the forks of Sulphide Creek.

The creek forks in four ways. The first year there were three of us—my brother Jack, George Lemmon and I. And we'd each take a fork and travel about a mile upstream every year and then prospect to the sides. So we'd gain about a mile a year. The last year I got up to Bruce-Jack Lake and that was as far as I went. That was in 1937. Then I got married, and the war came on and I never did get back.

But there were two Canadians—I don't know their names—but they were using Bruce-Jack Lake for a marker for the helicopter to pick them up. And when they got there, they used my camp and less than 100 yards from where I camped they found gold. There's over 500 men working there now. One of the richest gold mines in Canada!

If I'd gone back the next year I'd have found it within the first week. That's how close I was!

Bruce-Jack Lake was named for Jack and me.

The boat trip up the river was the easiest part. The hardest was the walking from the main river up Sulphide Creek, which is in a deep canyon for seven miles. Then it opens up into a nice valley. But near Twin John Peak there's only one place you can get around. There's a trail that goes across and a narrow shelf, and then it goes up to an overhang, and you just have to crawl along there. And you look down 1,000 feet on one side!

Ken Sampson was up there with us one year. And we took two lines together and put a line on his back and one on his front and a man on either side, and we pulled him back and forth to get him across there. Oh, what a trail that was!

But it was worth it when we got in there. It's the most beautiful country you've ever seen! After going through the canyon it opens out and there are red, mountains, green mountains and blue mountains. They're so many minerals in the mountains that they're all different colors in there.

At the foot of Mitchell Creek–that's the main fork–the face of the glacier is a mile wide. And there's a stream on one side, there's a blue and a green one here and one that's almost red over here. It's the prettiest place you've ever seen, and there's a lot of gold in there!

The Gingrass fork is richer than the main fork. We found more gold in it so somewhere there, there's a mine better than Bruce-Jack Lake, but it hasn't' been found yet. The reason they can't find it is there's too much gold. There's no way to trace it. You find gold everywhere. If you just found it in one stream, then you could trace it up. But every stream carries gold, a little bit.

The first date I found in there was 1884. There was a blaze on a tree that was put there by a member of the Chase family that lives in Wrangell now. And I found a milk bottle in that camp too.

McNeil Creek wasn't named when we first went in. But we found a blaze on a tree with an arrow pointing up. We climbed up and there was a cache–a tarp, some dishes, a pick and a shovel, and a little folding cup. There was also a note signed by McNeil and another fellow that said, "Take whatever you want. We're not coming back. We don't' even know where we're at."

I later had to go to Stewart, BC, to record my claims. I looked up McNeil and gave him back his cup and told him where he'd been. We later named the creek after him. McNeil Creek drains into the Sulphide, which drains into the Unuk.

The last year Jack, Bill Putvin and I went in. And I never went back after that.

After the Unuk years we started logging. Then the war came on and I went into the service while Jack stayed and ran the camp. At that time we were cutting spruce for airplanes–sixteen rings to the inch; they wouldn't let both of us go into the service. After the war we both went logging and guiding. Our company was called Johnstone Brothers.

We were logging in Smeaton Bay one time in 1948 when I found part of a skull in a cave. All that was left was the lower jaw and it was so big it would fit right over my face. It was definitely a human jaw.

And I was going to bring it to town. I brought it down to the boat and put it on the bunk opposite Jack's. Everything was fine until I turned the light out and there was enough phosphorous in the bone so that it glowed in the dark. And Jack was superstitious: "Get that thing outta here!" he said and made me take it back where I found it. Since then I've told other people where it was but they couldn't find it.

We never went back to the Unuk prospecting, though I went back years later guiding hunters. That's when the bear got me.

Must have been 1958. Three of us—Ed Roberts, Pete Bringsly and I—went moose hunting on the Unuk. There were no berries or fish that year and the bear were starving to death. They were killing and eating each other.

I was down on the river flats trying to get ducks for camp meat when three bear charged me at once. A male and a female and cub usually never get together. So what I think happened—the male met the female and cub and was going to kill them. But when they smelled me, they all ganged up on me.

I had a shotgun, regular number 4 shot, with shells that sometimes would not fire. Being legal I only had three shells in the shotgun and some in my pocket. When the bear charged me, I tried for the biggest one first and just as I shot at it, the female ran into me and juggled me. I couldn't get a good shot and only shot his eyes out. I was going to shoot the side of his head, but when she hit me, I just managed to shoot across his eyes.

The female then stood up and ran into me. I put the gun up under her throat, pulled the trigger and *click!* It was a dud. Then she knocked me down and threw me into the river. But the big male started making noise so she ran back and started chewing on him. The water was maybe 8-inches deep, but so muddy you couldn't see bottom. And the shotgun was underneath me. I pulled the shotgun up just as she came over the bank a second time.

I figured the gun would blow up. But I'd rather be blown up than chewed up so I shot and the gun held. I killed the female dead.

By that time the cub, a 2-year-old, had got into it. But that bear and I were making so much noise they could hear me back at camp over a mile away.

And one of the local guides, Del Richardson, was up there. And he got in our boat with Bringlsy and Roberts and came down to help. But by the time they got there the man with the gun was running so hard, he couldn't shoot straight. So the bear and I were wrestling and he shot and didn't hit either one of us. And the next shot hit the bear in the foot and made it worse yet. But the third shot he killed the bear.

The male was still bellowing up on the bank. Richardson finally went and shot it.

My gun was loaded and Roberts picked it up and said, "What'll I do with this?"

And I said, "Well, just shoot it up in the air and empty it." And he did and that shot was a dud too.

The river was just red with all the blood, mine and the bear's both. They dragged me into the boat and took me out to the yacht *Manana II.* Pete Bringsly said, "Now, if we just had some whiskey."

And the captain was a Seventh Day Adventist and he said, "There's no whiskey on this boat!"

But one of the hunters spoke up, "Well," he said, "I got to confess I smuggled some aboard so we do have some." So they went and got the whiskey. I was lying on the pilothouse floor and Pete Bringsly poured about a coffee cup full of whiskey. But instead of giving it to me, he drank it himself!

But there was still some left so they rolled me over and poured the holes in my legs full of raw whiskey and that did hurt! That did burn. It saved my leg though, I think.

I told the story later to a Seventh Day Adventist preacher and he said God helped me. But I don't know. I needed help and I had help, I think. But I don't know of anybody who's been charged by three bear at once and lived through it.

So maybe I did have help.

Bruce Johnstone met his bear on his terms, so did Johnny Morton and Ovid McKinley...but you might say, they had the "upper hand."

25

"THERE'S ONE!"

By
Ovid "Mac" McKinley as told to Larry Kaniut

I sewed him a row of buttonholes from his belly to his neck.

Anyone who's heard of the Old West range wars would likely be interested in the bear-cattle brouhaha on Kodiak Island in the mid-1960s. Jim Rearden apprised the public about it in his "Kodiak Bear Wars" piece in August 1964. The problem revolved around the argument of protecting cattle, bears or both.

One of the major complaints involved "strafing" grizzlies from the air with a "machine gun." It was a timely message that I do not wish to reiterate here. However I would like to share what it was like to be a "hired gun" for the game department, going aloft and gunning for brown bears from the cockpit of a Piper PA-18 rag wing aircraft.

Two guys, one plane, one bear. The Cub driver points out the brownie to his tandem partner. In the same microsecond he jams the stick forward, dumps the nose over and kicks the right rudder. The chase is on. The pilot grasps the dangers. There's a left cross wind and he's got to pick his way among the trees and low knobs to get his gunner close enough for a crack at bruin.

Johnny knows the area. He's flown it often. *We're on the deck. Bear's heading for that gully to hide. Got to watch that string of cotton-wood trees along the creek.* He reminds himself, *Keep an eye on that abrupt hill on the left in case the bear turns that way.*

The shooter also knows the dangers in his lap. *How many times have we done this?* Mac knows he'll get only one shot. *Don't hit the floats. Don't blow off the wing struts. Got to swing the Garand and aim behind him to compensate for our air speed. Jeez, he's bouncing like a top, humping across the grass and dodging around alder patches. Closer. Line up on the running bear. Just about there. Easy. Fire.*

Two guys, one plane, one DEAD bear.

That's how it ended…for the bear and for the hunters. But that's not how it started. Since the Russians arrived on the Emerald Isle with their cattle just prior to 1800, there has been trouble in paradise between them and bruin. In the 1960s cattle ranching was confined to a specific area of the island. Less than a dozen ranchers had leases, raising around 2500 cattle, something like 150-200 head apiece.

Most Americans don't even know where Kodiak is let alone what the island is like. All but kissing the root of the Alaska Peninsula 25-miles across the Shelikov Straits, Kodiak pokes her head out of the north Pacific. Alder patches, evergreen trees and mostly-rolling 2000-foot peaks blanket thousands of square miles of this archipelago fringed by numerous fjords. A dozen hamlets sprinkle the coastline. All told probably only a few thousand people populated the island in the 1960s.

Wondering what it must have been like to "strafe" a grizzly from a Super Cub, I contacted Johnny Morton and Ovid "Mac" McKinley to ask them how they did it. Both men had actively hunted bears for the ranchers. Until 1962 the conventional method of pursuing the stock killing bears was on foot or by horseback. Johnny and Mac lived in a different time and in a different world and did what was necessary to put bread on the table.

Johnny Morton, a WWII hero and experienced light aircraft pilot decorated by General George Patton, was a crack rifleman. He'd been a registered guide and outfitter until statehood in 1959 when he got out of the business because of the red tape. At that time bald eagles were considered nuisance birds and had a $3 bounty, so Johnny took advantage of that and periodically shot twenty or thirty a day. A 6-foot wing span was common but Mac tells of shooting one eagle with an 8-foot wingspan. Since dolly varden brought 3-cents per tail and seals had a $2 bounty per mask, Johnny harvested them, worked construction, continued flying and hunted for the ranchers because he knew them well.

John told me, "Not one bear out of a hundred will attack cattle. But when he starts killing, he'll never quit. One bear only ate off the ears. If it were a cow, he'd eat the udder. We killed some big ones. One of them was over ten-foot; some of the others were about 9-foot."

Mac came north from Seattle aboard the *Cordova*, an Alaska steamship plying its way across the Gulf of Alaska to Kodiak in 1946, during an era when a man's word was his bond. He could leave his door unlocked and borrow money from a local bar owner to send for his family in the States (which Mac did, enclosing $220 cash in an envelope. Mac told me, "Your credit was good till you proved otherwise."). He became a marshal, a chief of police and a fish hawk for the Department of Fish and Game.

Mac resembles an overgrown fire plug topped with half-inch grey-white hair. He is a bundle of energy and a compendium of Alaska adventure.

He said, "Those ranchers rode horseback and worked very hard ridding the range of problem bears. Hunting bears was not an every day thing, but something done when a bear was spotted. We chased around on foot over the ranches for several years off and on. John and I weren't hunting or flying together at that time."

In May 1963, Morton and McKinley teamed up, Johnny flying and Mac shooting from the back side window of an airplane. Mac explained the history and the action aloft.

The Process
Even though bears were hunted from the ground, eventually the plane was the way to go because it was the most efficient way to locate bears. Over those few years there were less than a dozen shooters who killed bears from the air. The primary four were Gilbert Jarvela, Dave Henley, Johnny and I. Gil and Dave, both commercial pilots, didn't have the work schedule to allow them time off therefore Johnny and I hunted the most. We eliminated several bears for the ranchers. They were glad to get our help and we were happy to provide it.

When the airplane come into the picture, it didn't come on real fast. We started in a J-3 Piper Cub with no flaps. Below 65-70 miles per hour it shivered and shook, affecting the shooter's success, but it was maneuverable at slower speeds. We also flew two Super Cubs, one a 90 horsepower and the other a 150 horse.

The smaller aircraft burned 5 to 7-gallons of fuel an hour if we worked it pretty hard. The 150 horse Super Cub burned 9-gallons an hour and it was the one best suited for shooting bears with a tail gunner—it was my favorite aircraft.

Joe Zentner bought the 90-horse power Super Cub and it was flown up to Kodiak from Outside. He paid for the fuel and perhaps some of the other ranchers helped out. As I recall, it was damaged later in a landing so it was laid up and couldn't be flown. It was hard to get parts and pieces. You couldn't just go down to the local store to buy them. This slowed down the aerial hunt for quite some time.

When Joe's Cub was re-rigged, they got her back to flying again. Meantime we had taken the door off the old J-3 so I could shoot out of it. I roped myself to the seat and tied a safety line to the .06 Garand—I could pull it back inside if all the movement from firing yanked it out of my hands.

We learned as we went along. Early on we had to have complete trust in the other guy's ability. John was the pilot; I was the gunner.

Disabling bears required practice and a lot of extra work. We used to throw out paper plates on a lake and make a run and shoot at those plates floating on the surface. You've got to get the angle, speed, lead the animal and so on. I got to where I could tear those plates up.

After a while, with experience I learned to shoot automatically. You don't necessarily aim through the sights or down the barrel, but you're pointing and judging when to fire when the bear is in that sight picture through the door.

When we were bear hunting, our work involved a lot of things and action. I don't know how you could tell a person how quick this all happened—that bird was popping along at 80, 85-miles an hour and just flying stable. You're coming up on the animal. John would say, "I can see him. Get ready."

I'm thinking, *I'll try to lead him. I've got to shoot under him.*

We had the top half of the door opened and fastened to the clip hanger beneath the right wing; the lower door hung open from its hinges. The bear's coming up underneath the wing struts.

I've got to judge the speed so that when I see him at a certain place through the open door, I can touch one off. I can't think as fast as the plane's moving, and by the time I think I should shoot, I should have shot because the target is behind us.

I'm canted just a little bit so that when the time comes and he's right here, I'll touch the trigger. By holding right behind the bear and a little low that ought to put it on him.

You've got to avoid hitting the wing struts and the floats. There are a whole lot of things hanging out on that airplane that's inconvenient. If the plane didn't have any wing struts, I might get off 8 rounds from the semiautomatic Garand M-1 while passing by that son of a gun. You have only a limited amount of space and time in which to shoot without damaging the plane before you're past the bear. If the bear's far enough away and I can get the sights on him, I might get off as many as three shots before he is out of sight. The fact that you could get three shots out increases your chances of hitting the bear by three.

Most times because of the range and the speed, you get only the one shot. The bear's running through alders and humps, trying to escape, and the cowboy up front is trying to keep it in sight and get close enough for a killing shot. The bear turns on a dime and reverses.

Johnny climbs to slow down, turns quickly and keeps up with the chase.

Never cut power. Keep it on so you can maneuver the plane. To stay in the vicinity, you've got to slow your speed. What better way than climbing? Make your turn up there, drop the nose so you don't stall, and you go right back down after the bruin. You're still in the same area. I load the rifle while we're coming back around. John puts her into a full slip and points the bird for the ground like a brick, flares out and we're on him again. Sometimes we'd get within 20-feet of the animal.

Sometimes I've shot over 60 rounds and never did a bit of good firing out the back window. Whenever the turbulence got to the point where it was bumping us around a bit, we were just wasting gas and ammo and went back home.

There were good days and bad days. You didn't just go out there and take them on like a flock of quail. You had to hunt for those rascals.

The Hunt

Johnny and I lived side by side just outside of town. Word of mouth was the way we got most of the information about a cattle-bear kill from the ranchers. Telephones were in town but they certainly weren't out on the ranches at that time. When word came in that a bear was spotted on a ranch, we'd get in the old pickup and drive down to the plane to begin our hunt.

Bears don't stay in the same place; they may be here today and several miles away tomorrow. But when a bear's traveling, he probably wouldn't kill a cow. He might go straight through a herd and just keep going.

On a typical day when it looked like we could get down amongst them, we'd go out early in the morning. Many guides will tell you that around 10 o'clock a bear heads for the brush and beds down. When they're bedded, they're hard to locate.

Gas was kept out at the hangar at the far end of Long Lake near town. We always got up on the plane and stuck a finger in that tank on each side to make sure we felt gasoline before we buzzed off the water. Because they weighed a fair amount, we didn't have a starter or a battery and it was a hand prop job.

Weather was always a factor. "Good" weather in Kodiak is generally rain with fog patches all through these little hills that time of day. If it's a real good weather day, we've got other work to do.

The radio was a little hand held thing about ten inches long. We carried it just in case. Even that wasn't a safe thing. If you hit the ground hard, the radio could come flying out of its holder and might hit you, beat you up if it didn't just pulverize you. For the radio to be effective we would have to talk to somebody on the ground. Of course, where we were, there was no one on the ground.

Most of our best hunting was done in the spring when the grass was first coming out. The sun hits the top of the hills first and you're probably going to find the cattle up where the fresh, green grass is and they're bunched together. That's a rule of thumb. Where you find the stock and they are moving around, that's when you'll find a lot of bears out and about.

Any time we were flying, we were prepared and looking for bears. I'd have some kind of a smoke pole sitting in the aircraft. Those Cubs have been known to quit and if you set her down the hard way and lived, the rifle would be a handy thing to have as a means of discussion in case you were accosted by a bear.

We flew high so we could see more country; we'd scoot and scout to see if we could find anything moving. We be-bopped around and flew down these little canyons and gullies.

We'd make a flyby over cattle. A bunch of spooky critters was a good sign of a bear's presence. We tried the rivers first, worked the creeks where bears walked these trails for centuries. It was always easiest to hunt the flats and avoid the hills, brush and trees. We took most bears where there weren't many trees.

If we couldn't see anything, we'd go back. We were very seldom out more than a couple of hours at the most.

Sometimes you're lucky.

When we located one, we'd go into high gear and get after this son of a gun. We'd get right down close to the deck. Being a rifleman, John knew what it took for me to hit that critter. He would do his level best to get me into a position where I'd have the rifle out that back window. He'd be coming up on this target and trying to stabilize that aircraft as much as possible.

The closer you get to a bear, the less time you've got to shoot him, but the bigger the target is. So you've got two or three ways of looking at this. If you get too far away and start shooting and there's no possibility of hitting it, you see ground flying up all over the place, and you've got to come back again.

When we got locked on a bear, we'd make a pass at it. An escaping brown bear could reverse direction in an instant and if the pilot didn't know how to fly, you'd be a half-mile away before you got turned around.

Even though it wasn't the easiest target to hit, coming up on a bear and missing him was annoying. You just figure, "What the heck did I do that for?" If there's a little burble in the flight of the aircraft when you touch the trigger, you're liable to be shooting out across the country...a little flip and that's all it takes to miss.

The planes were noisy and we couldn't talk much. I'd tap the pilot on the shoulder and point, or give hand signals to slow down. We understood each other and we carried on a pretty good conversation.

I'd signal "take it up" and up we went.

Once I fired the rifle, Johnny pulled up so we didn't get too far away from the target. Once you fire at that rascal, if he's ever been shot at, he's pretty cagey and he will run like a turkey to get to the brush.

John's flying the plane and I'm trying to keep track of the bear. If I signal for John to turn back, the turn can't be too tight or you get into trouble...moose hunter's stall, down she goes–it's killed lots of pilots.

Most of the time this method was successful.

All this excitement gets your blood pressure up.

One time Johnny and I were on a bear and I fired a couple of rounds from my .375 H&H Magnum. We made a turn out over the water to come back around on the bear and the rudder jammed. While he climbed, I got to work real quick pulling out the rear floorboards. I found a casing from the .375 wedged behind the rudder pedal. The casing was all crunched where he'd been stomping on it with the rudder pedal. Who would have ever thought a little slot in the floorboards would let a rifle shell casing go through and jam the controls?

I don't recall ever putting in a whole day of bear hunting unless Johnny plunked the plane down on a beach and I took the rifle up after some bear. That was a common method to hunt if we spotted a bear near a place to land. But a drop off hunter never knew what to expect with regards to the plane, whether the pilot would break it or not before the hunter and pilot saw each other again.

One hunt it was bumpy under the clouds coming up on Ron Hurst's place through the pass to Saltery Cove. We make the usual circle on the low hills part of the ranch. We flew out over the bay, didn't see anything and circled back toward Ron's cabin when we came to the creek going toward Hightower's place. We saw a big son of a gun along the creek by the trees. John spotted him first, "There's one down there!"

We were at 1000 feet and the bear was running toward the creek for an opening. John dropped down and flew alongside the bear and I popped him. I thought I got him, but the bear got up and run into these trees. We made two passes but we were on floats and couldn't land. We went to the saltwater bay a quarter mile away and touched down then taxied to the beach.

I told John, "You take care of the plane and I'll go up there and finish the rascal off."

I've got the .06 Garand and I'm on the cow trail going to where I thought the bear was. Rose bushes are thick with thorns as long as a hound's tooth. I'm ready to do battle, alert and looking everywhere for the bear.

About that time here comes Zentner in his plane. He flies over me and drops a note that flutters to the ground. I thought he was sig-naling me with the paper to show me where the bear was. I found out later from him that the note told me the bear got away. It turns out the note fell into the area where the wounded bear was. The bear couldn't see over the brush on all fours so it stood up since he could hear me moving in on him through those thorny rose bushes.

About then I heard the bear click his teeth. That son of a gun rose up and up and up, kept going up to the sky. He was huge. I've had bears stand up but never that close. I sewed him a row of but-tonholes from his belly to his neck. And he fell back in a pile. After I calmed down, I cut his head off to take back to Joe. It weighed at least thirty pounds. I got back to the plane and John said, "I see you got him." I threw the head into the plane and we took off from some real choppy waves.

We went over to Joe's ranch, flew by his house and landed on the lake. Joe came down soon and told us he knew where the bear was that got away from us. Then I took the head out of the plane and said, "He didn't get away from us."

Wanting us to know there was more than one, he said, "There's another one."

We discussed the bear that he'd dropped a note to tell me about. He asked me if I rode a horse and I told him, "I'm not much of a horse rider but I'll try."

Since John had to go to town to refuel the plane and return, I told him we'd be on the hill by 3; it was 11 then. The horse I rode was named Jughead and was well named.

We came over the hilltop at 2:30 and still had a ways to go. We followed a cow trail when we could–there were 2-foot wide paths on every hilltop around. Joe said, "We're there. That bear's right in those alders," and he points down hill. I'm going to tie this nag up and hopefully this bear will run uphill like most do when they are jumped.

As I walked down, I could hear the plane approaching from the north. I wanted to stay in the open because John was going to shoot the area up from the plane. John's son Reilly was with him and he's no slouch with any firearm. He leans out the door with a .44 magnum six-shooter to make noise. *Boom! Boom! Boom!*

Here comes the bear. It come right across this field and I pumped 6 Government Issue slugs out and he didn't even slow down. Joe heard me shooting and came riding down the hilltop trail. The bear ran right up to Joe's horse–he's as big as the bronc–and Joe tried to get his rifle up to shoot but the horse went nuts with fear. He got a shot off before the bear turned. Now it's coming back to me and there wasn't a blade of grass to hide behind.

Joe rode back up the hill to be above the bear just in case he got away from me. The animal's 200 feet away and coming right at me. I shot twice. Hit him but it didn't even slow him down. He's getting closer. I loaded a new clip and fired six rounds. I must have hit him in the front leg with the sixth one. He went down and was trying to get up. I had only two rounds left.

I ran at him like a P-38 and shot him twice from about 2-feet away in the back of the head before he quit. The bear was full of holes but wouldn't go down.

Then I waved John off and he took Reilly back to town and later he returned for me. He was at the lake when Joe and I got back.

John had warned me to be careful because this was a big bear and asked me why I charged the bear like a marine. He was in a box seat watching the event. I told him that I was out of shells and had the last two rounds in the rifle and wanted them to count.

The Mounted Rifle

Dave Henley came to the island the same time John Morton did in 1946 and had a ranch at Kalsin Bay. He was a World War II fighter pilot who flew P-51 Mustangs. Conversation eventually got around to combining the fighter pilot's skill with the ranchers' need to eliminate problem bears. The logical, if not, controversial solution was a "fighter plane" to strafe the animals. They teamed up to develop a means of increasing the cattle's chances of surviving.

Then it started to take root, that there was a better, faster way to go after bears...you didn't have to go out and kill yourself. Henley was the man. What he said, you paid attention to. And with his guidance a whole lot of us are still around here.

I don't know of anyone in the group other than Dave Henley with the experience and know how to come up with the M-1 Garand mounted on the Super Cub. It was an effective one-man operation–there was usually only one guy in that airplane. Why carry another 200 pounds when you're going to be maneuvering?

They mounted the rifle on a tripod, front and back, on the top of Zentner's 90 horse Super Cub on wheels. It was set up high because you've got a propeller to worry about out here. It shot above the prop about an inch. Your sight ran horizontally between the cabanes just aft of the windscreen, set dead on the target at 125 yards. Even at 200 yards the bullet had only a 3-inch drop.

The weapon was rigged so that the pilot could fire it from the cockpit like the old fighter planes. Attention was paid to the mechanism to allow room to facilitate operation. A button on the stick activated the trigger. Wiring ran up beneath the fabric on the side of the aircraft and through the greenhouse, the roof "window" of the aircraft, to a solenoid attached to the trigger.

A slot was cut in the greenhouse and allowed the pilot to reload while in flight. When the last shell was fired, the pilot could reach his hand to the ammo clip from the cloth bandoleer. He slid the clip through the opening and pushed the end of the clip into the rifle magazine, gave the rifle bolt a yank to release the ejector and slide in the first round. The Garand was ready with a round in the chamber. It would take care of itself until you needed to put in another clip.

He put that clip in, charged the weapon and put the bird back on the target.

John was perfect for the mounted rifle. He had a long arm where he could reach up to the open slide and replace the clip. He was fast.

If you're shooting the Garand at a bear and you miss, you can see the mud fly or a tree branch fall, and you keep right on peppering and go right in there after him. Everything's happening so damn fast. Dave was telling us about the P-51 Mustang. He was doing some low-level flying and was getting about 450 mph and he felt like he was in a wedge. Of course, this doesn't feel like a wedge. Optically everything is out there and you can see it. It's stopped and you aren't. Depends on the plane and the pilot. A guy like Henley got on a bear and there was feathers. He did a lot of damage.

The mounted rifle was the most effective means of getting a bear that they ever come up with. It's hard to pin down the exact number taken by this means because many weren't counted, and we didn't make a lot of noise about taking them.

It was only a matter of time, however, before the bear-cattle volcano in Paradise erupted and overflowed.

Mac told me, "I didn't think we'd get by as long as we did. The main thing that we were concerned with, is just what happened. We got publicity."

Morton added, "If you have to kill a bear, you might as well do it with a P-51 or something similar instead of fooling around in the brush for a month and maybe not get it. Jim Rearden didn't like the machine gun. He didn't have anything bad to say about Mac and me, just how good I could fly the airplane…that we did what we had to do and all that. The machine gun on the airplane was all legal. Fish and Game and FAA approved it. This was the only time the game department ever sanctioned shooting bears with an automatic weapon from the air over Kodiak.

"Once *Outdoor Life* got hold of it, the people read about it and had a screaming fit. The pressure from the guides shut it down. They used the mounted Garand only a short time. After that Mac and me started shooting bears out of the side of a Super cub."

And so a truly a historic period passed from Alaska, and, probably, from the planet.

Mac added:
Very few of today's readers will ever know or even care about those old original ranchers. This day and age will never produce their breed again—men like Sid Olds, Joe Zentner, Tom Nelson and Tom Felton.

No doubt, Joe Nana would like to have had an airplane from which to do business. But all he had were his hands and his knife to fight his bears.

Mac McKinley and Paul Callahan in 1948 with 7-8-foot eagle
worth $3.00 bounty.

Photo from Mac's personal collection

26

A BRAVE BRAVE

Joe grabbed a handful of hair and jumped into the air toward the beast's back.

Mike Cramond published a story in the October *Saga* magazine, and titled it "The Fearless One." It's an extremely unusual–and some would say, unbelievable–tale of a man, a bear and a knife. Joseph Nana is one of a handful of men who has knifed a grizzly and survived.

Mike vouched for this story's credibility by stating that Indians are a proud people and would be totally humiliated if they were discovered in a lie.

I've rewritten the event here.

Take a batch of fierce determination, toss in a heap of courage and add a bunch of toughness, and you have Joseph Nana. Though small in stature, he was wiry. Combine the powerful proportions of his wrists and forearms with the rest of the package in this coastal Canadian Indian and you have one capable hombre, a man who desired to be known as a great hunter.

He respected the cunning and ability of his ancestral hunters but he wanted more. He planned to acquire a rifle on the order of the white man's thunder stick so that he could be a more efficient hunter. He spent one winter and spring toward that end trapping and curing beaver and marten pelts in the Rocky Mountains with his wife.

When the Chinook, the Indian word for snow eater, came in the spring, he loaded up their catch and headed to the Hudson's Bay trading post near the modern town of Windermere, B.C.

As Little Joe looked on, the Scotch trader piled the furs high. They made a trade and Joe left the post with a rifle, cradling it fondly in his arms as he would a baby. His trade included powder, horn and patches.

Before long Joe was hunting all manner of game including deer, elk and moose while acquiring game for the Indian village. When fall rolled around, he decided that a grizzly would provide food for his family and some needed warmth in the form of a bear skin rug. So he went bear hunting.

Evening shadows tip toed across the valley when he approached a rock slide scarring the face of a mountain. Knowing that grizzlies inhabited the area, Joe decided to climb the 2,000 slide to look for *ursus horribilis*.

Within a short period of time the sunset would bathe the mountains in red and the bears would leave the mountain junipers in search of their groceries. Joe laid out his muzzle loading kit as he sat on a fallen pine tree. He discovered he had but a trace of black powder in his powder horn. Using half the suggested amount would stretch the powder and should be enough to kill a grizzly–he'd done so with elk and moose.

Measuring out the powder, he poured it into the chamber along with a patch and a ball, tamping them home with the ramrod to complete the task.

Prepared now to take on a bear Joe headed up the slide as quickly as possible. With rifle in hand he reached the top, stopped at the edge of the woods and listened. He heard the faint trickle of sliding shale. Listening intently, he then heard more of the same sound and then the deeper *clunk* of a heavy boulder rumbling downhill. *A bear is digging above me!*

Circling some wild thimbleberry and raspberry bushes, he came to a patch of pine trees. He moved quickly through the thicket, the layer of needles and moss muffling the sound of his movement. When he reached the area of the noise's origin, he stopped behind a juniper clump. From there he spotted a grizzly working above him on the slope. He watched it paw rocks and earth aside, ducking its head periodically to lick roots from its paws. It was unaware of his presence.

Joe wet both his cheeks with saliva and turned his head slowly. The breeze tipped its hand when one side of his face chilled slightly from the draft, telling Joe what he needed to know before proceeding. *I can approach the bear on its level.*

He retreated into the pines and climbed higher. When he reached the bear's elevation, he peeked around the brush and discovered that the grizzly had also moved uphill. It dug near a clump of junipers on a flat spot between large boulders.

Since his charge consisted of such a small amount of powder, Joe chose to get closer to ensure pushing the ball through the bear's hide, ribs and heart. He knew he'd get only one shot because there would be no time to reload.

Using a twisted pine and juniper bushes for cover, he moved stealthily toward the bear until he was within twenty yards.

The bear looked up, pointed its snout into the air and blasted his breath and dirt from its mud caked nostrils. It sniffed the air with its rubbery, black nose then stuck its head down and resumed digging and feeding.

On pins and needles, Joe stalked closer. His chest was tight and he was nearly breathless when he stopped only five steps from the bear. He shouldered the long barreled rifle, poked it out of the juniper bush and drew a bead just behind the beast's shoulder.

At the moment that Joe pulled the trigger, the animal shuffled backward. The rifle barked, and the ball slammed into the brute's massive shoulder muscles.

An earth-shaking roar filled the air as the bear rose on its hind legs while swinging its front paws wildly. Then it whipped its massive head around and bit repeatedly at its shoulder, tearing out chunks of fur with its teeth.

Fear gripped Joe in an iron hand. He knew he couldn't move even if he wanted to.

Suddenly he saw the bear raise its head and heard the animal squeal. With quivering lips extended the bear's coal red eyes burned into the bushes that shielded Joe. The Indian knew that the bear's sensitive nose had picked up his man scent.

The beast dropped to the ground and lunged toward Joe then stopped its bluff charge.

The Indian knew the maneuver was designed to cause fright and flight in the pursued, at which time the bear would close in for the kill. But the man held his ground.

The bear moved slowly and in a determined manner in a direct line toward him.

Knowing that his chances of survival were futile should the bear catch him in the bushes and before the bear could reach him, Joe jumped from his hide toward the flat spot of ground before him, pulling his 10-inch knife from his belt in mid-air.

No sooner had he hit the ground than the bear was on him. Joe knew the animal would bite the closest object to him so he stuck out his left hand. Instantly the bear clamped its jaws onto his hand and Joe lunged in as close to the animal as he could get in order to clear its paws and to get within stabbing range. Then Joe went to work with the sharpened knife blade. He stuck the knife into the bear's side as hard as he could, sticking it between the ribs.

With Joe's hand still in its mouth, the grizzly grunted and rose on its hind legs. The man repeatedly thrust the knife into the side of the bear while standing as close to it as he could, trying desperately to stab the life out of it while keeping away from the paws that could decapitate or disembowel him with a single swipe.

Hoping that the Gods-of-the-Hunter were with him, he prayed.

Blood streamed from its nose and mouth as the bear dropped onto its haunches. It released its grip on his hand.

Joe grabbed a handful of hair and jumped into the air toward the beast's back. He landed squarely on it as easily as a trick rider mounting his horse. Joe swung his arm in an arc over and over, slamming the blade into the side of the bear's chest. It spun around like a Brahma bull in a rodeo contest, crow hopping, grunting, roaring and trying to toss the man from its back. But Joe held on as the bear tired.

Maybe I'll survive this after all. That's when he saw the second bear!

From the corner of his eye he spotted a tawny object and realized it was standing close by. The second animal was only 10-feet away, working its nose and watching the spectacle before it.

Suddenly the brute beneath Joe relaxed and dropped to its shoulders. It twitched and heaved, rolling over onto and pinning Joe under it.

Joe observed the second bear's pig-like eyes watch him as he tried to free himself.

In a final effort to rise, the dying animal gathered itself. Joe jammed his knife into the bear's side again and pushed against the animal at the same time. It dropped to the ground, coughing blood and unable to continue the battle.

He was free from it.

Joe considered jumping out onto the slide to avoid the second bear. But he had seen bears move quickly on rockslides, even somersaulting to gain speed. Before he could make up his mind, the second bear closed in, from only six feet away.

Joe took a deep breath and also offered this bear his left hand. Without waiting for a second invitation the bear grabbed it above the wrist.

The Indian lunged against the bear and jabbed his knife into its side. Reasoning that his balance was as good as the bear's and that he'd fare better by staying erect, Joe hoped he could push it against a tree. He let go of his knife and grasped the hair on its back while pulling himself into the bear.

Feeling his leg muscles bulging against his buckskin pants, somehow he managed to move the bear backward. Hot blood poured from the bear's mouth down the back of Joe's neck.

The bear lunged sideways and Joe lost his grip on the fur. His wrist came free and he grabbed for the knife handle. He was unable to hold onto it because his sweaty hands were too slick.

Just then he fell to his knees as the grizzly dropped beside him.

Joe tried to scramble away but slipped when a stone dislodged beneath his moccasins.

The bear lunged toward him, coughing bloody bubbles from its mouth.

Even though Joe thought the end was near, he rolled quickly away and scrambled to his feet.

But the bear was quicker. In the flick of an eye it opened its mouth and grabbed his wrist again, crunching his hand.

Joe kicked the knife handle with his foot and the bear coughed, releasing his wrist.

In an instant Joe was airborne, sailing out and over the slide. He landed sliding and tumbling down the loose rocks. He turned to look back and saw the bear swaying its massive head from side to side and he heard it coughing from deep within its chest. Joe knew his knife blade was buried in its lungs.

He continued down the mountain and toward the river. When he reached the lowland, he came to a beaver pond and washed the blood and gore from his hand. He then pulled off dock leaves and plastered his wounds with them, securing them with a spider web.

Although exhausted from the battle and thinking his hand would be useless in the future, he reveled in the thought that his reputation as a great hunter was established. He had taken two Great Grey Bears with a knife. Not even the Medicine Man had accomplished that.

The next day the able bodied villagers followed him up the rock-slide to the site of the battle. There they found the first bear dead and bloated. They heard the dying moans of the second bear where it lay in the bushes nearby.

Joe saw his knife and stepped toward the near dead animal to retrieve it. With a final effort the bear tried to rise, blood coming afresh from its mouth. But it was not to be. With a twitching spasm and great sigh, the bear lay still.

The villagers skinned the bears, parceled out the meat and returned to their village where they feasted for two days, toasting Joseph Nana as the mightiest hunter of all the tribes.

Joe survived by using his head and primitive weapon. The two animals that strove for survival in the next story relied upon the weapons of their kind and their wild ways.

RANGE BULL
AND RENEGADE BEAR

Blaze pawed the ground with a front hoof, tossing dirt skyward.
He then flung his head defiantly and snorted.

In his chapter "The Longhorn and the Grizzly" W.P. Hubbard treats the reader to a story of two wild animals bent on survival–one, a grizzly attempting to procure food and the other, a bull trying to stay off the bear's dinner menu. A heap of rowdy in the bear got it into serious trouble with the longhorn. Professional hunter Lon Duncan told Hubbard about the battle between the bear and the beef.

In the late 1890's a marauding grizzly had a price tag placed on his head. In addition to the numerous elk and deer he'd killed in normal day to day grizzly bear living, he had destroyed eighty cattle, a hundred sheep and several horses. The loss of many imported cattle contributed to the high reward of $750 to be paid the person who dispatched the rogue. Because of the bear's buff-colored pelage, Colorado Stockmen called him Buff.

So many ranchers were losing cattle to Buff that they hired professional hunter Lon Duncan to track down and kill the bruin. In short order Duncan learned that every time Buff visited one particular area of his range, he spent a few days near a mineral spring. The spring was located at the head of a blind canyon, and entry could be gained only through a narrow gap between sheer rock walls sixty feet high.

When Duncan learned that Buff was headed to the area encompassing the spring, he took a shortcut, hoping to beat bruin to the waterhole. He arrived in the dark, and daybreak the next morning discovered the hunter hidden among boulders on the rim near the canyon entrance overlooking the spring. The small, flat area of the spring was nearly devoid of brush. Scattered bushes covered the ground near the wall opposite him and a long since fallen, dead tree lay on the ground, gray-white, jagged limbs poking out from its trunk.

He saw Buff's tracks at the spring and realized the bear had beaten him after all. It had slipped in sometime during the night. Even though Lon was disappointed that he'd missed the animal, he was confident that the bear would visit the spring again, as was his custom before passing on to other areas of his range. That assumption and the direction of the wind encouraged him to sit tight to see what might develop.

Before long Duncan heard an animal approaching the spring entrance. As he watched, a big, blaze-faced, roan-colored wild longhorn with white hindquarters and legs shuffled through the opening and ambled halfway across the flat area near the spring, muscles rippling beneath his tough skin.

The hunter recognized the animal immediately as Blaze, a cross-bred Hereford-Longhorn bull, five-eighths Longhorn, three-eighths Hereford. Blaze was as wild an animal as roamed the territory. The 12-year-old bull had avoided being rounded up by hiding out in remote ranges. Scars tattooed his hide, evidence of fights with other bulls. A battle with a bear or mountain lion left healed-over claw marks on his neck. As rugged, wily and wild as they come was this critter.

For some time the bull stood scanning the spring area before approaching the bear tracks and sniffing them. Then he moved to the waterhole. Ever alert, he lifted his head and tested the wind with his nostrils. Then he lowered his head to drink. However, before he could take in water, he whirled around and snorted. He took two long leaps forward, stopped quickly and jerked his head up.

Blaze's tail shot up stiffly in an arc. Muscles bulged all over his body, the picture of pure strength and defiance. He stared across the opening.

Duncan's eyes followed the bull's gaze. There stood Buff on his hind legs almost directly below him. So quietly had the bear arrived, that Lon hadn't heard him. Buff's head was tilted slightly forward. His tongue lolled from his mouth. Cocked at his sides were his claw festooned forepaws. He seemed to know that he had the advantage and appeared satisfied with the prospect facing him.

Blaze pawed the ground with a front hoof, tossing dirt skyward. He then flung his head defiantly and snorted.

Buff dropped to all fours and advanced slowly toward the bull. Facing the bear with eyes riveted on his approach, Blaze backed up until his rear hooves were in the waterhole. Then he moved sideways toward the bear, eyeing his every move.

When the combatants were within a few feet, Blaze charged the bear. Simultaneously Buff reared onto his hind legs. As they met, the bear swung swiftly with both forepaws.

His left forepaw ripped deep gashes in Blaze's chest below the neck while his right forepaw struck a solid blow behind the bull's shoulder. The left-right combination knocked Blaze into the brush and resulted in a thunderous *crash*, clapping off the canyon walls.

No sooner had Blaze hit the ground than he instinctively twisted his hindquarters and struck out at the charging bear with both sledgehammer-like rear hooves. They connected and sliced deeply into the bear's chest, knocking him over backwards and eliciting a bellow of pain and anger.

Blaze jumped to his feet before Buff could react. As the bear rose, Blaze rushed him and drove a horn into his shoulder. The bull effortlessly flipped his head and freed the horn but not before the bear bit a chunk from his shoulder.

They circled, feinting several times toward the other before the bull followed through. Buff rose on hind legs and turned sideways in an effort to avoid Blaze. He was too slow, however, as one horn caught him under the left front leg, piercing the muscle and exiting near the shoulder.

The bear's weight and movements forced Blaze's head down and sideways. Buff bawled in rage and hooked his claws into Blaze's side and back while biting at the top of the bull's neck back of the head. With the decided advantage of his horn in the bear, Blaze moved constantly, keeping Buff off balance. For fifteen seconds the two were locked in mortal combat.

Buff was able only to bawl his rage and to claw and bite at Blaze's shoulder and side, inflicting minimal damage. Had Buff been able to bite the bull's neck solidly, it would likely have ended the battle.

Blaze pivoted on his front hooves and continued moving quickly enough to keep his hindquarters away from the bear's teeth and claws, and deterring the bear's climbing onto his shoulders.

Blaze then jerked his head up and turned to the side, freeing his horn from the bear's body. Simultaneously he struck out at the bear with his front hooves. Failing to connect, he moved backward from the bruin.

Blood flowed freely from both beasts. Blaze's neck and shoulder exhibited torn and mutilated flesh from the bear's raking claws and chomping fangs while Buff's chest, sides and shoulders revealed gashes and puncture wounds

There was a brief pause in the action.

Then Buff charged headlong on all fours. Blaze lunged to meet his charge and swung his head toward the bear just as Buff rose again on hind legs. Once more the bear's movement was too late, as one of Blaze's horns penetrated Buff's chest, driving up through the chest and into the bear's mouth from beneath its lower jaw.

The action forced the bear's head back, rendering him useless for the moment. Blaze pushed forward. Buff was at a definite disadvantage as Blaze drove him backward–he could only paw futilely at the bull's head.

Their harried action carried them to the downed, dead tree where Blaze bellowed and tossed his head, sending the bear upward and freeing the bull's horn again. So great was the bovine's effort that the grizzly flew backward and smashed into the tree. The crisp *crack* of breaking branches and the bear's bawl of pain rang out simultaneously.

As Buff hit the tree, a short, pointed limb, rock hard from years of heat and exposure, penetrated his side like a lance behind the rib area and exited back of his left shoulder. The force of the fall snapped the limb off and it stuck out either side of his body, just aft of his shoulders. Blood spurted from the new wounds.

Blaze stood nearby, his nose all but torn away, his face, shredded flesh. In what appeared an effort to clear blood from his eyes in order to improve his vision, he kept tossing his head. He bellowed in pain.

After lying beside the tree for several minutes, Buff rose groggily to his feet, popping his teeth in rage. He wobbled limply toward the wild longhorn. Blaze charged him, hooking a horn into his upper right hind leg. The horn pierced through the body and poked out the opposite side.

The weight of the bear on his horn held Blaze's head down allowing Buff to stand on his hooked leg and to bring his other hind leg into play, reaching up and forward in an attempt to rip the bull's ribs from the shoulder to the hind quarters.

The bear's loss of blood had weakened him enough that his movements were slowed and Blaze was able to pivot on his front legs to free himself from Buff before the bear could enact his plan.

However as they parted, Buff's claws tore Blaze's throat badly under his neck.

Blaze struck quickly twice at the bear with a hoof, ripping a gash in his belly and causing Buff to expel a pained *woof* and to stagger blindly. By now parts of his intestines were trailing on the sun baked earth. Suddenly Buff dropped to the ground. Gainfully he tried to rise, but his life's blood was gone. His head slumped forward onto the parched earth. The renegade grizzly would kill no more.

Blaze stood with his head down, wobbling spraddle-legged and trembling all over. At length Blaze stumbled forward and looked down at the bear. He snorted in anguish, poked the bear with a horn, turned and stumbled away through the canyon's opening.

Lon grabbed his rifle and ran down to the canyon mouth. When he reached it, he happened onto Blaze, lying dead beside a large boulder.

The area of the battle covered a 50-foot diameter circle.

The hunter skinned both animals and had their heads mounted as they were.

Blaze weighed 1500 pounds. He was clawed from the end of his nose to the middle of his back. Great quantities of his neck skin, muscle and tissue were missing. His throat had been torn half open. One eye was ripped out and gone. His horns measured three-feet and ten-inches across and were thick at the bases, with a good outward and upward curve near the pointed ends.

Buff was between 15 and 18-years old and weighed 887 pounds. Twenty-seven gashes covered his body. Several claws on each paw were broken off, a fact that figured strongly in the bull's favor and, no doubt, greatly reduced the damage to him.

The broken limb imbedded in Buff measured three feet one inch in length. The limb broke two of Buff's ribs and tore a vein that led to his heart.

These two powerful and mortal, wild enemies put on quite a display for Lon Duncan who was privileged to witness it. He was able to record the action with his eyes, ears and memory and later to tell his story so others could better understand God's creatures in life and in death—their power, determination and way of life. Perhaps Duncan should have paid the stockholders for his front row seat at the event.

If a wild range bull with all its power fell to a grizzly, how could a mere man, unarmed, survive a ferocious attack by the horrible bear?

THIS BEAR
WAS ALL BUSINESS

*Flame stabbed the darkness; the recoil jolted Forest
to the core of his being; and the bear fled,
a strangled bawl trailing off into the night.*

This is one of my three all time favorite bear stories, one of the most incredible I've ever encountered. Forest Young endured some of the most severe injuries of any man who lived. Although he was the primary victim, this story "belongs" to a number of people. Foremost is his hunting pal Marty Cordes, to whom Forest's rescue became paramount. Next, is Forest's wife Retha who lived with the pain of Forest's recovery and nursed him back to health. Lastly, those who ventured out that dark night to rescue Forest–Carl Heinmiller, Walt Dueman, Tommy Ward and Marty Kings; the men who flew rescue and the medical professionals.

Although this tale appeared in *Some Bears Kill*, I wanted to share interviews with Forest's wife and partner.

F orest reached the cache, glanced back at the kill site a hundred yards away and saw two grizzlies. Moments later he saw a bear coming for him. Assuming it was a bluff charge, he waved his arms and shouted. At the last moment Forest realized this was no bluff. He lunged for a tree limb and started to climb out of harm's way. He never made it.

The grizzly snatched him from the tree. Hitting the ground on his back, Forest quickly rose to a sitting position. The bear's left foreleg pinned his legs. Man and beast were nose to nose, the hapless hunter at the bear's mercy as its blood-red eyes bored into his.

Expecting the beast to grab him by the throat and snap his neck, Forest pummeled the bear's face until he broke his hand. Forest felt his clothing grind into his flesh while the bear chewed. Every bite registered intense pain as the animal systematically stripped flesh and clothes from the hunter.

An eternity later Forest chose to play dead and the bear immediately broke off its attack. But then Forest groaned, and the bear nailed him again, slashing a hole in his side that exposed his bladder. Forest remained motionless while the grizzly tried to put his lights out, ripping three ribs from his spine and tearing a hole into his chest cavity. Then the grizzly left.

Being mauled by a bear was the least of Forest's concerns in late September 1955. A patchwork of green and gold mantled the hillsides, signaling winter's approach. Forest and his hunting buddy Marty Cordes assaulted the hills on a moose hunt. The men shot two respectable bulls, field dressed them, cached the hides and some meat in a birch tree and packed part of their take two miles to the cabin.

The following day the pair loaded the canoe with meat and Marty headed for Haines, 45 miles down the Chilkat River. By the time Marty returned the following afternoon, Forest had everything in camp except Marty's moose hide.

On October 2, Marty took the shotgun to gather a batch of grouse while Forest targeted Marty's moose hide. They planned to rendezvous at the cabin around noon.

When Forest neared the kill site, he noticed two mounds of debris covering the moose remains, confirming that bears had taken over. The discovery neither alerted nor scared Forest to the dangers of a bear attack because he'd encountered bears for years. But he'd waited too long to leap for the protection of the tree, thinking this was a false charge.

After the initial mauling and the bear's departure, Forest hoped the beast would not return. But then he heard a strange panting noise and felt the muskeg shake. The bear stood only a yard from his face. Time crawled. Finally the bear moved off.

In spite of the pain Forest managed to roll onto his stomach, allowing body fluids to drain from his nose and mouth and to facilitate his breathing. Later Forest heard that queer panting sound and felt the ground shake again. No sound could have caused him greater fear.

Perhaps the animal sensed he'd moved because it roared its rage. The grizzly lifted Forest off the ground in its jaws and shook him until he thought his back would break. The brute ripped out one rib and left two exiting the skin, mangled his right hand, opened a hole revealing his lung cavity, tore flesh from the inside of his legs and ripped his buttocks. As abruptly as it had appeared, the bear dropped Forest and departed again.

Cold water filtered up through the muskeg and chilled Forest to the bone. He agonized...*even if Marty finds me when he returns*, I might be dead. Believing his plight hopeless he determined to take his life.

After several minutes of painful and frustrating fumbling, Forest retrieved his pocketknife. He cut his left wrist, exposing tendons. Seeing no blood and fearing a crippled hand should he survive, Forest stopped. Before long he considered cutting his jugular vein. As Forest felt for his jugular, Marty hailed.

Later Marty said, "I came to Alaska when I was 19-years old and spent 6 years in Kodiak. I don't shock easy. When I saw Forest, I knew he was hurt badly. Forest said, 'Shoot me.' Then he warned me, 'Watch out, the bears are still here.'

"I had a shotgun, the most vicious thing around at short range. We were in a heap of trouble and a long ways from help. We had to play it from the word go. I took my jacket off and covered him up and left the shotgun with him, even though I didn't think he could fire it."

Shocked and unable to carry Forest because of his injuries, Marty headed as fast as possible to camp.

Marty continued, "I ran back to the cabin and fired 3x3 from the top of the valley (close to the Canadian border), laid out an X on the river bank, loaded up gear and ran back to Forest. I blew up an air mattress and rolled him-eased him into a sleeping bag–making him as comfortable as possible. I built a shelter over his head, hung his outer clothing from limbs to fend off the drizzle and laid the loaded shotgun beside him. Then I lit the lantern and placed it within Forest's reach and headed back to camp preparatory to heading downstream for Haines."

Forest knew that the soonest he could expect Marty was midnight, if all went well. But his main concern was whether he'd live that long.

Marty left immediately for Forest's truck, knowing that he had another 30 miles to cover by road to reach Haines. Marty said, "It was 10-20 miles to Forest's truck. I knew the river well and my only handicaps were the late fall's low river and the 8-horse kicker on the canoe."

When Marty finally reached town, he said, "I ran in here and grabbed Retha and told her the bad news and got hold of the Troopers. There was no plane in town."

Marty needed to round up a rescue party and cover the same mileage on his return.

"I rounded up Carl Heinmiller–he was our 'doctor', a major in the army during World War II. I got hold of Walt Dueman, Marty Kings and Tommy Ward (he knew the country inside out)–all three were skookum guys.

"We grabbed Tommy's boat and another. It was darker than the inside of a hat and hard to tell where the sides of the river were, let alone how much water was in the river. We sheared a pin and pulled into an old camp nearby where I got a nail from a tree. We replaced the pin and went upriver like the wind."

An hour after Marty's departure Forest began feeling better. *Maybe I'll make it.* He'd nearly forgotten the bear and had fought the urge to doze when he heard that queer panting and felt the ground beneath him shake.

Forest lay motionless in the bag, the top covering his head. His tormentor approached. Perhaps confused by the light, the sleeping bag and Marty's clothes, the animal vented a blood-curdling roar and lumbered off.

Sweet relief flooded Forest.

As darkness fell, the lantern burned out and Forest panicked. He fully expected the bear to jump him once it realized the light was gone. And his fear was realized.

Forest heard the beast coming for him. Then it was there, near his head. Forest pointed the shotgun in the bear's direction, held high so no pellets would strike it and fired. Yellow-orange flame stabbed the darkness; the recoil jolted Forest to his core; and the bear fled, a strangled bawl trailing off into the night.

About midnight, as Forest focused on Marty's return, the bear came back. Forest decided if it got within ten feet he'd shoot it–*if it doesn't kill it, maybe the shot will drive him off.*

For ten minutes the bear snuffled twenty-five feet away before leaving.

Just after that Forest heard the welcome sound of an outboard. He figured rescuers had reached the cabin. Since his lantern had gone out, he prepared to strike matches to signal the rescuers to his location. When he heard voices, Forest lit all the matches. Voices responded and, fifteen hours after the attack, Forest finally felt free.

Carl Heinmiller injected him with penicillin and morphine.

Marty recalled, "Nobody but I knew where we were. One guy went ahead with the lantern. He steered us that way. We went 50 steps and our arms were on fire. We rested, lit another cigarette for Forest and BS'd. He was conscious and thought he'd make it.

"We hauled him 2-3 hours. One place I got lost. We set him on the ground and I'd go look for a recognizable landmark. I spotted some white moss. Then I knew where I was. About that time a bear let out a growl and Carl fired off a round."

It proved that the bear that mauled Forest was reluctant to give up his victim, but the men were more determined to get Forest to medical attention.

Marty continued, "We got to the cabin and met the guys who'd left 15-minutes behind us–they'd become lost on the river.

"During the night Carl worked on Forest.

"The next morning in daylight a plane flew over watching for our signal. We had agreed that if Forest was alive, we'd jump up and down; if not, we'd lay on the ground. We all jumped up and down. Then a helicopter came in from Whitehorse and landed a mile away.

"When the chopper came in, Forest opened his eyes and said, 'Cordes, your eyes look like two pee holes in the snow.'

"I said, 'You don't look so good yourself.'"

As it turned out Marty, Carl and Walt Dueman struggled in the dark nearly four hours carrying Forest to the cabin.

The next morning Forest was loaded aboard a Royal Canadian Air Force helicopter and flown to Juneau's St. Anne's Hospital. He arrived in critical condition twenty-seven hours after his ordeal had begun.

While Forest was on his way to the hospital, Marty said, "We went back to the sight of the attack and picked up gear and tried to memorize the bear track in order to extract revenge; but we never saw it again."

Retha later said, "I heard about it that evening because they had to get some fellas that were here to go back upriver with Marty. It was awful. I didn't know how badly he was hurt until they got home. They had to get a helicopter to send Forest to Juneau. Dr. Carter was on call and gave me the whole dope. Forest was gonna live or else.

"He never wanted to kill bears. He's not going to shoot them.

"It took a year before he could sit down. He mostly rested on a bed the entire year after the mauling. He had a sore that came right where the chair hit his leg. He kept complaining about it and he wanted to see the doctor and he went to the doctor and had it removed. There was a clump of grass the size of a quarter as green as grass. The chair aggravated the lump. At least a year or two after the mauling he had one the same size in his neck where his shirt collar is.

"He had no mental problems connected with the attack. For a long time the three ribs torn out gave him a problem, but they seemed to heal up."

Forest spent nine weeks in the hospital, lost 30 pounds, three ribs, a half-inch off his third finger on his right hand and acquired some nasty scars. But he survived.

Going unarmed and believing the charge was a bluff nearly cost Forest his life.

Parting comments:

We enjoyed working on these stories for you and your family and friends. You can look forward to another bear book, What's Bruin? It will include Larry's bear cartoons, humor and light-hearted bear anecdotes and information. The web site will give you advance notice of publication date.
A children's coloring book, Alaska's Fun Bears, will be our next offering. Our daughter Jill and Larry have put together this extraordinary book for children that would make anyone fall in love with bears.
See you then.

–Pam Kaniut

Man's Experience in Bear Country

All too many people have very little experience with bears. Therefore when a person encounters a bear, he normally overreacts, usually in panic. For all practical purposes the bear is probably just curious. It wanders around the campsite sniffing and wondering about the smells or other things. It has no interest in the person but the man thinks that because a bear showed up in his presence it is going to eat him.

–The author

A BAD ONE

"Death in the Night," Ben East, *Survival*, Pages 266-275, Outdoor Life, E.P. Dutton & Co., New York, 1967

BATTLE OF GIANTS

Man Meets Grizzly, F.M. Young, Pages 183-186, Houghton Mifflin Co., Boston, 1980

"THE LORD'S ON MY SIDE"

Personal interview with Gene Moe and his wife Shirley at their Anchorage home, April 25, 2000 and successive visits

LIFE FOR LIFE

"The Dog Who Forgot to Fear," Jim Rearden, Pages 265-270, *The Outdoor Life Bear Book*, Edited by Chet Fish, Outdoor Life Books, New York, 1983

PROTAGONIST OF ANTAGONIST?

Grizzly Country, Andy Russell, Pages 63 and 64, Alfred A. Knopf, New York, 1972

DEATH STALKED THE ICE

"Death in the Ice," Ben East, *Survival*, Pages 113-128, An Outdoor Life Book, E.P. Dutton & Co., Inc., New York, 1967

TWO, CLOSE TO DEATH

Alaska Bear Tales, Larry Kaniut, Pages 92-93, Alaska Northwest Publishing Co., 1983
All About Bears, Don DeHart, Pages 15 and 16, Johnson Publishing Co., Boulder, CO, 1971

A BAD MISTAKE

Grizzly Country, Andy Russell, Alfred A. Knopf, Inc., New York, 1967

BEAR AND BULL FIGHTS

California Grizzly, Tracy I. Storer and Lloyd P. Tevis, Jr., Pages 141-162, University of Nebraska Press, Lincoln/London, 1978
The Grizzly Bear, Bessie Doak Haynes and Edgar Haynes, University of Oklahoma Press, Norman, OK, 1966

HE TALKED TO THE BEAR

"When Life Stopped," Ben East, *Survival*, Pages 1-14, E.P. Dutton & Co., Inc., New York, 1967

TWO BEARS, TOO CLOSE

"Black Bears Attack, Too," Ben East, *Survival*, Pages 129 141, E.P. Dutton & Co., Inc., New York, 1967

BUD'S FAITHFUL KENAI

"Stone Deaf Discard," Niska Elwell, *The Alaska Book*, Pages 242-245, J.G. Ferguson Publishing Company, Chicago, 1960

IN SEARCH OF A MAN-KILLER

Alaska Bear Tales, Larry Kaniut, Alaska Northwest Publishing Company, Edmonds, WA, 1983

No Room for Bears, Frank Dufresne, Pages 31-36, Holt, Rinehart and Winston, New York, 1965

"Jack Thayer was killed by a bear," Harold E. Smith, *ALASKA Magazine*, Pages 23, 62-63, August 1971

Forest Service account, Fred Herring, Pages 28-32, from R.N. DeArmond, Juneau, AK

BETWEEN A HARD PLACE AND A ROCK

A Fight With A Grizzly Bear, George G. Spurr, Boston, 1886

SHOOT STRAIGHT

"Of Terrible Courage," Bud Helmericks, February 1956, *The Outdoor Life Bear Book*, Pages 156-163, Outdoor Life Books, New York, 1983

A BEAR FROM NOWHERE

All About Bears, Don DeHart, pages 21-25, Johnson Publishing Co., Boulder, CO, 1971

"Look out for Grizzly Bears," *When Alaska Was Free*, Knut D. Peterson, Pages 58-66 and Pages 67-71, Ashley Books, Inc., Port Washington, NY, 1977

Old Sourdough, Knut Peterson, The Lettershop, Fairbanks, Alaska, 1982

Personal correspondence with Knut D. Peterson 1976 and 1977

ALMOST TOO MUCH GRIZZLY

"My Last Grizzly," Dan Ludington as told to James Doherty, Pages 290-295, *Outdoor Life Bear Book*, Outdoor Life Books, 1983

BURIED ALIVE...TWICE

Bear Attacks, Kathy Etling, Pages 48-52, Safari Press, Long Beach, CA, 1997

The Grizzly Book, Jack Samson, Pages 135 and pages 209-210, The Amwell Press, New Jersey, 1981

Killer Bears, Mike Cramond, pages 200-212, Outdoor Life Books, New York, 1981

"Big Land, Big Game," Ran Lake, *The ALASKA SPORTSMAN*, pages 14, 15, 29-33, October 1945

DETERMINED TO LIVE

The Book of the American West, Jay Monaghan, Bonanza Books, New York, 1963

The Grizzly Bear, Bessie Doak Haynes and Edgar, Pages 50-53, University of Oklahoma Press, Norman, 1966

Grizzly Country, Andy Russell, Alfred A. Knopf, Inc., New York, 1967

Hugh Glass, Mountain Man, Robert M. McClung, Morrow Junior Books, New York, 1990

Man Meets Grizzly, F.M. Young, edited by Coralie Beyers, Houghton Mifflin Co., Boston, 1980

Notorious Grizzly Bears, W.P. Hubbard, Sage Books, Denver, 1960

Pirate, Pawnee and Mountain Man: The Saga of Hugh Glass, John Myers Myers, Little, Brown and Company, Boston, 1953

"The Man who would not Die," Winfred Blevins, *Reader's Digest*, Pages 138-142, (condensed from *Give Your Heart to the Hawks*), October 1978

A MAN'S MAN

All About Bears, Don DeHart, page 9 plus, Johnson Publishing Co., Boulder, CO, 1971
Bear! Clyde Ormond, Pages 93-108, The Stackpole Company, Harrisburg, PA, 1961

ONE TOUGH COOKIE

"Kibbee," Thomas Martindale as told to Mae T. Krouse, *The Alaska Book,* Pages 247-248, J.G. Ferguson Publishing Co., Chicago, 1960

EVER THE WOMAN

Hunting the Alaska Brown Bear, John W. Eddy, G.P. Putnam's Sons, New York, London, 1930

TOE TO TOE WITH A GRIZZLY

"A Record Grizzly Fight," James Bryce, Pages 48-50, A *Treasury of Outdoor Life,* edited by William E. Rae, New York, 1975

OLD GROANER

"The Moaning Marauder of Cripple Creek," by W.H. "Handlogger" Jackson (brother-in-law to the two principals in this story), Pages 191-199, *The Alaska Book,* J.G. Ferguson Publishing Company, Chicago, 1960
Personal correspondence from Bruce Johnstone and Louise Harrington, January 24, 2001.

"THERE'S ONE!"

"Kodiak Bear Wars," Jim Rearden, *Outdoor Life Bear Book,* Outdoor Life Books, New York, 1983
Personal (taped) interviews with:
    1. Johnny Morton, at his Kodiak home on Mill Bay Road, summer 1988
    2. Ovid McKinley—at his Anchorage home, Friday 26, January, 2001; my home February 9 and his home February 19, 2001

A BRAVE BRAVE

A Bear Behind, Mike Cramond, Pages 159-165, Trendex Publications, North Vancouver, B.C., Canada, 1973

RANGE BULL AND RENEGADE BEAR

Notorious Grizzly Bears, W.P. Hubbard, Pages 59-65, Sage Books, Denver, 1960

THIS BEAR WAS ALL BUSINESS

Interviews with Retha Young and Marty Cordes, last week of June, 1989 at Retha's home in Haines, AK

Since the spelling of some names varied in sources, I chose one, or in some cases, listed variants.

MY PERSONAL BEAR BOOK COLLECTION

Over the years I've collected some great bear books and I want to share the most interesting and helpful ones with you.

Those <u>underlined</u> are outstanding for one reason or another.

The asterisk * before the title indicates that the book is still in print (to the best of my knowledge). If one of the following IS in print and I've failed to note it, please advise so that I may correct my oversight. (Perhaps if enough readers contact publishers requesting these out of print books, they will be reprinted.)

Should you wish input on these or others that may not be listed, I invite your call; (907) 868-3437 or your correspondence —
web site: www.kaniut.com;
e-mail: larry@kanuit.com;
snail mail: 4800 Natrona, Anchorage, AK 99516

A Bear Behind, Mike Cramond, Trendez Publications, North Vancouver, B.C., Canada, 1973
Mike shares childhood experiences including his pet brown bear, kids and bears, some stories and some scarey experiences.

A Boy Scout in Grizzly Country, Dick Douglas, Jr., G.P. Putnam's Sons, New York, London, 1929
Information about Kodiak and experiences with its bears.

* *The Adventures of James Capen Adams, Mountaineer and Grizzly Bear Hunter of California,* Theodore H. Hittell, Crosby, Nichols, Lee and Co. Boston, 1860
Biography of mountain man and adventurer "Grizzly Adams" who captured and raised grizzly bears. Other subjects include trap building, camp life, hunting antelope and elk, mountains—the Coast Range Rockies and Sierra Nevadas and, of course, James' bears, Lady Washington, Ben Franklin and Samson.

A Fight With A Grizzly Bear, George G. Spurr, George C. Spurr, Boston, 1886
An old timer shares his fight with a Sierra Nevada grizzly. He was severely mauled and later lost an arm, but was able to climb to safety in a tree after throwing a stone into the charging bear's mouth. She choked on it and fell over a cliff in her effort to reach him.

* _Alaska Bear Tales_, Larry Kaniut, Alaska Northwest Publishing Co., Edmonds, WA, 1983
> Comprehensive book detailing bear-man encounters in Alaska—false charge, close calls, maulings and fatalities (involving the victims, their rescuers, family and medical professionals), humor, hunting methods, tall tales and advice for safe travel in bear country. Annotated bibliography is worth the price of the book.

Alaska Bear Trails, Harold McCracken, Doubleday, Doran & Co., Inc., Garden City, New York, 1931
> Explorer and photographer McCracken discusses his early days in British Columbia, his initial trip to Alaska, the _Dirty Dora_, legendary bear hunting guide Captain Charlie Madsen, gold prospecting, caribou, grizzlies and moose and going to Siberia.

Alaska's Mammoth Brown Bears, Will H. Chase, Burton Publishing Co., Kansas City, MO, 1947
> The first half of the book portrays a biographical sketch of Tyee from cubhood through his death at the eruption of a volcano. Chase describes the brown bear's easy going nature, a brownie-black bear fight, a close call in the Yukon, the destruction of brownies in the 1800s, fire power and a plea for co-existence/conservation with/of the species. A good book.

All About Bears, Don DeHart, Johnson Publishing Co., Boulder, CO, 1971
> Don covers Alaska's bears, hunting, close calls and maulings, stories of the hunt, tips for successful hunting, weapons and field glasses.

Bear!, Clyde Ormond, The Stackpole Company, Harrisburg, PA, 1961
> General information about North American bears, hunting and weapon and ammunition choice. Introduction by Joe Foss.

* _Bear Attacks (Vols. 1 & 2)_, Kathy Etling, Safari Press, Long Beach, CA, 1997
> North American bears, bear myths, grizzly history and early American encounters with mountain men and other outdoorsmen, black and polar bear attacks and avoidance of maulings.

* _Bear Attacks The Deadly Truth_, James Gary Shelton, Shelton Productions, Box 355, Hagensborg, B.C. Canada V0T 1H0, 1998
  In his second book Shelton stands up for human safety in bear country. He denounces the popular preservationist philosophy and provides examples of the increasing bear density in British Columbia. He talks about a "new" kind of bear, that is more habituated to and less fearful of humans, greatly due to the pro-bear save-the-animal mentality. A must read for anyone wishing to save self, family or friends in bear country.

* _Bear Attacks II_, James Gary Shelton, Shelton Productions, Box 355, Hagensborg, B.C. Canada V0T 1H0, 2001 ($20 U.S. includes S&H for each Shelton book–above & below)
  This is Gary Shelton's third in a series of publications providing realistic information about bears. This book contains over 30 first-hand accounts of bear attacks that are analyzed to determine the causes for these terrible events. In addition, this material presents new concepts regarding how bears perceive humans. As in his past works, the author exposes myths in our belief systems aboutnature and examines how science is influenced by environmental politics.

* _Bear Encounter Survival Guide_, James Gary Shelton, printed in Canada, 1994
  Shelton provides information on bear-man conflict including general and predatory attacks, bear avoidance, survival strategy, polar bears, bear management and conservationism vs. preservationism. An excellent book providing tips for staying uninjured in bear country.

Bear Hunting, Jerry Meyer, Stackpole Books, Harrisburg, PA, 1983
  Black bear hunting in America and Canada—the hunt, preparations, with dogs, from bait stations, methods, suitable weaponry, strategies, care of game, table fare, wounded bears and the animal's future.

Bears, Ben East, Outdoor Life, New York, 1977
  A look at North America's three bears and their habits and numbers. Some good stories.

* _The Bears of Manley_, Sarkis Atamian, Publication Consultants, Anchorage, Alaska, 1995
  In addition to black, grizzly and polar bears, this book of profound philosophy discusses manhood and hunting—two essentials to saving the world. Truly a wonderful book.

The Beast That Walks Like Man, Harold McCracken, Oldbourne Press, London, 1957

> The grizzly from days of the Indians and explorers to modern times including adventures, birth and nature, stories about man and bear, sporting with bears, classification and distribution.

* *The Ben Lilly Legend,* Frank Dobie, Little, Brown and Co., Boston, 1950

> Biography of the legendary Texas outdoorsman and bear hunter.

The Biggest Bear on Earth, Harold McCracken, J.B. Lippincott Co., New York, 1943

> The life story of a brown bear, not unlike Roger Caras' *Monarch of Deadman Bay.*

* *California Grizzly,* Traci I. Storer and Lloyd P. Tevis, Jr., University of Nebraska Press, Lincoln, London, 1978

> A historical account of the grizzly of California and those who encountered it—Indians, frontiersmen, Spaniards and Grizzly Adams. A thorough bibliography and appendices.

* *The Education of a Bear Hunter,* Ralph Flowers, Winchester Press, New York, 1975

> Hunting black bears in Washington for tree damage control, adventures and close calls, blacks in logging country and some bear meat recipes.

<u>*The Grizzly Bear*</u>, Bessie Doak Haynes and Edgar, Universtiy of Oklahoma Press, Norman, 1966

> This comprehensive collection of stories begins in the 1600s and includes explorers, mountain men, California bears, pets, naturalists, cattlemen, Mexican, Alaskan, Yellowstone, folklore and legend. Superb bibliography included in great book.

* *The Grizzly Bear,* Thomas McNamee, Alfred A. Knopf, New York, 1984

> Seven months in the life of a sow grizzly and infant cubs. A view of the bear, its nature and habitat.

<u>*The Grizzly Bear*</u>, William H. Wright, University of Nebraska Press, Lincoln and London, 1909

> One of the classic studies of grizzly bears including history, personal observations, nature and distribution.

The Grizzly Book, Jack Samson, The Amwell Press, New Jersey, 1981
   Anthology of grizzly stories.

* <u>Grizzly Country</u>, Andy Russell, Alfred A. Knopf, Inc., New York, 1967
   Russell talks about the grizzly in western Canada and in Mt. McKinley
   National Park in Alaska—habitat, character, habits, nature, social life, as
   an adversary, history and camera hunting. <u>A superb book.</u>

*<u>The Grizzly Our Greatest Wild Animal</u>, Enos A. Mills, Houghton Mifflin Co.,
Boston and New York, 1919
   Mills covers the bear's nature and habits while making a plea for man to
   consider the character of the grizzly and to preserve the animal.

* <u>Grizzlies Don't Come Easy</u>, Ralph W. Young, Winchester Press, Tulsa,
Oklahoma, 1981
   Young details his arrival in Alaska, his guiding career and famous clients,
   bear information, good stories and his love of the giant omnivores. A pitch
   for saving brown bear habitat and a great read.

*Hunting the Alaskan Brown Bear, John W. Eddy, G.P. Putnam's Sons, New
York, London, 1930
   A detailed account of a brown bear hunt on the Alaska Peninsula—
   steamship transport followed by walk-in 30-mile each way, 30-day hunt
   with legendary Master Guide Andy Simons.

<u>Killer Bears</u>, Mike Cramond, Outdoor Life Books, New York, 1981
   Collection of man-bear encounters—mostly maulings—and assorted-
   thoughts. Excellent book with detailed charts on bear mauling statistics.
   The charts alone are worth the price of the book.

The King Bear of Kadiak Island, Elliott Whitney, The Reilly & Britton Co.,
Chicago, 1912
   From the Boys' Big Game Series, an account of bow hunting brown bears
   on Kodiak Island.

The Kodiak Bear, Jim Woodworth, The Stackpole Company, Harrisburg, PA,
1958
   Brown bears of Kodiak, hunting stories and information on bears including
   hunting, photographing, proper weaponry and trophy care.

Kodiak Bear Hunt, J. Frederick Palmer, Exposition Press, New York, 1958
   Brown bear hunting Kodiak Island with Captain Charlie Madsen.

* *Last of the Great Brown Bear Men*, Marvin H. Clark, Jr., Great Northwest Publishing and Distributing Co., Spokane, WA, 1980
    Kodiak brown bear guides Bill Pinnell and Morris Talifson, their guiding, hunting methods and stories, bear information, the politics involved and old guides still guide.

* *Lords of the Arctic*, Richard C. Davids, MacMillan Publishing Co., New York, 1982
    The polar bear in history and in geography, his environment, habits, nature, relationships with other bears and man, Nanook's intelligence, his nearest neighbor the Eskimo, the Eskimo hunt, comments about danger in bears land, Churchill and the animal's future.

Man and Bear, edited by Jack Samson, The Amwell Press, New Jersey, 1979
    Bears from the time of Lewis and Clark includes stories by literary types, outdoor writers and world renowned hunters.

<u>Man Meets Grizzly</u>, F.M. Young, Edited by Coralie Beyers, Houghton Mifflin Co., Boston, 1980
    Without a doubt, one of the best collections of bear information and stories ever assembled. Formatted from morning years to the heydays, hard times, sundown, afterglow and nightfall, stories cover mostly up through the early 1900s and touch on explorers, mountain men, cattlemen and stock killing grizzlies, maulings and fights between bears and other beasts. <u>A superb read</u>.

* <u>Monarch of Deadman Bay</u>, Roger A. Caras, Little, Brown and Company, Boston, Toronto, 1969.
    Roger's extremely realistic fictional account presents the biography of a monster brown bear, his life and death on Kodiak Island and brown bear nature. A long-time classic in the bear book world.

* <u>More Alaska Bear Tales</u>, Larry Kaniut, Sammamish Press, Issaquah, WA, 1989
    Collection of serious and humorous man-bear encounters in Alaska—the hunt, close calls, humor, bears in man's world, mauling chart (most comprehensive one available when published) and advice.

* *Night of the Grizzlies*, Jack Olsen, Signet Book, New York, 1969
  Compelling account of numerous bear incidents in Glacier National Park
  during the summer of 1967, which contributed to the attack and deaths of
  two 19-year-old college women on the same night. Olsen's excellent, sad-
  but-necessary book castigates park officials for their apathetic and ineffec-
  tive methods of addressing the man-bear problem and proposes better ones
  for the future.

* *No Room For Bears*, Frank Dufresne, Holt, Rinehart and Winston, New
York, Chicago San Francisco, 1965
  All three North American bears, their nature, adventure and humor ooze
  from its pages. More noticeable is the author's depiction of the importance
  of recognizing the need to question mankind's relationship to and responsibility for bears and their habitat. Super book.

Notorious Grizzly Bears, W.P. Hubbard, Sage Books, Denver, 1960
  Very good book discussing grizzly nature, characteristics and habits. A
  number of man grizzly encounters, historic bears and bear incidents in
  several western states. Good book for the library.

Of Bears and Men, Mike Cramond, University of Oklahoma Press, Norman and
London, 1986
  A collection of bear information, hunting, maulings, fatalities, general
  knowledge and hunting methods.

The Outdoor Life Bear Book, edited by Chet Fish, Outdoor Life Books, 1983
  Great collection of some of the best bear stories ever gathered, including
  some top guides' stories as well as outdoor writers'. Encompasses bear
  attacks, observing and managing bears, myths, brown/grizzlies, hunting,
  bear dogs, archery hunting, the unexpected, and experts' answers.

* *Some Bears Kill*, Larry Kaniut, Safari Press, Long Beach, CA, 1997
  Thirty-eight of the best stories ever collected, primarily bear maulings and
  fatalities and man's refusal to give up. Eleven appendixes and bear mauling
  avoidance advice are worth the price of the book.

* *Tales of a Bear Hunter*, Dalton Carr, Safari Press Inc., Long Beach, California,
2001
  Seventeen chapters capture over four decades of bear hunting and reflect
  Carr's love of nature and respect for bears. Beneficial information about the
  bear's behavior and anatomy as well as calibers and cartridges for bruin.

* *Track of the Grizzly*, Frank C. Craighead, Jr., Sierra Club Books, San Francisco, 1979.
   Culmination of Frank's extensive study of the Yellowstone grizzly— objective look at the bear's history, man's relation to him, park service mistakes and thought provoking questions regarding the bruin and man's responsibility to him.

True Bear Stories, Joaquin Miller, Rand McNally & Co., Chicago and New York, 1900
   Seventeen American bear stories in this 250-plus page book.

The Wild Grizzlies of Alaska, John M. Holzworth, G.P. Putnam's Sons, New York, London, 1930
   A comprehensive account of Admiralty Island grizzlies— classification, hibernation, food, intelligence, breeding habits and ferocity—descriptions of their country and history, encounters and attacks, literary history, conservation and photography—value and methods. And, of course, information about Allen Hasselborg, long time "bear man of Admiralty Island."

Where the Grizzly Walks, Bill Schneider, Mountain Press Publishing Co., Missoula, 1977
   Man's callous disregard for grizzlies since the days of Lewis and Clark raises the questions of man's need to protect the bruin's existence in our ecosystem (he includes Craighead's battle with Yellowstone mismanagement).

White Bear, Charles T. Feazel, Henry Holt and Co. New York, 1990
   Comprehensive book about polar bears includes their habitat, nature, the bear today and tomorrow. Some good stories and information about Churchill, where the bears live among townspeople—interesting chapter with numerous incidents highlighting bears' intrusion into man's dwellings. Very good read.

The World of the Polar Bear, Richard Perry, University of Washington Press, 1966
   Polar bears, the sow's den, the world of the polar bear including cubs, hunting seals, bears and walruses, nomadic lifestyle, bears and men, and past and future.

Perhaps you'd like to read another of Kaniut's books:

ALASKA BEAR TALES

Published in 1983 this 318-page collection became an instant best-seller, achieving its 3rd printing the first year. This comprehensive book looks at man-bear encounters in Alaska–from false charges to fatalities. Chapters include Alaska's "three bears" and their nature; comments by mauling victims as well as their rescuers, family and medical professionals; humor and advice for avoiding bear mauling. A rich, annotated bibliography is worth the price of the book.

"*Alaska Bear Tales* is **one of the best ever done** on bear-human contacts."
—John Williard, *Billings Gazette*

"I simply <u>COULD NOT</u> put this book down. **Stephen King, eat your heart out!**"
—(Amazon.com) zakmartin from Seattle, WA

"...considerable success of *Alaska Bear Tales*... 'going back to press this week for 20,000 more, bringing the in-print total to 37,000."
—*Publisher's Weekly*, November 18, 1983

MORE ALASKA BEAR TALES

More Alaska Bear Tales provides the reader with all-new Alaskan bear stories. This 285-page volume was selected from 900 pages of material sent to the publisher in 1989. Nineteen-page chronological chart of bear mauling information lists person, place, type bear, cause and person action.

"...it's difficult...to study the compelling stories of the first book and not be terrified. The second volume has a lighter touch. The stories are longer and do not always end with...blood being spilled."
—Alaska Magazine, January 1991

"As in *Alaska Bear Tales* **this one picks up where it left off**. The book is much more than a blood and guts thriller. It affords the reader an open minded look at the attacks and as you read you find yourself second guessing the victims. Larry has put forth alot of effort in his research. I enjoyed the book and <u>hope that there is a book three in the works</u>..."
—Amazon.com reader jdmiles@worldnet.att.net from Arizona October 28, 1998

"The saga continues from the first book. Spine tingling reading full of chills, thrills, and even some laughs. **Do not pass this book up** but be prepared to <u>not be able to put this book down</u>!"
—Amazon.com reader from San Luis Obispo, CA August 12, 1999

CHEATING DEATH

Kaniut captures the triumph of the human spirit. He provides a ringside seat to such adventure as smashing into the side of a mountain in an aircraft in sub-freezing weather, cascading down a vertical icefall amidst tons of fractured ice and attempting to unravel rope around a leg 30-feet beneath the water's surface. The publisher selected 18 stories for this 174-page book that presents survival stories from the Great Land.

Volume after volume, people continually shake their heads in wonder, "How does Kaniut keep producing these great books?"

"All 18 episodes roil the blood and chill the imagination. Yet beyond the unrelieved grimness of the book, one savors the triumph and giddiness of survival when survival seems out of the question."
                    —Cliff Cernick, *General Aviation News & Flyer*, Septermber 1994

"For author Larry Kaniut and other Alaskans, stories of disaster and near-disaster are a staple of each day's news. Here, Kaniut brings together some of the most **exceptional stories**–true tales of men and women who find within themselves the courage and ingenuity to cheat death."
                    —Barnes & Noble, Bellevue, Washington, September 1994

SOME BEARS KILL

In an effort to apprise the reader that "bears aren't bad; people need education," Larry Kaniut offers *Some Bears Kill*. This, his third bear book, captures 39 new bear-man stories. The appendix, which discusses proper people etiquette in bear country, is worth the price of the book.

"*Some Bears Kill* is **one of the most fascinating books** I've ever read…your books are better than anything on TV…FASCINATING. I'm one of your biggest fans. Just keep them coming.
                    —Spencer Ward, personal correspondence, September 26, 1997

"I was <u>unable to put the book down</u> until I finished it. These books are terrific."
                    —Diane Tayman, from correspondence sent BASS Pro Shops, May 2, 2000

"Larry Kaniut is an authority on Alaska's bears and the destruction they cause. Safari Press is proud to publish his latest–*Some Bears Kill*–313 pages of pure terror. *Some Bears Kill* **is the best yet.**"
                    —Promo from Safari Press brochure with book's release

DANGER STALKS THE LAND

Kaniut pulls no punches as he relates 42-stories depicting the worst that Alaska dishes out. A survival preparedness checklist AND great advice for safe return from outdoor activities could save your life.

"…absolutely the **best stories I have ever read!**"
—Anonymous, www.kaniut.com web site

"…last night I invited my wife to the hot tub to soak and talk but NO she was too busy reading *Danger Stalks the Land*! Congratulations on **another fantastic book.**"
—Tom Smith, biologist USGS

"By far, Larry Kaniut's best book."
—Amazon.com reader Ernest W. Hedrick, Collegeville, PA

"Mind numbing true adventure! This is easily the **best collection of true adventure tales ever assembled**…run to your nearest bookstore and BUY THIS BOOK!"
—Amazon.com reader Jim Walters, Washington State

For autographed copies or to learn more about the author visit
www.kanuit.com

KANIUT WAS HERE !